"In *Worshiping with the Reformers,* K
practices that resulted from the Ref
the sixteenth century. Outlining the
tantism and with Roman Catholicis
ideal starting point for anyone curiou ... ... historical development of worship
practices that are still important today."

Amy Nelson Burnett, Varner Professor of History at the University of Nebraska-Lincoln

"Karin Maag's deft presentation gives voice to ordinary worshipers across the Reformation's broad confessional spectrum as they gathered for prayer, song, sermon, service, and the Eucharist. Maag explores the Reformation's complex liturgical landscape with precision and aplomb. The faithful have rarely been heard in such clear tones. It is a profoundly human account that continues to resonate in our contemporary society."

Raymond A. Mentzer, Daniel J. Krumm Family Chair in Reformation Studies at the University of Iowa

"*Worshiping with the Reformers* is a sheer delight! Karin Maag has synthesized scholarly insights and a wide array of personal stories to offer a wonderfully helpful and engaging account of key facets of worship from a variety of perspectives. What we learn from this splendid volume is intrinsically valuable as well as deepening our understanding of the historical roots of our ways of worshiping today."

Suzanne McDonald, professor of systematic and historical theology at Western Theological Seminary, Holland, Michigan

"This invaluable book takes us right into the experience of worship in the age of the Reformation. Professor Maag's mastery of the theological issues is impressive, but what is most compelling about the book is how human it is: she never forgets that worship is something that people do and find meaning in, and she always gives us the view from the pew as well as the pulpit."

Alec Ryrie, professor of theology and religion, Durham University

"The Reformation meant millions of people gained new understandings of the church and what it means to 'be' church. In this highly interesting and informative book, Karin Maag helps us understand what worship came to mean for those experiencing Protestant faith. Elements of church worship including preaching, prayer, and sacraments come alive as being vital while voices and stories of worshipers bring us into their experiences in their newfound faith. Maag is a superb scholar whose stimulating study helps us understand Reformation worship. It also motivates us to deepened worship practices of our own."

Donald K. McKim, author *of Everyday Prayer with the Reformers* and *Reformation Questions, Reformation Answers*

"Karin Maag provides an expert view of the lived experience of religion in the Reformation era. Illustrated by an array of vivid examples, this book analyzes the role of states, clergy, and communities in the formation of religious cultures. This very readable account of the complex and fluid religious landscape of early modern Europe will be of great interest to those interested in the Reformation as well as those reflecting on the roots of contemporary debates about worship."

Graeme Murdock, associate professor of European history at Trinity College Dublin

"Karin Maag's engaging, wide-reaching, and instructive overview of worship in the Reformation era examines ritual and devotional practices in churches, homes, schools, and other settings. It is the perfect point of departure for those eager to understand how the emergence of new forms of Christianity in the sixteenth century involved not just theological doctrines but also real people's lived experience. Maag's insightful study paves the way for richer conversation about worship in the church today."

Barbara Pitkin, senior lecturer in religious studies at Stanford University, and author of *Calvin, the Bible, and History*

"For early modern Christians, debates regarding 'right worship' laid bare foundational differences in theological belief, communal identity, and personal devotion. In this outstanding book, Karin Maag explores the rich variety of worship practices—and inevitable 'worship wars'—that characterized Protestant and Catholic churches during the Reformation era. Maag tells an important story—and does so with meticulous detail and vibrant color."

Scott Manetsch, professor of church history at Trinity Evangelical Divinity School, associate general editor of the Reformation Commentary on Scripture

"*Worshiping with the Reformers* not only fills a lacuna in historical scholarship but also offers an indispensable resource for the church. Maag is an expert guide whose rich illustrations bring readers into the sanctuaries, chapels, homes, and public spaces of early modern life. This book helps us to understand the various contours of devotion demonstrating how various patterns of worship have become markers of Christian identity that endure to the present. Highly recommended!"

Chris Castaldo, lead pastor of New Covenant Church, Naperville, Illinois, and author of *Talking with Catholics About the Gospel*

"A masterful overview of worship traditions in the Reformation. Drawing richly on primary sources, Karin Maag presents a coherent account of liturgical life from mainline Protestant, Anabaptist, and Catholic churches. Highly recommended!"

Timothy George, distinguished professor at Beeson Divinity School of Samford University, general editor of the Reformation Commentary on Scripture

KARIN MAAG

WORSHIPING WITH THE REFORMERS

Academic

An imprint of InterVarsity Press
Downers Grove, Illinois

InterVarsity Press
P.O. Box 1400, Downers Grove, IL 60515-1426
ivpress.com
email@ivpress.com

InterVarsity Press® is the book-publishing division of InterVarsity Christian Fellowship/USA®, a movement of students and faculty active on campus at hundreds of universities, colleges, and schools of nursing in the United States of America, and a member movement of the International Fellowship of Evangelical Students. For information about local and regional activities, visit intervarsity.org.

All Scripture quotations, unless otherwise indicated, are taken from The Holy Bible, New International Version®, NIV®. Copyright © 1973, 1978, 1984, 2011 by Biblica, Inc.™ Used by permission of Zondervan. All rights reserved worldwide. www.zondervan.com. The "NIV" and "New International Version" are trademarks registered in the United States Patent and Trademark Office by Biblica, Inc.™

Figure 2.1: Jean Perrissin, Le Temple de Paradis / Wikimedia Commons
Figure 6.1: Lucas Cranach the Elder, Reformation altarpiece, photographer: W. Bulach / Wikimedia Commons
Figure 7.1: Lucas Cranach the Elder, Martin Luther, St. Anne's Church, Augsburg / Wikimedia Commons

Cover design and image composite: David Fassett
Interior design: Cindy Kiple
Image: Luther preaching: © Bridgeman Images

ISBN 978-0-8308-5302-1 (print)
ISBN 978-0-8308-5303-8 (digital)

Printed in the United States of America ♾

InterVarsity Press is committed to ecological stewardship and to the conservation of natural resources in all our operations. This book was printed using sustainably sourced paper.

Library of Congress Cataloging-in-Publication Data
A catalog record for this book is available from the Library of Congress.

P	20	19	18	17	16	15	14	13	12	11	10	9	8	7	6	5	4	3	2	1
Y	37	36	35	34	33	32	31	30	29	28	27	26	25	24	23	22	21			

For my beloved siblings

Liane Clark and Eric Maag,

and with heartfelt appreciation to my

longtime colleague and friend Paul Fields,

curator of the H. Henry Meeter

Center for Calvin Studies.

Contents

ACKNOWLEDGMENTS

AT THE END OF A PROJECT OF THIS SIZE, it is good to take a moment to express appreciation to all those who have helped along the way. My thanks go first to Dr. David McNutt, associate editor at IVP Academic, who originally approached me with this project and convinced me to go ahead with it. His encouragement and quiet good sense have been heartening. Thanks also to everyone at InterVarsity Press for their stellar work. I am delighted to have this work included as a companion volume to the Reformation Commentary on Scripture series. I am also grateful to the two external readers who provided me with helpful feedback.

I am also grateful to colleagues at Calvin University and Calvin Theological Seminary for their friendship and support, including John Witvliet, Susan Felch, Laura Smit, Kate van Liere, Frans van Liere, Dan Miller, William Van Vugt, Ronald Feenstra, Lyle Bierma, and Richard Muller. These, alongside my other colleagues in the History Department at Calvin University and my seminary colleagues, have made teaching and working at these two institutions a joy.

I am particularly grateful to my colleagues at Hekman Library—I have been constantly impressed at how many of the resources I have needed for this project have been available in hard copy or as an electronic resource through the Hekman Library website or through interlibrary loan. I was also able to access a wide range of articles through the databases to which Hekman Library subscribes. Without excellent academic libraries like Hekman Library, this book and so many others could not be written. My special thanks go to Kaitlyn van Kampen, who cheerfully filled all my interlibrary loan requests.

I have relied extensively on the collaboration and good humor of my Meeter Center colleagues, including program coordinators Laura Beer and most recently Deborah Snider. Deborah in particular has been invaluable in reading through the manuscript of this book, checking and rechecking the footnotes, and building the indexes and "For Further Reading" lists. I am also profoundly grateful to my long-time colleague and friend Paul Fields, the Meeter Center curator. We have happily worked side by side for well over two decades. I could not ask for a finer colleague.

Finally, I am deeply grateful for the interest and support of friends and family, including Shirlene and Mike Abma, whose warm friendship has been a wonderful gift in my life; Jim and Andrea Turner, who always have an interest in my recounting of Reformation doings; and Susanna Phillippo for her stalwart transoceanic friendship. My husband, Chris, has lovingly supported me at every turn, as have my parents. But I dedicate this book to my sister, Liane, and my brother, Eric. Our interests and professional lives have gone in very different directions, but I could not be more proud to be their sister.

INTRODUCTION

IN 1545, A YOUNG MAN FROM ANTWERP arrived in Strasbourg to begin his studies. Since he was a French speaker and a Protestant, he began to attend the French Reformed church in Strasbourg where John Calvin had served as a pastor until his return to Geneva in 1541. For his own safety and that of his relatives still in Catholic Antwerp, the young man adopted the pseudonym Martin du Mont and wrote letters under that name to his relatives in the Low Countries about his experiences. He gave a particularly detailed report about Reformed worship in Strasbourg, recounting not only what took place but also its emotional and spiritual impact on him:

> For the first five or six times, when I saw this small gathering of people expelled from every land for having upheld the honor of God and of his gospel, I began to weep, not out of sadness but out of joy, in hearing them sing as willingly as they did, thanking God for having brought them to a place where his name is honored and glorified. No one can fathom the joy of singing the praises and marvels of the Lord in one's mother tongue as we do here. On Sundays, instead of a mass, we sing two psalms or prayers and afterwards there's the sermon. . . . The pastor faces the people and prays for the people in their mother tongue, loud and clear, so that everyone can hear. After the prayers, he

climbs into the pulpit and preaches, from seven-thirty to nine
o'clock, and these sermons are wonderful to hear.[1]

This eyewitness account captures many of the aspects of Reformation-
era worship that form the heart of this volume: preaching, praying,
singing, and spiritual fellowship. The letter from the young man
from Antwerp also highlights the effect of these activities on the
participants, including him, to the point of bringing him to tears.
For this student far from home, the experience of worship among
other religious exiles helped make sense of what was otherwise a
difficult experience.

In 1562, the Swiss reformer Heinrich Bullinger laid out his vision of corporate worship in a text that later became known as the
Second Helvetic Confession. Bullinger underscored the importance of communal worship alongside private reading of Scripture
and exhortation:

> In order that the Word of God may be properly preached to the
> people, and prayers and supplications properly made, also that
> the sacraments be rightly administered, and that collections
> may be made for the poor, and to pay the costs of all the
> Church's expenses, and in order to maintain social intercourse,
> it is most necessary that religious or Church gatherings be held.
> For it is certain that in the apostolic and primitive Church,
> there were such assemblies frequented by all the godly.[2]

Bullinger held that public worship was a normative practice rooted in
the early church that filled a considerable range of important roles,
not least of which was maintaining bonds of fellowship among
worshipers. Although this text is more prescriptive than descriptive,

[1]Letter published in Alfred Erichson, L'Eglise française de Strasbourg au seizième siècle d'après
des documents inédits (Strasbourg: Schmidt, 1886), 22-23 (translation mine).
[2]Heinrich Bullinger, Second Helvetic Confession (1562), chapter 22, "Of Religious and Ecclesiastical Meetings," Christian Classics Ethereal Library, www.ccel.org/creeds/helvetic.htm.

Bullinger, like du Mont, highlighted the vital importance of communal worship for the faithful.

It is fair to say, however, that not everyone experienced worship as positively as did young Martin du Mont or in the way described by Bullinger. Indeed, many of the vignettes and first-person accounts that appear in the following chapters highlight the reactions of early modern men and women who for a range of reasons found the experience of worship difficult or off-putting or confrontational. How could it be otherwise, given the dramatic changes that took place in many aspects of worship in the Reformation era? If nothing else, this study highlights the challenges of making changes in a community's worship practice. Furthermore, although some readers may be surprised to realize how frequently social conflicts flared up in worship services, it is worth remembering that—as is often the case today—tensions in the broader society inevitably found their way into church, since neither the building nor the practice of worship was hermetically sealed off from the rest of people's lives. It is also true that the historical record has mostly preserved accounts of problems and protests—the voices of the quietly contented rarely surface, especially in judicial or consistorial records.

Whether appreciative or hostile, these early modern accounts of worship and its effects also underscore a key reality of the Reformation—namely, that people noticed and took to heart any changes that affected their worship practice. Many of the people whose voices are heard in the chapters of this book may not have been able to explain the theological distinctions between transubstantiation and consubstantiation, for instance, but they knew and valued the different parts of the Communion liturgy in their own tradition and were quick to protest any changes they opposed. Today's worship wars have parallels in early modern churches, where individuals and communities fought over the correct way to celebrate the sacraments, or whether congregational singing should be accompanied by instruments, or whether those leading prayers during worship should pray extemporaneously or use set texts. Worship offered both an opportunity for individuals and communities to turn to God, but also a chance to make clear statements about identity, belonging, and the power of ritual.

This book, a companion volume for the Reformation Commentary on Scripture series published by IVP Academic, is aimed at those who want to know more about the experience of worship in the Reformation era, both to get a better sense of the worship lives of early modern Christians and to understand the roots of current-day worship practices. However, a volume of this length cannot hope to be comprehensive. The field of research in early modern worship, liturgy, iconography, musicology, sacred space, and popular religion is ever-expanding. It would be best, therefore, to read this book as part of a broader conversation rather than as the definitive word on any of the topics covered in this work. Readers wanting to know more are encouraged to consult the footnotes and "For Further Reading" lists at the end of each chapter to find further resources. Decisions also had to be made as to which confessional groups to include in comparing early modern worship practices. Broadly speaking, the five main confessional families included in this work are Catholics, Lutherans, Anglicans, Reformed, and Anabaptists, though not all appear in equal proportions in each chapter.[3] Although the primary focus of this book is on the practice of worship, most of the chapters include some background on the theological approach adopted by Reformation-era church leaders on these various topics. Finally, it is worth noting that worship practices were not set in stone within any one confessional

---

[3]Throughout this book, the term *Anglican* refers to the Church of England. Theologically, under Edward VI and then under Elizabeth, the Church of England was Reformed, but its ecclesiology and style of worship retained many more traditionally medieval aspects than did the Reformed churches on the European continent. Because this book focuses primarily on the practice of worship, both the term *Anglican* and the distinctive worship style of the Church of England will constitute a distinctive category.

group, nor were confessional borders rigorously policed. In other words, there was more flexibility and diversity in Reformation-era worship practice than one might think.

One of the aims of this book is to help current-day clergy and laypeople think more deeply about various aspects of worship practice. Why do some churches pass the plates of bread and the trays of cups from person to person along the pews, while others ask their members to come forward to the front of the sanctuary to receive the bread and the wine or grape juice? What lies at the root of some Protestant churches' deep discomfort with set prayers? Why are some European Lutheran churches virtually indistinguishable from Catholic churches in terms of the amount of religious images in their worship spaces, whereas Reformed churches at first glance seem so devoid of images? This book offers insights into the practice of early modern churches that lay bare the roots of these divergent aspects of contemporary worship.

Yet in building connections between worship in the Reformation era and today, it is important to remember the very significant points of contrast between these two eras. One of the biggest differences between early modern Europe and today, and one that current readers should bear in mind from the start, is the key role played by the government in regulating the practice of worship. Governments in areas that had officially adopted Protestantism saw it not only as their right but also as their duty to ensure that populations gathered regularly for worship. In Lutheran areas, for instance, governments prepared prescriptive documents known as church orders, laying out their expectations regarding attendance, behavior, the format of the worship services on Sundays and weekdays, and so on. In officially Protestant areas, the government paid the salaries of the pastors, once again ensuring that the regulation of worship fell within the civil authorities' remit. To a modern ear, the injunctions ordering people to attend church and threatening fines for those who refused to comply may seem both harsh and counterproductive. But it is worth remembering that regulations on paper and enforcement in practice are two different things. If nothing else, the authorities' repeated reminders that church attendance was expected of everyone in the community suggests that reluctant churchgoers found various ways to evade the requirement.

The other key point to emphasize before delving into the subject is that uniformity in worship practice, even within one confessional group, was more of an aspiration than a reality in the early modern era. Except in the very smallest territories, such as city-states (and even there), the practice of worship depended very much on the clergy and the laypeople who were present. Carefully crafted and beautifully worded liturgies, detailed church orders, and regular visitations designed to stir hearts and shape lives around worship were no match for pastors who preached week by week in a monotone or parishioners who fell asleep as soon as the sermon got underway. Conversely, creative pastors might find new ways to prepare youngsters for their first Communion, or congregation members might find ingenious ways to retain elements of worship from previous eras that they still held dear. Although the regulations surrounding early modern worship offer a vision of uniformity (as highlighted in the Second Helvetic Confession), the reality (as described by Martin du Mont) was much more varied—and more interesting.

ONE

GOING TO CHURCH

Meetings of the Church are enjoined upon us by God's Word;
and from our everyday experience we well know how we need them.

JOHN CALVIN, *INSTITUTES OF THE CHRISTIAN RELIGION*

PICTURE THE SCENE: IT IS SUNDAY MORNING in your community. Some people are getting up and getting ready for church. Depending on their denomination and its worship practices, they are collecting their Bibles, making sure they have a contribution for the offering, wearing their best clothes (or perhaps just ordinary clothes), looking over the Scripture readings for the day, or ensuring they have their choir folder or praise band music to hand. Or perhaps, as during the pandemic, families and individuals are gathering around their laptops for a streaming worship service led from their pastor's living room. Non-churchgoing neighbors, meanwhile, are sleeping in, getting groceries, having a leisurely breakfast, or taking care of the thousand and one household tasks that have accumulated over the week. For them, Sunday is like any other day. Within any one community, the range of practices and activities on any given Sunday is immense.

John Calvin, *Institutes of the Christian Religion*, ed. John T. McNeill, trans. Ford Lewis Battles (Philadelphia: Westminster, 1960), 2.8.33.

When we turn to the sixteenth century, the picture is very different. Whether Reformed, Anglican, Lutheran, or Catholic, the emphasis on going to church on Sunday (and often on other days of the week as well) was strong and was mandated by religious and political authorities across the whole of the community. In Anabaptist circles, the focus on gathering for worship was equally strong but did not have the force of political authorities behind it. Community pressures might shape expectations that everyone would come together for worship, but attendance at Anabaptist worship gatherings was not mandated by government leaders. Anabaptist worship in the early modern era meant gatherings in private homes, barns, or even in fields or forest clearings.[1] The pressure of persecution also often meant that the time and place of worship was not set but was passed on by word of mouth, making enforcement of attendance very challenging. Hence this chapter will focus more on the other confessional groups, leaving the Anabaptists aside for now.

From a theological perspective, church attendance on Sundays was part of the Sabbath observance as laid out in the Ten Commandments (Ex 20:8; Deut 5:12). Church leaders from across the confessional spectrum emphasized the importance of Sunday church attendance to honor God both individually and as a community of believers. In this chapter, we will explore both the theology and the practice of going to church in the Reformation era. Most of the information on the practice of church attendance in this chapter comes from church orders, which were texts that laid out how worship should take place for a given confessional group. These documents are prescriptive: they lay out what is supposed to happen. One cannot, however, conclude that these texts match the reality of what actually took place. The church orders therefore need to be paired with other documents, including

---

[1] See for instance the testimony of early Dutch Anabaptists reported in Piet Visser, "'Wherever Christ Is Among Us We Will Gather': Mennonite Worship Places in the Netherlands," *Mennonite Quarterly Review* 73, no. 2 (1999): 215-33, esp. 218-19.

church court and consistory records, which shed light on the challenges religious leaders faced in getting individuals and populations to go to church. The practice of going to church also raises a number of questions: In an era before people had watches, how did believers know when it was time to gather for worship? Who went to church? Was anyone excused from attendance? What happened to those who failed to attend? Did participation vary depending on gender or age? How often did people go to church over the course of a week: Only on Sunday mornings or at other times as well? What were the worship-attendance expectations for an average layperson in different confessional groups? Was strict Sabbath observance a reality for sixteenth-century Christians? Were there special times of year or particular days in the church year when church attendance was more important or more prevalent than at other times? Readers are encouraged to read and reflect on this chapter alongside the next one, "At Church," to gain a fuller understanding of what churchgoing meant in the sixteenth century.

The Challenges Surrounding Church Attendance

To many twenty-first-century people, the idea of coercing faith practice by compelling individuals to attend communal worship services seems both counterproductive and wrong. Yet the sixteenth-century approach was different. Because faith commitments were understood as applying to the community as a whole, rather than to individuals, religious and political authorities were in agreement that everyone in a given community should go to church and should practice corporate worship in the same way. To allow for variations or disregard individual nonattendance was dangerous and would lead to God's anger against the whole community.

Our first account sheds light both on communal expectations and on individuals' responses to the mandate to go to church.

～

On March 12, 1582, a woman named Bessie Glass appeared before the kirk session in the Scottish city of Perth. The kirk session was the body of pastors, elders, and deacons charged with church discipline in Presbyterian Scotland, equivalent to a consistory in Reformed France, the Netherlands, or Geneva. Bessie Glass, wife of William Duncan, was in trouble for a number of reasons, including her fundamental lack of knowledge of the Christian faith, her propensity to spend time in taverns, her vulgar talk, and her absence from Sunday worship. The fact that the kirk session knew she was skipping worship highlights a strong neighborhood or community awareness as to who was or was not in attendance on any given Sunday, a fairly impressive feat given that the town had five thousand to six thousand inhabitants.[2] In subsequent appearances before the kirk session, after she was widowed, she faced charges of begging, vagrancy, and causing a public scandal.[3] The records also suggest Bessie Glass was a woman who ended up living on the margins of her community, causing upset to her seemingly more respectable neighbors. Yet in March 1582, at least, the kirk session seemed to have no qualms about her participation and presence at worship. In fact, they demanded it. She was ordered to come daily to church to be instructed in the faith, steer clear of taverns, and attend church twice every Sunday, under penalty of public repentance and a fine (or an hour in the public stocks if she was unable to pay).[4] Here we have a woman whose outward behavior at least suggests little interest in communal worship, yet because she lived in Perth and the community as a whole was meant to live according to the teachings of the Reformed faith, Bessie Glass, too, was to come to church, and even attend more frequently.

---

[2]Margo Todd, introduction to *The Perth Kirk Session Books 1577–1590*, ed. Margo Todd (Woodbridge, UK: Boydell, 2008), 9-14.
[3]*Perth Kirk Session Books*, 377-78. Scottish women who were married did not take their husband's name. Instead, they kept their family name at birth throughout their lives.
[4]*Perth Kirk Session Books*, 215-16.

༄

The second vignette stems from a very different confessional context—namely, early seventeenth-century Catholic France, where Reformed Protestants were an officially tolerated but hardly welcome minority. The Edict of Nantes of 1598 had brought peace to France after years of religious civil wars. Under the terms of the edict, French Huguenots had the right to worship in a number of French cities, but crucially not any closer than five leagues (ten miles) from Paris. Parisian Huguenots thus had to travel by water or by road to attend worship in Ablon or later in Charenton, as described in the diary of the leading Huguenot classical scholar Isaac Casaubon, who lived in Paris between 1604 and 1610. He recounted how one Sunday he and his wife, his sister, and two sons planned to take a boat to attend the two Sunday worship services at the Reformed church in Charenton. However, even though they got to the dock in Paris at seven in the morning, nearly all the available boats were full, and they ended up in a small and leaky vessel, hauled by a man trudging along the riverbank. The boat was in such poor shape that they hesitated and wondered about staying home, but their eagerness to hear the sermons and be part of the worshiping community overcame their anxiety. As they neared their destination, however, their craft was accidentally rammed by a larger boat. The smaller vessel began taking on water and the whole family risked drowning. Although everyone was eventually rescued, Casaubon did lose the psalter he had been holding at the time of the crash. The psalter had been his wedding gift to his wife some twenty-two years earlier. His wife, as was her usual practice, had begun singing two psalms, one after the other, as soon as they left the dock. Casaubon recalled that they had finished Psalm 91 and were on the seventh verse of Psalm 92 when the accident occurred.[5] Here we have a family so eager to attend worship that they were willing to make use of substandard transportation to get there. We also have a picture of families preparing for worship along the way, in this instance by singing psalms.

↪

Clearly, early modern church attendance met with varying levels of enthusiasm, apathy, or active resistance. Some members of the various confessional groups eagerly looked forward to going to church and were profoundly shaped by their attendance practice, even including the journey to church. In fact, going to church could be a risky business, particularly for those who were part of minority religious groups within a larger, often hostile, community that held to a different understanding of the Christian faith. Some had to cross political borders, traveling every Sunday from a Lutheran to a Catholic area (or vice versa) to attend church.[6] Others, as indicated in the second vignette, had to travel considerable distances through hazardous conditions within their own country to find the closest place of worship that matched their confessional outlook.

These two accounts from very different ends of the spectrum in terms of a person's response to going to church underscore the importance of bearing in mind how wide-ranging the response to church attendance could be, from disaffection to enthusiasm. As we consider various facets of the experience of going to church in the Reformation era, we should remember that the difference between authorities' expectations and the lived reality of ordinary people could be significant.

---

[5]L. J. Nazelle, *Isaac Casaubon: sa vie et son temps (1559–1614)* (Geneva: Slatkine Reprints, 1897), 117-20.
[6]For an enthralling account of how confessional tensions disrupted journeys to church for those living in confessional borderlands in a somewhat later period, see Benjamin Kaplan, *Cunegonde's Kidnapping: A Story of Religious Conflict in the Age of the Enlightenment* (New Haven, CT: Yale University Press, 2014).

THE THEOLOGICAL CASE FOR GATHERING FOR WORSHIP

The bulk of early modern theological reflections on why Christians should come together for worship is rooted in discussions and debates about the nature of the Sabbath and the importance of Sabbath observance.[7]

In his 1529 *Large Catechism*, Martin Luther laid out the reasons for Sabbath observance in his presentation of the (for Lutherans) third commandment.[8] His entire discussion was framed by his emphasis on the centrality of the Word of God. The Word preached, explained, or meditated on sanctified the Sabbath. For Luther, the Sabbath was definitely not a human-centered observance. At the same time, he noted the importance of a regular recurrence of rest for human beings, especially for manual workers, servants, and others who otherwise had no opportunity to take a break from their labors. He highlighted the importance of Sabbath in proving an opportunity for the faithful to gather for worship. Since Sunday was traditionally the day for this rest and worship, Luther advocated keeping to this practice. He observed that while any day of the week would do for this rest and worship opportunity, it was fitting to select one day so that everyone would follow the same pattern, and "so no disorder be caused by unnecessary innovations."[9]

In his *Institutes of the Christian Religion*, as well as his commentaries and sermons, John Calvin also addressed the issue of Sabbath

---

[7]This chapter will focus above all else on the arguments advanced by church leaders to encourage the faithful to gather together for corporate worship, leaving aside the interesting but often complex discussions about what other activities may or may not be permitted on the Sabbath.

[8]Lutherans and Roman Catholics, unlike the Reformed, combine the commandment stating "You shall have no other gods before me" and the commandment against idol-making into one. They then subdivide the later commandment about coveting into two separate ones: one against coveting someone else's wife, and a separate one on coveting anything or anyone else belonging to a neighbor. Each confessional group still holds to ten commandments, but the division into clauses is not identical.

[9]*Luther's Large Catechism*, trans. J. N. Lenker (Minneapolis: Augsburg, 1967), 15-30, esp. 27.

observance.[10] In the *Institutes*, he highlighted the importance of the Sabbath as an opportunity for humans to rest from their sins, allowing room for God's grace to work in their lives, both on the Sabbath and on other days. Calvin pushed back against the strongly ceremonial understanding of the Jewish Sabbath as depicted in Scripture. Like Luther, Calvin emphasized both the importance of Sunday as a day for corporate worship and as an occasion for physical rest for those who might otherwise be oppressed by their employers or by the more powerful in society.[11]

Other reformers including Heinrich Bullinger and Martin Bucer largely shared these views, emphasizing the importance of gathering for corporate worship on Sundays and condemning activities that might draw people away from going to church. Both men recommended stringent penalties for those who failed to observe the Sabbath.[12] Bullinger, however, did not believe that the practice of observing the Sabbath on Sunday was commanded in the New Testament. Instead, he agreed with Calvin and Luther that it made sense to select Sunday as the day of worship to honor Christ's resurrection day and to maintain uniformity and good order in the church.[13] He also allowed for necessary work on the Sabbath, even including bringing in crops at risk of spoiling if they remained too long in the fields.[14] Later Reformed theologians including Franciscus Junius and Jerome Zanchi echoed many of these views on the Sabbath, yet these two men

---

[10]See especially Calvin's *Institutes of the Christian Religion* 2.8 and his 34th and 35th sermons on the book of Deuteronomy: John Calvin, *Sermons on Deuteronomy* (London: H. Middleton, 1583).

[11]For a helpful overview of Calvin's understanding of the Sabbath, see John Primus, *Holy Time: Moderate Puritanism and the Sabbath* (Macon, GA: Mercer University Press, 1989), 121-34.

[12]Primus, *Holy Time*, 135, 137-38.

[13]Primus, *Holy Time*, 134-38.

[14]For Bullinger's treatment of Sabbath observance, see "Of the fourth precept of the first table, that is, of the order and keeping of the Sabbath-Day," in Heinrich Bullinger, *The Decades of Heinrich Bullinger*, ed. Thomas Harding (Grand Rapids, MI: Reformation Heritage Books, 2004), 1:253-67.

also went further in that they saw the observance of the Sabbath as part of God's original creation ordinance. Junius stated that the switch from the Jewish Sabbath on Saturday to the Christian Sabbath on Sunday was done with the authority of Christ, while Zanchi gave substantive weight to the fourth commandment in shaping the ecclesiology of the present-day church.[15]

Theological reflections and debates over Sabbath observance were particularly prevalent in early modern England, where traditionalist members of the Church of England and Puritans clashed repeatedly over their differing understandings as to how strictly the Sabbath should be kept. Both sides agreed, however, that the most important aspect of Sunday was going to church. Bishop Hugh Latimer, later executed for his Protestant views during the reign of Mary Tudor, preached a sermon in 1553 in which he described the purpose of Sunday as follows: "The holy day is ordained and appointed to none other thing, but that we should at that day hear the Word of God, and exercise ourselves in all godliness. . . . [It is] a day appointed of God that we should hear his word, and learn his laws, and so serve him."[16] For the Anglicans as for the Puritans, hearing God's Word, learning, and growing in godliness all took place first and foremost in church, thus reinforcing the need for regular church worship attendance for all.

THE AUTHORITIES' PUSH FOR SUNDAY-MORNING CHURCH ATTENDANCE

As noted in the account of Bessie Glass's tribulations, the standard expectation in all early modern communities, whatever their confessional outlook, was that everyone in the community would attend worship on Sunday mornings. In state-church systems, religious and political leaders worked together to mandate church attendance. In England under Edward VI, for instance, the Act of Uniformity of

---

[15]Primus, *Holy Time*, 138-44.
[16]Quotation from Latimer's sermon in Primus, *Holy Time*, 23.

1552 stated that everyone living in the king's realm was to attend
their local church on Sunday and on "other days ordained and used
to be kept as holy days." In his half-sister Elizabeth's reign, this
ordinance was reasserted and strengthened by the imposition of
increasingly heavy fines for those who would not comply.[17] In practice, it seems the elderly, the sick, youngsters under sixteen, the very
poor, and servants were not pursued for nonattendance. Instead,
the English authorities concentrated on prosecuting those with a
higher social status, usually men, to make a bigger impact and signal
the seriousness of their intent to enforce church attendance on all.[18]
Indeed, one of their main targets was recusant (Roman Catholic)
families, who did not join their Anglican neighbors in the parish
church, and instead fostered attendance at covert Catholic Masses
in the privacy of their homes. One way to limit the impact of penalties for refusal to conform to Anglican public worship was for
the leading member of the household to attend worship services in
the parish church, leaving his family to maintain Catholic worship
in the home setting. Although these men could be accused by fellow Catholics of being "Church Papists"—in other words, of con-
formity to Anglican worship under pressure—this approach could
be sufficient to divert the authorities' attention toward more un-
yielding targets.[19]

In smaller communities, such as city-states, church attendance
on Sundays was easier to enforce, simply due to smaller numbers
and closer communal bonds. Magistrates in the Reformed Swiss
cities regularly issued mandates regarding church attendance,

---

[17]Clive Field, "A Shilling for Queen Elizabeth: The Era of State Regulation of Church Attendance in England, 1552–1969," *Journal of Church and State* 50 (2008): 213-50, esp. 214-15.
[18]Field, "A Shilling for Queen Elizabeth," 217.
[19]For more on patterns of church attendance and religious practice among English Catholics,
whether recusants or those willing to conform at least outwardly to parish church-attendance
requirements, see Andrew Muldoon, "Recusants, Church-Papists, and 'Comfortable'
Missionaries: Assessing the Post-Reformation English Catholic Community," *The Catholic Historical Review* 86, no. 2 (2000): 242-57, esp. 250-53.

from the early Reformation onward. In Zurich, for instance, the city council issued a lengthy ordinance in 1530 about the importance of going to church. The ordinance stated that "everyone, whether noble or commoner, of high or low social rank, women and men, children and servants, along with all those who live and dwell in our city, territory, dominion, and area" had to attend worship "at least every Sunday."[20] The only ones who were excused were those who were sick or who presented other valid reasons for their nonattendance to the guilds or the communal authorities.[21] In other words, all absences from communal worship services had to be justified. In Geneva, the 1547 ordinances to regulate worship in the countryside took a similar approach when regulating attendance at Sunday worship:

> Everyone in each house is to come on Sundays, unless it be necessary to leave someone behind to take care of children or animals, under penalty of 3 sous. . . . Those who have man or maid servants, are to bring them or have them conveyed when possible, so that they do not live like cattle without instruction.[22]

The Genevan authorities, like their Zurich counterparts, expected that church attendance would cut across social classes—no one was exempt except in cases of necessity. Small fines were to be levied against those who did not comply. The requirement to go to church applied not only to household servants but also to those at the top: in 1545, the Genevan Small Council decided to pass an ordinance

---

[20]"Christenlich ansehung des gemeinen Kilchganngs . . . (1530)," in *Zürcher Kirchenordnungen 1520–1675*, ed. Emidio Campi and Philipp Wälchli (Zurich: Theologischer Verlag, 2011), 1:94-95 (translation mine).

[21]"Christenlich ansehung," 95.

[22]"Ordinances for the Supervision of Churches in the Country February 3, 1547," in *Calvin: Theological Treatises*, ed. J. K. S. Reid (Philadelphia: Westminster, 1977), 77. For purposes of comparison, Genevan farm laborers were paid fifteen sous a day at the height of harvest season in 1600.

mandating the leading magistrates and officers of the city to attend
Sunday sermons in the city's churches.[23]

The Swiss Reformed ordinances made clear connections between a
population's unwillingness to attend worship and divine anger mani-
fested through natural or human-made calamities.[24] For instance, the
city fathers of Basel in 1588 ascribed the current uncertain times featuring terrible wars and rising prices to God's outstretched rod of
punishment due to people's profound ungratefulness and sins. The
primary remedy offered was for everyone (husbands and wives, children and servants) to attend church more faithfully and more fervently
than before.[25] It is worth pointing out that the regular repetition of
such ordinances enjoining church attendance suggests that the population as a whole never managed to live up to these expectations.

Like the Anglicans and the Reformed, Lutheran church and state
leaders also mandated regular Sunday attendance at church. The
1573 church order of Oldenburg, in what is now Lower Saxony, for
instance, reminded people of the obligation to go to worship services,
and to make sure that their children and servants attended as well.[26]
In Lutheran Scandinavia, people were also told to attend church on
Sundays as part of their duty to observe the Sabbath. In the kingdom
of Sweden, for instance, the Church Order of 1571 mandated church
attendance on Sundays for everyone. Those who did not attend were
to be warned in the first instance, and if they subsequently failed to
come to Sunday worship, they were subject to a small fine.[27] In these

---

[23]*Les Sources du droit du canton de Genève,* ed. Emile Rivoire and Victor van Berchem (Aarau:
H. R. Sauerländer, 1930), 2:470.

[24]The term *Swiss Reformed* refers to the Protestant churches and communities who belonged
to the Swiss Confederation or its territories. Geneva did not join the Swiss Confederation
until 1815, and thus Geneva is not included in this group.

[25]"Sammelmandat (1588)," in *Basler Kirchenordnungen 1528–1675,* ed. Emidio Campi and
Philipp Wälchli (Zurich: Theologischer Verlag, 2012), 85-86.

[26]*Die evangelische Kirchenordnungen des XVI. Jahrhunderts: Niedersachsen,* ed. Emil Sehling
(Tübingen: J. C. B. Mohr, 1980), VII/2:1095.

[27]Mila Kuha, "Popular Religion in the Periphery: Church Attendance in 17th Century Eastern Finland," *Perichoresis* 13, no. 2 (2015): 17-33, esp. 20.

state churches, as in the Reformed and Anglican communities, these ordinances were issued by government leaders and carried the weight of state-enforced penalties for those who did not conform.

Catholics too were meant to be going to church Sunday by Sunday. Canon law gathered together in a compendium known as the *Decretals* during the papacy of Gregory IX in 1230 required Catholics to attend Mass on Sundays and on feast days in their own parish church.[28] By the sixteenth century, the canons or decrees of the Council of Trent underscored the importance of weekly attendance at Mass and sought to encourage attendance at parish churches by limiting the possibility of having Masses in other venues, such as in private homes. In its twenty-second session, held in September 1562, the Council of Trent ordered that bishops were to "admonish their people to go frequently to their own parish churches, at least on Sundays and the greater feast days."[29] At the local level, bishops and other Catholic church leaders implemented a range of strategies to push for more regular attendance at Mass. For instance, visitation records for Catholic communities in Galicia in early modern Spain uncovered persistent nonattendance at Mass, which not only contravened canon law but also harmed the parishioners' chances of learning more about their faith. In response, the visitors appointed by the bishop advocated fines for those who came late to Mass or did not come at all. To reduce the chances of temptations waylaying people who might otherwise come to Mass, the episcopal visitors also ordered that taverns that remained open during Mass be fined.[30]

---

[28] See Norman Tanner, *The Church in Medieval Norwich, 1370–1532* (Toronto: Pontifical Institute of Medieval Studies, 1984), 2.

[29] *The Canons and Decrees of the Council of Trent*, trans. H. J. Schroeder (Charlotte: TAN Books, 1978), session 22, "Decree concerning the things to be observed and avoided in the celebration of Mass," 152.

[30] Allyson Poska, *Regulating the People: The Catholic Reformation in Seventeenth-Century Spain* (Leiden: Brill, 1998), 61, 67.

Thus Catholic, Lutheran, Anglican, and Reformed church leaders in state churches shared the conviction that church attendance was vital and used fines or other penalties to make recalcitrant churchgoers conform. The authorities' complaints about reluctant attendance and the draw of competing activities masks the presence of faithful churchgoers, whose ready assent to going to worship was rarely formally noted. In other words, the complaints about nonattendance may paint an overly negative picture only because it was precisely those who skipped church who left traces in the records.

Yet in some instances at least, the barriers to going to church seemed less to do with unwillingness to come to worship and more to do with practical obstacles making it difficult for a person to attend. Take, for example, the cases of Pernette Roget and of Françoise, daughter of Amyed Danel. In both instances, the women were questioned by the Genevan Consistory because of their absence from worship. The two women responded that they did not come to church because they did not have appropriate clothes to wear. Pernette Roget's clothes were at the pawnshop, while Françoise said she "did not receive Communion because she is badly dressed and does not dare go with the others."[31] Indeed, the social distinctions affecting church attendance that these accounts highlight were even more severe in the case of another Françoise, the widow of Jean de La Barre. In 1560, when called before the Consistory for her absence from worship, she said "she did not go to sermons because when she does people spit on her and avoid her and it seems that this is because she is poor."[32]

Apparently, these women felt they could not join other Christians at worship because of their lack of appropriate clothing or their poverty.

---

[31]Pernette's sons were ordered to help their mother financially so she could retrieve her clothes from the pawnshop in the neighboring town of Evian. There is no record of the Consistory's response to Françoise Danel's concerns. *Registers of the Consistory of Geneva in the Time of Calvin*, ed. Robert Kingdon et al. (Grand Rapids, MI: Eerdmans, 2000), 104, 236.

[32]Thomas Lambert, "Preaching, Praying and Policing the Reform in Sixteenth-Century Geneva" (PhD diss., University of Wisconsin-Madison, 1998), 313.

Yet in most cases, the grounds for absence from church were not due to class distinctions or unkindness on the part of other congregants. Instead, ordinances and mandates on church attendance are full of the authorities' complaints about people who preferred to work or stay home or wander the streets or hang out in taverns or play cards and gamble than to join fellow believers in corporate worship.[33] Reasons not to go to church also included a preference for hunting, or target-shooting, or other outdoor recreations conflicting with worship times.[34] The pressure of sports schedules overlapping with Sunday-morning worship is nothing new! Solutions included ordering all businesses, especially taverns, to close their doors and cease serving customers during worship time. Already by 1537 the Genevan authorities told all shop owners to close their doors and keep them closed on Sunday morning during the time of the morning worship service.[35] To help businesses know when to shut up shop and parishioners know that it was time to head to worship, church bells rang in advance of the start of the worship service. In Zurich, for instance, the city's inhabitants were to assemble in church for Sunday worship by the time the bells had rung for the third time.[36] In Geneva, the practice was to ring the bells twice: once at least a half hour before the worship was due to begin, and a second time just before the worship service started.[37]

---

[33]Irrespective of their confessional outlook, authorities had the same complaints about the reasons for nonattendance. See Spanish Catholic leaders' complaints in Poska, *Regulating the People*, 66-67, and very similar complaints on the part of Reformed authorities in the Swiss lands in Alfred Ehrensperger, *Der Gottesdienst in Stadt und Landschaft Basel im 16. und 17. Jahrhundert* (Zurich: Theologischer Verlag, 2010), 127.

[34]"Sonntagsheiligung. Pflicht zum Predigtbesuch (1540?)," in *Zürcher Kirchenordnungen* 1:193.

[35]See Lambert, "Preaching, Praying," 306.

[36]"Christenlich ansehung," 95.

[37]Elsie McKee, *The Pastoral Ministry and Worship in Calvin's Geneva* (Geneva: Droz, 2016), 233.

SUNDAY-AFTERNOON AND WEEKDAY CHURCH ATTENDANCE

While church and state leaders expended considerable energy in making sure their populations attended church on Sunday mornings, they faced equal or greater challenges in getting people to show up for worship services at other times and on other days. On paper at least, the number of worship services in a given community over the course of a week could be quite large. By the time of Calvin's death in 1564, for instance, Geneva's three churches each offered between nine and thirteen services a week, including either three or four on Sundays.[38] The Swiss city of Basel held four services on Sundays, and two every weekday (at five o'clock and nine o'clock in the morning), as well as a prayer service on Tuesdays.[39] In Lutheran Württemberg, the figure was a more manageable five worship services a week in urban areas, and three in the countryside.[40] Across the board, however, church leaders clearly wanted to make sure that there were sufficient corporate worship opportunities for the faithful on a daily basis, at least in the urban areas, as well as multiple times of worship on Sundays.

Some of the Sunday-afternoon worship services were directed at young people and had a catechetical focus. Not surprisingly, getting youngsters to come back to church in the afternoon following the morning church service could be an uphill task. In the Lutheran territory of Württemberg, for instance, church visitation records between 1581 and 1621 showed that while the population's church-attendance record on Sunday morning was good, attendance rates fell away when it came to the midday catechism service. In principle, all servants and all inhabitants aged six to thirty (if still unmarried) were to attend the noontime teaching. Yet other attractions at times proved stronger, especially during the summer months, when young people preferred

---

[38]McKee, *The Pastoral Ministry*, 104-5.

[39]Amy Nelson Burnett, *Teaching the Reformation: Ministers and Their Message in Basel, 1529-1629* (Oxford: Oxford University Press, 2006), 56.

[40]Bruce Tolley, *Pastors & Parishioners in Württemberg During the Late Reformation, 1581-1621* (Stanford: Stanford University Press, 1995), 73.

to be out picking berries or socializing over coming back to church for the catechism service.[41] The youngsters were not the only ones to be reluctant—indeed, across German Lutheran territories, the authorities found that the population did not warm to the idea of coming back for an afternoon service on Sundays.[42]

Church and state leaders were aware of the challenges that stringent requirements for church attendance posed, especially when it came to weekday services. In many cases, rules for attendance at these other services were less strict than the ones governing the Sunday-morning worship. For instance, in the Genevan countryside the rule was that at minimum one member from each household should attend weekday services, leaving the others free to work or attend to household matters.[43] In Geneva itself, the main focus during the week was the Wednesday-morning worship service, which everyone was supposed to attend. As was the case on Sundays, shops were to close on Wednesday mornings until the worship service was over, thus preventing Genevans from being distracted by everyday activities when they were supposed to be going to church.[44] In Strasbourg from 1542 onward, the main weekday worship service took place on Tuesdays— again, everyone was meant to go, and work ceased during the worship time.[45] By offering options for daily worship for the pious, but concentrating efforts on getting the wider community to attend worship on one other day apart from Sundays, church and state leaders sought to find a workable compromise.

---

[41]Tolley, *Pastors & Parishioners*, 73-76.

[42]Tolley, *Pastors & Parishioners*, 77.

[43]"Ordinances for the Supervision of Churches in the Country," 77.

[44]Lambert, "Preaching, Praying," 306; *Les Sources du droit* (Ordinances dated March 1, 1549), 2:526-27. By 1581, the main weekday prayer service shifted from Wednesday to Thursday. See McKee, *The Pastoral Ministry*, 308.

[45]René Bornert, *La Réforme protestante du culte à Strasbourg au xvie siècle (1523–1598)* (Leiden: Brill, 1981), 186.

High Days and Holy Days

One particular challenge for church authorities in Protestant areas was how to manage the transition from Catholic to Protestant worship when it came to feast days. Catholics and Protestants agreed that the people should come together for worship on Sundays, but what about other key dates of the Christian calendar that fell on different days of the week, like Ascension Day (celebrated on a Thursday, forty days after Easter Sunday), or Good Friday, or Christmas in years when December 25 did not coincide with a Sunday? Early modern Catholics observed a wide range of feast days, from days honoring local saints to days associated with the life of the Virgin Mary, as well as the major traditional feast days of the Christian calendar, including Epiphany, Ash Wednesday, Maundy Thursday, Good Friday, Easter, Ascension Day, Pentecost, All Saints/All Souls, and the four Sundays of Advent leading up to Christmas.[46]

Martin Luther's early writings on liturgy and worship cut back on the traditional observance of many of the church's feast days. In his 1523 text *Concerning the Order of Public Worship*, Luther spoke out in favor of pruning the church calendar, though he did leave room for some optional observances:

> All the festivals of saints are to be discontinued. Where there is a good Christian legend, it may be inserted as an example after the Gospel on Sunday. The festivals of the Purification and Annunciation of Mary may be continued, and for the time being also her assumption and Nativity, although the songs in them are not pure. The festival of John the Baptist is also pure. Not one of the legends of the apostles is pure, except St. Paul's.

---

[46]For more on Catholic feast days, see Göran Malmstedt, "In Defence of Holy Days: The Peasantry's Opposition to the Reduction of Holy Days in Early Modern Sweden," *Cultural History* 3, no. 2 (2014): 103-25, esp. 105-6.

They may either be transferred to the [closest] Sunday or be celebrated separately, if one so desires.[47]

Thus in spite of his strong initial statement, Luther left room for some continued observance of traditional feast days. The various church orders testify that Lutherans retained many of the Catholic feast days. The list of feast days observed in Lutheran territories differed, however, depending on each ruler's preference. For instance, in the Palatinate under the Elector Ottheinrich, Lutherans were expected to be in church on all Sundays and on the following feast days: Christmas Eve and Christmas Day, New Year's Day, Epiphany, Easter Monday, Ascension Day, the Monday after Pentecost, three Marian feast days (her Purification, Annunciation, and Assumption), and the feast days for John the Baptist, Michael the Archangel, and for all the apostles.[48] Other areas made different choices: Sweden retained over thirty holy days apart from Sundays, whereas Denmark only kept sixteen.[49]

In England, the liturgical calendar was pared down significantly, beginning under Henry VIII, and continuing under both Edward VI and Elizabeth. By Elizabeth's reign, the Church of England officially marked the milestones of Christ's life as feast days, and the feast days of the apostles and Evangelists. Work was supposed to cease on these days, even if the feasts occurred on a weekday, and people were meant to be in church. Those who failed to honor these feast days could expect a reprimand from church leaders. The English also added new feast days to the calendar, especially ones marking the coronation of their monarchs and commemorations of major deliverances, such as the foiling of the Gunpowder Plot against James I, commemorated on

---

[47]Martin Luther, *Concerning the Order of Public Worship*, in *Luther's Works*, vol. 53, *Liturgy and Hymns*, ed. Ulrich S. Leopold (Philadelphia: Fortress, 1965), 14.

[48]Ottheinrich, "Kirchenordnung" (1556), in *Die Evangelischen Kirchenordnungen des XVIe Jahrhunderts*, ed. Emil Sehling (Tübingen: J. C. B. Mohr, 1969), 14:163.

[49]Malmstedt, "In Defence of Holy Days," 106-7.

November 5 each year.[50] This day of remembrance and thanksgiving expressed in worship services was particularly popular among English Puritans, who otherwise objected to worship observances for feast days other than Sundays. In this instance, the commemoration of the defeat of the Gunpowder Plot offered a golden opportunity for Puritan preachers to warn congregations about the ongoing dangers of resurgent Catholicism.[51]

Reformed areas tended to pare down the number of feast days drastically—in Scotland, for instance, the *First Book of Discipline* of 1561 threw out any observance of feast days whether associated with saints, with the Virgin Mary, or even with Christ.[52] The Scottish population, however, continued to want to celebrate many of these feast days, especially Christmas.[53] Because Reformed church leaders were worried about any possible persistence of what they saw as Catholic superstition, they tended to criticize any increased attendance at worship on days previously hallowed as major feast days for the church. For instance on December 25, 1551, during his sermon on Micah 5:7-14, Calvin took time to condemn those who had come to church specially on that day to mark the feast of Christmas, warning them of the dangers of marking one specific day in the church calendar.

> Now, I see here more people than I am accustomed to having at the sermon. Why is that? It is Christmas day. . . . But if you think that Jesus Christ was born today, you are as crazed as wild beasts. For when you elevate one day alone for the purpose of worshipping

---

[50]For more on this commemoration see Dennis H. Richardson, "Ever Remember Gunpowder, Treason and Plot!," *British Heritage* 9, no. 6 (1988): 40-46.

[51]For more on feast days and their observance in the English church in the sixteenth and seventeenth centuries, see David Cressy, "God's Time, Rome's Time, and the Calendar of the English Protestant Regime," *Viator* 34 (2003): 392-406.

[52]*The First Book of Discipline*, ed. James Cameron (Edinburgh: Saint Andrew Press, 1972), 88-89.

[53]See *The First Book of Discipline*, 88 (footnote) and a longer analysis by Margo Todd in *The Culture of Protestantism in Early Modern Scotland* (New Haven, CT: Yale University Press, 2002), 183-88.

God, you have just turned it into an idol. . . . It matters not whether
we recall our Lord's nativity on a Wednesday, Thursday, or some
other day. But when we insist on establishing a service of worship
based on our whim, we blaspheme God, and create an idol, though
we have done it all in the name of God.[54]

In Calvin's eyes, celebrating Christmas or other feasts of the church
year that did not fall on a Sunday was to reopen the door to Catholic
superstition rather than the true worship of God.

Although the Reformed are mostly known for doing away with feast
days or other dates in the church calendar in favor of a focus on Sunday
worship, they did expand the range of communal worship offerings in
one way—namely, by mandating popular attendance at special mid-
week services called together on an irregular basis. These gatherings
were known as days of prayer and fasting. People were summoned to
attend these special worship services at times of local or national threat,
whether natural (epidemics, drought, floods, etc.) or human-made
(wars, persecutions, threats of invasion, etc.). In Strasbourg beginning
in 1531, the pastors asked the magistrates to order special days of prayer.
In August of that year, the first such prayer service was held, calling on
God for help in the war against the Turks. By 1542, the practice became monthly: on Tuesdays once a month the population gathered for
a special time of prayer and preaching, sometimes accompanied by a
celebration of the Lord's Supper. All work and trade was to cease during such times of worship.[55] The Genevans also held special services of
prayer and fasting when human-made or natural disasters threatened
beginning in 1567, when they received news of the start of the second
French religious war.[56] Around fifteen such special worship services of

---

[54]John Calvin, *Sermons on the Book of Micah*, trans. and ed. Benjamin Farley (Phillipsburg,
NJ: P&R, 2003), 302-3.
[55]Bornert, *La Réforme protestante*, 185-86.
[56]*Registres de la compagnie des pasteurs de Genève*, ed. Olivier Fatio and Olivier Labarthe
(Geneva: Droz, 1969) 3:17.

prayer and fasting took place in Geneva between 1567 and 1620. The reasons for these gatherings included the Saint Bartholomew's Day Massacre in France in 1572, the war between Geneva and Savoy in 1589, the failed attack by Savoy against Geneva in 1602, and the outbreak of plague in 1615.[57] These occasional worship services took place on Wednesdays, the main weekday worship day in Geneva, and work ceased during the worship time, allowing everyone to participate. As the Company of Pastors noted after the 1578 prayer and fasting service, "a large number of people attended, both morning and evening."[58]

CONCLUSION

While the reformers altered many of the liturgical and worship practices, the fundamental importance of regular and faithful attendance at worship was one consistent feature. Whether Catholic, Lutheran, Reformed, or Anglican, church and state leaders agreed that it was vital for their populations to come to worship on Sunday mornings, and ideally also at other times as well. Reformers highlighted the theological importance of Sunday worship and upheld the duty of worship attendance for everyone across social classes and age groups. The popular response to this obligation varied, however, from wholehearted enthusiasm to reluctance, due to preferences for other leisure activities rather than going to church. As we shall see in the next chapter, the clash of expectations versus reality continued when parishioners finally made it to church—here too the authorities repeatedly complained about inattentiveness, misbehavior, and disruption. Yet in the Reformation era, parish pastors could still count on having the majority of their flock present at church services, having left their day-to-day obligations aside to join with others in the community in

---

[57]Olivier Fatio, "Le Jeûne genevois: réalité et mythe," *Bulletin de la société d'histoire et d'archéologie de Genève* 14 (1971): 391-494, esp. 392-93.

[58]See the account of the 1578 fast in Max Engammare, *Time, Punctuality, and Discipline* (Cambridge: Cambridge University Press, 2010), 74.

communal worship. In the subsequent chapters, we will explore what actually took place during these worship services.

For Further Reading

Field, Clive. "A Shilling for Queen Elizabeth: The Era of State Regulation of Church Attendance in England, 1552–1969." *Journal of Church and State* 50 (2008): 213-50.

Lambert, Thomas. "Preaching, Praying and Policing in Sixteenth-Century Geneva." PhD diss., University of Wisconsin-Madison, 1998.

Malmstedt, Göran. "In Defence of Holy Days: The Peasantry's Opposition to the Reduction of Holy Days in Early Modern Sweden." *Cultural History* 3.2 (2014): 103-25.

McKee, Elsie. *The Pastoral Ministry and Worship in Calvin's Geneva.* Geneva: Droz, 2016.

Poska, Allyson. *Regulating the People: The Catholic Reformation in Seventeenth-Century Spain.* Leiden: Brill, 1998.

Primus, John. *Holy Time: Moderate Puritanism and the Sabbath.* Macon, GA: Mercer University Press, 1989.

Tolley, Bruce. *Pastors and Parishioners in Württemberg During the Late Reformation, 1581–1621.* Stanford: Stanford University Press, 1995.

Two

At Church

The Public Worship being begun, the people are wholly to attend upon it, forbearing to read anything, except what the Minister is then reading or citing; and abstaining much more from all private whisperings, conferences, salutations, or doing reverence to any person present, or coming in; as also from all gazing, sleeping, and other undecent behavior, which may disturb the Minister or people, or hinder themselves or others in the service of God.

A Directory for the Public Worship of God (1645)

IMAGINE ARRIVING AT CHURCH for worship during the Reformation era. You enter through the door, and then what? What were the customs and practices regarding sitting, standing, kneeling, or making ritual gestures before or during the worship service? What were the authorities' expectations regarding appropriate behavior in church, and how far were these challenged by practices of popular sociability in the worship space? Did families sit together, or not? Was there any role or place for children in worship? Were marriages and

---

Text included in the *Book of Common Order of the Church of Scotland commonly known as John Knox's liturgy: and the Directory for the Public Worship of God agreed upon by the Assembly of Divines at Winchester*, ed. George Washington Sprott and Thomas Leishman (Edinburgh: Blackwood, 1868), 292.

funerals conducted as part of the regular worship service or separately? Beyond singing and joining in prayers, what role did lay people play in worship? How were worship leaders trained, and what characteristics did effective worship leaders display? This chapter will focus primarily on the practice of worship, drawing evidence from a wide range of sources, including eyewitness accounts, to provide a multidimensional account of how congregations experienced worship in the early modern period.

ᴗ

In 1556, an anonymous Catholic writer published a polemical dialogue in which he recounted what he had seen and heard during his time in Reformed Lausanne, near Geneva. He described the Reformed churches and their worship practices as follows:

> Inside, it is just like a college or a school. It is full of benches, and in the middle there is a pulpit for the preacher. In front of it, the low benches are for the women and small children, and further around the high benches are for the men, with no distinction of rank. Almost all the stained-glass windows are already destroyed, and thick dust up to the ankles is everywhere. . . . As soon as they come into church, each person chooses a spot and sits down, as in a school, and there they wait until the preacher goes into the pulpit. As soon as the preacher appears, they all kneel down except for him. He stands with his head uncovered and his hands folded together to pray. He prays a prayer he makes up out of his own mind, ending it with the *Pater Noster* but no *Ave Maria*, and does the whole thing in French, and the people quietly answer *So be it*. And twice a week (only in the cities), they sing a Psalm or part of a Psalm before the sermon. Everyone sings together: men, women, girls, and children, all of them sitting down. And if anyone prays

when he comes into church, people point their fingers at him and mock him, and hold him to be a Papist and an idolater.[1]

Not surprisingly, the author disagreed with much of what he saw in the worship services he attended, but his account offers a unique window both into the practice of Reformed worship at the time and into his own expectations for worship from a Catholic perspective. He felt that the setting for these worship services was all wrong: the images, even including in stained-glass windows, were all gone. The behavior of the worshipers startled him as well: from his perspective, the focus was too much on teaching and not enough on devotion.

A PLACE FOR COMMUNAL WORSHIP

One way to understand the worship priorities of early modern Christians is to consider how their places of worship were laid out in the interior, particularly when communities had the opportunity to construct a new building for worship, set up according to their specifications. For instance, in the Lutheran city of Ulm, a new parish church, known as the Holy Trinity Church, was built between 1617 and 1621. The building was rectangular and had a flat ceiling rather than a vaulted one. The pulpit stood in the center of the northern wall, and the seating was laid out on the ground level and on a balcony on two sides of the building. The inauguration sermon, preached by the Lutheran superintendent Conrad Dieterich, praised the building's interior. He highlighted the presence of a "splendid altar" and accompanying religious artwork, the large windows that let in the light, and the comfortable seating. An inauguration poem also survives, describing the central crucifix topped by a sun and the tetragrammaton for the name of God. A further document from a church architect in Ulm, Joseph Furttenbach the elder, outlined his

---

[1] *Passevent Parisien* (1556) in Karin Maag, ed., *Lifting Hearts to the Lord: Worship with John Calvin in Sixteenth-Century Geneva* (Grand Rapids, MI: Eerdmans, 2016), 63.

plans for the ideal Lutheran church. This 1649 document called for a flat ceiling in the church, to limit the problems pastors faced in terms of excessive reverberation when preaching in churches with vaulted ceilings. It also rejected the use of pillars, because these tended to block lines of sight between the congregation and the pulpit. Finally, in a move designed to make church attendance more comfortable for everyone, the architect recommended the use of wood paneling to insulate the building's interior and even suggested that the pulpit be built with a special box to provide a means of heat to keep the preacher's feet warm![2]

In Reformed areas, new church buildings were also erected in the early modern period that reflected the confessional group's worship priorities. In Scotland, the town of Burntisland, north of Edinburgh, built a church at the very end of the sixteenth century. This square-shaped building features the pulpit in the center, and rising tiers of pews and benches all around it. In a second phase of building, an upper story of galleries was built at the expense of the various guilds, so that their members "commodiously . . . may hear and see the minister at preaching and prayers."[3] The same desire to have the pulpit as the focal point and to have the seating arranged around it held true in France, where Huguenots constructed places of worship for their own use. Although these buildings have not survived due to the vicissitudes of the civil wars and the pattern of deliberate destruction following the revocation of the Edict of Nantes in 1685, enough evidence survives in texts and images from the time to provide a clear understanding of their interior layout. For example, a well-known painting of the Temple de Paradis, built in Lyon for Huguenot worship in 1564, depicts an oval interior centered on a tall

---

[2]Philip Hahn, "Sensing Sacred Space: Ulm Minster, the Reformation, and Parishioners' Sensory Perception, c. 1470 to 1640," *Archiv für Reformationsgeschichte* 105 (2014): 55-91, esp. 84-86.
[3]Andrew Spicer, *Calvinist Churches in Early Modern Europe* (Manchester: Manchester University Press, 2007), 57-60.

pulpit. The building offered seating both on the main floor and on an upper level.[4] The church itself was torn down in 1567, but the survival of the painting provides insight into the way the worship space was set up. Other Huguenot places of worship built in the later sixteenth and early seventeenth centuries shared common features: they were rectangular or polygonal, with the pulpit placed in the center, and with as few architectural obstacles to people's sightlines as possible. Wealthier Huguenot communities ensured that their places of worship had large windows with clear glass to let in sufficient light, and constructed galleries, sometimes on two floors, to accommodate everyone in the congregation.[5]

Both these Lutheran and Reformed new constructions provided places of worship that to a Catholic would look very much like a school, as in the first vignette. The pulpit stood in the center, and the furnishings and interior architecture were all designed to encourage congregations to focus on the preacher with their eyes and especially with their ears. Yet even though the layout might have suggested that the aim was simply to impart instruction from the pastor-teacher to the congregants-students, the church building still retained its holy character, both among church leaders and for the population.

A SACRED SPACE

Before turning to the practice of worship in church buildings, it is worth taking a moment to understand how church buildings and their immediate surroundings, such as adjacent graveyards, were viewed by religious authorities and laypeople in the late medieval and early modern world. In the medieval world, and in Catholic churches in the Reformation era and beyond, the sacred character of church buildings came from their consecration: a ritual of blessing and anointing carried out by bishops, which transferred the space from the secular to

---

[4]Spicer, *Calvinist Churches*, 172-73.
[5]Spicer, *Calvinist Churches*, 184-200.

Figure 2.1. Jean Perissin, *Le Temple de Paradis* (1569-70)

the spiritual realm. The ritual of consecration included the use of holy water, incense, and signs of the cross, as well as the dedication of relics associated with the lives of saints, the Virgin Mary, or Christ. These relics were usually placed in or on the high altar.[6]

The reformers also had to address the issue of sacred space—this reality surfaced in a number of ways, not least when it came time to dedicate a new church building for worship. In 1544, Luther preached at the first worship service in the newly built chapel of the Electors of Saxony in Torgau. In his sermon, he specifically addressed the issue

---

[6]Hellmut Zschoch, "Was macht die Kirche zum 'Gotteshaus'? Wie sich die Bedeutung des Kirchgebäudes durch die Reformation wandelt," *Luther* 87, no. 1 (2016): 35-44, esp. 35.

of consecration of places of worship, and made clear distinctions between the Catholic and Lutheran understanding of that practice.

> My dear friends! Now we want to consecrate this new house
> and dedicate it to our Lord Jesus Christ. But this is not my task
> alone. You too should reach for the aspergillum and the censer,
> so that this house will therefore be set up for nothing other
> than our loving Lord speaking to us himself through his holy
> Word, and we in turn speaking to him through prayer and
> praise. Therefore, to ensure that [this space] is blessed and ded-
> icated in a Christian fashion, not like the Papist churches, with
> their episcopal anointings and censings, we want to proceed ac-
> cording to God's command and will, in hearing and reflecting
> on God's Word.[7]

According to Luther, church buildings needed to be consecrated as
sacred space, but the focal point that ensured their holiness was not
the ritual of consecration but the presence of Word-centered worship.
Subsequent Lutheran pastors continued the practice of consecrating
churches, and developed a repertoire of sermons for the occasion,
mostly referencing the dedication of the temple in Jerusalem during
the reign of Solomon (1 Kings 8).[8] By the 1630s, Lutheran church
consecrations could become large-scale events, as in Regensburg in
December 1631, involving city-wide processions, a morning worship
service with a sermon and Communion, and an afternoon worship
service with another sermon and the celebration of the sacrament
of baptism.[9]

---

[7]Martin Luther, "Sermon for the Dedication of the Church at Torgau," 1544, quoted in
Zschoch, "Was macht die Kirche zum 'Gotteshaus'?" 39 (translation mine).
[8]Vera Isaiasz, "Early Modern Lutheran Churches: Redefining the Boundaries of the Holy
and the Profane," in *Lutheran Churches in Early Modern Europe*, ed. Andrew Spicer (Farnham, UK: Ashgate, 2012), 17-37, esp. 26-27.
[9]Isaiasz, "Early Modern Lutheran Churches," 31-32.

Although the presence of buildings set aside for worship continued to be important for Lutheran and Reformed communities, so
much so that they were willing to invest significant amounts of time
and money to refurbish existing churches or set up new ones, religious leaders had to tread carefully. Luther and other reformers
agreed that Word-centered worship could take place anywhere and
was not restricted to church buildings. But for practical reasons, and
because prayers and praises gained in strength and power when the
entire community was present, church buildings were needed as a
place to bring the worshiping community together.[10] On the one
hand, they wanted to ensure reverent and devout behavior in these
spaces, but on the other hand, they wanted to make sure that their
communities did not venerate the space itself or misuse it for "superstitious" practices. In Geneva, for instance, all church buildings were
locked outside of service times. As the church ordinances for the
Genevan countryside noted in 1547,

> Of Times of Meeting at Church
> Buildings are to remain shut for the rest of the time, in order
> that no one outside the hours may enter for superstitious rea-
> sons. If anyone be found making any particular devotion inside
> or nearby, he is to be admonished: if it appears to be a supersti-
> tion which he will not amend, he is to be chastised.[11]

The Genevan authorities thus signaled their desire to control access
to the church building in order to deter unsanctioned individual lay
devotional actions that might have hearkened back to Catholicism.
Individual devotional practices that deviated from the norms could
be caught and corrected more effectively when the whole community
gathered for worship.

---

[10]Zschoch, "Was macht die Kirche zum 'Gotteshaus'?," 41.
[11]"Ordinances for the Supervision of Churches in the Country," in *Calvin: Theological Treatises*, ed. J. K. S. Reid (Philadelphia: Westminster, 1954), 79.

Furthermore, the reformers agreed that what made the church holy was the action of communal worship itself, oriented around the preaching and hearing of God's Word. Outside of the worship services, the building itself did not contain the presence of God.[12] However, this rejection of the intrinsic holiness of the church building itself was difficult to sustain, particularly given the importance placed on consecrations. In their sermons, seventeenth-century Lutheran pastors definitely described their churches as intrinsically sacred. The Lutheran superintendent Christoph Schleupner declared in his consecration sermon at Hildesheim in 1603 that the church building was "not a common house for citizens, not a town hall or a chancery, not a princely palace or a royal castle, even less a drinking house, but a temple, a church, a house of God which, because of its inhabitant, is preferable to all earthly living quarters and profane buildings."[13] The presence of God made the building into a church—in this sermon, at least, the shift away from Luther's emphasis on the preaching of the Word and the presence of the congregation as the two markers defining a consecrated church is very noticeable.

Yet whether the church edifice was intrinsically holy, or made holy by the community gathering for worship, religious authorities agreed that the space was worthy of respect. From the perspective of medieval church leaders, both the church building itself and the adjoining graveyard were sacred spaces, thus restricting the kinds of activities that could take place there. In 1451, for instance, the bishop of Exeter Edmund Lacy ruled that

> places consecrated to God [should] be venerated by all, and by no means profaned or in any way violated by a jarring or unsuitable activity, whether in working, jesting, or playing . . . ; there should be no laughter, shouting, immoderate mirth, indecent

---

[12]Zschoch, "Was macht die Kirche zum 'Gotteshaus'?," 42.
[13]Quoted in Isaiasz, "Early Modern Lutheran Churches," 35.

and indiscreet dances, indecent mockeries and harmful plays
proper to the market-place or the stage.[14]

These rules were not unique to the pre-Reformation era: in fact
church leaders in the Reformation period continue to issue ordinances in the same vein, barring any kind of sales, dancing, noise,
quarrels, games, plays, or other secular activities in churchyards, especially if these activities took place during worship time and disrupted the services.[15]

These expectations, however, clashed with the laity's understanding as to how the space should be used, both on practical and spiritual
bases. Lay Christians highlighted their understanding of the power of
sacred spaces by favoring them for certain activities. For instance,
making an agreement by shaking hands in a graveyard was thought to
hold more power than making an agreement elsewhere.[16] Because
they provided access to open space, which could be at a premium especially in walled cities and towns, churchyards also continued to be the
venue for various games and sports. Furthermore, the presence of
people coming and going to church meant that peddlers, sellers, and
fairs made use of churchyards for their activities, in some instances
right through the Reformation era.

Training the Worship Leaders

Before considering both the theory of appropriate worship behavior
and the lived experiences of worshipers in church, it is worth spend-
ing a moment on the training of those entrusted with leading worship. In most instances, early modern clergy who led worship learned
their skills by observation and by practice, rather than through formal courses in worship. Clergy in several confessional groups could

---

[14]Quoted in David Dymond, "God's Disputed Acre," *Journal of Ecclesiastical History* 50, no. 3 (1999): 464-97, esp. 464.
[15]Dymond, "God's Disputed Acre," 484.
[16]Dymond, "God's Disputed Acre," 471.

turn to printed liturgies, which laid out the various component parts of a worship service in order. Medieval Catholic clergy made use of a range of missals or liturgical service books containing the text of the liturgy of the Mass and other sacraments, Scripture readings, antiphons, and so on. Although the core content was the same, variant editions proved popular in different regions, such as the Sarum rite in England or the rite of Breslau in the German lands. In 1570, these variant editions were replaced by one authoritative volume, the Roman Missal, promulgated by Pope Pius V. Lutheran territorial churches established orders of worship and laid these out in their church orders, basing them on Luther's order for a Latin Mass (1523) and a German Mass (1526). For their part, Anglican clergy used successive editions of the Book of Common Prayer, whereas Reformed clergy turned to liturgies authorized by their churches, including the *Forme des Prieres* (1542) for Geneva or the Book of Common Order (1562) in Scotland.[17] In many instances, these texts not only provided the words of the liturgy but also offered rubrics that guided the pastor's actions and that laid out expectations concerning the role of the congregation.

THE AUTHORITIES' EXPECTATIONS FOR WORSHIPERS

Across the confessional spectrum, civil and religious authorities agreed: congregations attending worship were to be quiet, attentive, and focused on the liturgy. They were not to chat to their neighbors, wander about, or get distracted by others. They were also not supposed to fall asleep. They were to arrive on time and make sure to remain all the way to the end of the worship service. To ensure that standards of proper behavior in worship services were being met, religious authorities regularly investigated these matters, laying out both their expectations and the

---

[17]Frank Senn, *Christian Liturgy: Catholic and Evangelical* (Minneapolis: Fortress, 1997), 267-380.

problems that could arise. For instance, the churchwardens who inspected English churches in the early seventeenth century were to ask,

> Whether any of your parishioners . . . do not reverently behave themselves during the time of divine service, devoutly kneeling, when the general confession of sins, the litany, the ten commandments, and all the prayers and collects are read, and using all due and lowly reverence, when the blessed name of the Lord Jesus is mentioned, and standing up when the articles of the belief are read?[18]

In this instance, the authorities clearly associated reverent posture with devout attentiveness, and they wanted to ensure that congregation members marked the transitions from one holy moment of the worship service to another by kneeling, bowing, or rising to their feet.

In the Catholic churches of early modern Spain, the authorities were equally keen to regulate parishioners' behavior during Mass, placing particular emphasis on the importance of silence during communal worship:

> The sacred temples, places dedicated to God Our Lord and his saints, where the faithful Christians congregate particularly to invoke and serve him and to be heard, have to be very revered, and in them one has to be very quiet and one must stop all things which might disturb the divine offices or impede the devotion of the ministers who say them or of the rest who hear them.[19]

This emphasis on reverent silence clashed, however, with congregations' own expectations about how to behave during worship.

---

[18] Visitation articles of the early Stuart church (spelling modernized), cited in Christopher Marsh, "Sacred Space in England, 1560–1640: The View from the Pew," *Journal of Ecclesiastical History* 53, no. 2 (2002): 286-311, esp. 290.

[19] Instructions from Bishop Valdivieso in 1622, quoted in Allyson Poska, *Regulating the People: The Catholic Reformation in Seventeenth-Century Spain* (Leiden: Brill, 1998), 62.

The People's Behavior in Church

One facet of the difficulties in regulating congregations' behavior in church, in Protestant areas at least, was that the expectations for congregational behavior during worship had undergone a significant shift. Whereas during a Catholic Mass the faithful could and did move around the worship space, engaging in personal devotions and prayers before various altars and statues, Protestant congregations, especially in Reformed areas, were meant to stay put in their seats and listen with quiet attentiveness, an especially challenging undertaking during sermons that could last an hour or more. This transition from Catholic to Protestant worship practices did not always go smoothly, especially in the first generation. For instance, in the first years of the Genevan Reformation, the Genevan Consistory admonished several people for continuing to engage in their Catholic devotions in an undertone during the sermon. The same complaint surfaced in England, where the collection of authorized sermons during the reign of Elizabeth included the "Homily on the Right Use of the Church." This sermon contrasted Paul's admonition to encourage "glorifying with one spirit and mouth" (Rom 15:6) with the contemporary practice of the English church, "when every man and woman, in several pretence of devotion, prayeth privately; one asking, another giving thanks, another reading doctrine, and not regarding to hear the common prayer of the minister."[20]

Another problem church leaders in all confessional groups faced was simply trying to maintain the attention and worshipful focus of the congregation. The religious authorities' injunctions about reverent behavior and silence persistently ran into difficulties, largely because gathering for worship was as much a social occasion as a devotional one for many in early modern Europe. In seventeenth-century Spain, for instance, people conversed with one another, even stepping

---

[20]"On the Right Use of the Church," in *Certain Sermons or Homilies, appointed to be read in churches* (London: printed for the Prayerbook and Homily Society, 1852), 152-53.

outside the building during Mass to continue their conversation.[21] Other aspects of worship led to movement among the congregants, rather than stillness, particularly when the consecrated Communion hosts were elevated or when relics were displayed. People would surge forward to get as close as possible to these holy elements, leading to concerns about crowd control.[22]

In Lutheran Finland, the religious authorities complained about people who stood silently, without participating in the worship service or making any effort to join in the singing. Meanwhile, others were sitting on the floor and gossiping or chatting with their neighbors while apprentices caused havoc in the galleries.[23] Things were no better in the German Lutheran churches: complaints from the clergy in Ulm from the 1560s onward listed the noise made by peasants taking shortcuts through the church building to get from one side of town to the other, the chatter and laughter of members of baptismal or wedding parties, children's screams, and dogs' jingling collars and barking.[24]

As noted in chapter one, the authorities' ordinances requiring everyone to attend worship on Sundays, and perhaps one other time during the week, conflicted with the difficulties in maintaining order and quiet in a church filled with the entire generational spectrum, from older people down to small children. There was no Sunday school or separate program or space for children during the worship service, and the challenges of staying awake, quiet, and focused were, not surprisingly, profound. In many locations, boys who were in school attended worship with their classmates, sitting on reserved benches under the eye of their teacher. As highlighted later in chapter seven, some schoolboys also played an active role in

---

[21]Poska, *Regulating the People*, 62.

[22]Poska, *Regulating the People*, 65-66.

[23]Riitta Laitinen, "Church Furnishings and Rituals in a Swedish Provincial Cathedral from 1527 to c. 1660," in Spicer, *Lutheran Churches in Early Modern Europe*, 311-31, esp. 328-29.

[24]Hahn, "Sensing Sacred Space," 78.

the worship service by helping the cantor to lead the congregational singing. Some churches tried a seating arrangement by which children sat together on benches toward the back of the sanctuary and upstairs in the balcony, as in Castres in France from 1640 to 1650, but this plan was quickly abandoned, because the children made too much noise, preventing others from hearing the sermon. Instead, most churches reserved seating for children in the front, where their behavior could be monitored under the eyes of the adults in the congregation.[25]

BAD BEHAVIOR IN CHURCH

Apart from not paying attention, congregation members also got in trouble for their dramatic reactions to what they heard or witnessed during worship services. Most often, the people in question were reacting to a sermon to which they objected. For instance, in 1679, Elizabeth Finchett from the parish of Eccleston in Cheshire took strong exception to the preacher's sermon one Sunday. As noted in the deposition against her,

> And particularly one Lord's Day the curate there earnestly in his sermon exhorting the people to peace and passing Amity and Christian Affection to each other you the said Elizabeth as one offended and enraged at the said Wholesome doctrine did in a very uncivil and irreverent manner throw away your Bible and spectacles from you and in the greatest haste and rage you could rise up from the seat or pew, rushed by the rest in the seat, and clamorously muttering as you passed along hastened through the alley [aisle] and so out of the Church.[26]

---

[25]Raymond Mentzer, "Les débats sur les bancs dans les Églises réformées de France," *Bulletin de la société de l'histoire du protestantisme français* 152 (2006): 393-406, esp. 394.

[26]Quoted in Marsh, "Sacred Space in England," 303 (spelling modernized).

Although the account does not specify exactly what upset Elizabeth Finchett, her actions that Sunday were sufficiently disruptive to the rest of the congregation and to the orderly process of worship that her case was brought to a church court.

More seriously, acts of violence could take place in the worship space, even during worship services, when long-standing feuds or quarrels came to a head. In early modern Scotland, for instance, pastors and kirk sessions had to deal repeatedly with repercussions of violence that broke out as congregations gathered for worship. In 1579 the Wednesday-afternoon worship service in the main church of St Andrews was disrupted when two sailors armed with swords attacked James Cuthbert as he sat listening to the sermon, leaving him with a head injury. In 1591, a brawl broke out between two feuding groups at the end of a worship service in Stow, near Edinburgh, leaving one man dead and another wounded. In 1593, in a church near Stirling, William Sinclair and his two sons were killed as they left the building after worship. These deaths came as the result of a long-standing feud between William Sinclair and Sir Archibald Stirling of Keir, originally due to a dispute over land, but progressing to the death of Sir Archibald's brother James at the hands of William Sinclair, and now these three murders on the Sabbath in the churchyard.[27] It is worth wondering whether the Reformed move away from considering the church building as an intrinsically sacred space made people less inhibited about carrying out such acts in churches or churchyards. Not surprisingly, church leaders worked diligently to prevent these feuds from erupting into violence by striving to reconcile quarreling parties at the earliest possible stage. Church and state also cooperated in creating rituals of reconciliation between aggressor and victim, usually mandating that these rituals take place in the location of the original offense—namely, within the perimeter of the church. So for instance,

---

[27]Michael Graham, "Conflict and Sacred Space in Reformation-Era Scotland," *Albion* 33, no. 3 (2001): 371-87, esp. 371-73.

Allan and Patrick Carstairs, who had wounded James Cuthbert during the sermon in 1579, were made to participate in an atonement ritual in the very same spot during a worship service, sitting on the stools of repentance in front of the whole community, and then kneeling in front of James Cuthbert in apology, offering him their swords that had wounded him. They were also made to pay for his medical care.[28] This public ritual of repentance and apology, enacted at the very spot where the original offense had taken place, both acknowledged the wrong done to James Cuthbert and repaired the breach in the community gathered before the face of God.

SEATING ARRANGEMENTS

Although there is evidence of various kinds of seating in pre-Reformation churches,[29] the increasing focus on the sermon in Protestant worship led to an expansion in the provision of fixed seating around the pulpit for the congregation. Evidence from England, for instance, suggests that the installation or renovation of pews and benches was one main way that wealthier members of congregations invested in their church buildings after the Reformation.[30] This development gave rise to a number of challenges. One simply had to do with the rational use of space: one person's seating was not supposed to block access or prevent others from having adequate sightlines to the pulpit or the chancel (the location for the celebration of the Lord's Supper in early modern English churches). The other main challenge involved conflicts between members of the congregation as to who should sit where: were all seats equally open to everyone, or did individuals and families have rights to certain seats, whether due to custom, habit, or payment? In England, individuals and families claimed exclusive rights to occupy pews that they had erected or paid for, an

---

[28]Graham, "Conflict and Sacred Space," 384-85.
[29]Marsh, "Sacred Space in England," 291.
[30]Marsh, "Sacred Space in England," 297-98.

attitude that conflicted with the churchwardens' conviction that they had the authority to assign seats in church. In 1607, for instance, the churchwardens at Chatteris near Ely tried to get Robert Phickas to move from his seat, because they wanted to assign it to Agnes Key. Phickas, however, refused to move or make room for her beside him, asserting that the seat was his own.[31] Similar conflicts took place in Reformed France, where French consistories spent endless hours trying to establish seating charts and determining which person or family had an assigned seat in which place. Most of the quarrels that surface in the records involve women, whose seating was usually located near the pulpit. Conflicts ranged from women nailing cushions in place to mark the spot they considered their own to rivalries and quarrels over the positioning of a bench for one family that meant someone else's bench had to be moved over.[32] The most protracted case, from 1639 to 1642, involved two rival families in Alès, and featured multiple appeals and counterappeals, all the way to the provincial synod. In the end, all the protagonists were barred from the Lord's Supper because of their refusal to come to terms, and both families ended up no longer attending the weekly worship services.[33]

Apart from conflict between individuals and families over their seating location, the other main effect of the installation of seating was the setting aside of reserved seating for the most prominent members of the congregation. In other words, while officially all seating was equal and there were no reserved seats, in practice, the social hierarchies that prevailed outside the church building were replicated inside the worship space. In France, both Catholic and Reformed places of worship set aside reserved seating for royal officials, nobles, church patrons, and magistrates. These seats could be wider, deeper, raised up, and certainly more comfortable than the benches set out

[31]Marsh, "Sacred Space in England," 300-301.
[32]Mentzer, "Les débats sur les bancs," 395.
[33]Mentzer, "Les débats sur les bancs," 396-97.

for ordinary members of the congregation. Seats for royal officials usually featured cloth or tapestry displaying the fleur-de-lis (the symbol of the French king), whereas civic leaders' seating could display the community's coat of arms. Nobles and patrons of local churches could also display their coats of arms on or around their seats.[34]

Although the processes and controversies over seating arrangements in early modern churches might seem peculiar to a modern audience, they provide clear evidence of the hybrid character of these sacred spaces. On the one hand, church services brought the entire community together to worship God. On the other hand, the social distinctions that divided people in their everyday lives persisted even when they crossed the church's threshold.

The intersection between corporate worship and day-to-day life also surfaced at key moments of individual Christians' existence, most notably at the time of their marriages and their funerals. These two instances were marked by church rituals, albeit in varied forms.

MARRIAGE SERVICES

Across the confessional spectrum, religious leaders insisted that for a marriage to be fully valid, the wedding ceremony had to take place in church. This insistence on a church ceremony cut across popular practice, which held that the engagement—that is, reciprocal promises to marry made in front of witnesses—was what made for a valid marriage, and couples could live together as husband and wife after that point. From this popular standpoint, specific religious rituals, from the very simple, such as a clerical blessing of the parties and of the rings, all the way to a nuptial Mass, were not mandatory.[35]

---

[34]Andrew Spicer, "The Huguenots and Marks of Honor and Distinction in the Parish Church and Reformed Temple," in *Emancipating Calvin: Culture and Confessional Identity in Francophone Reformed Communities*, ed. Karen Spierling, Erik de Boer, and R. Ward Holder (Leiden: Brill, 2018), 230–49, esp. 233–40.

[35]Bryan Spinks, "Conservation and Innovation in Sixteenth-Century Marriage Rites," in *Worship in Medieval and Early Modern Europe: Change and Continuity in Religious Practice,*

Yet from the clergy's point of view, a wedding ceremony conducted at church was the necessary step in declaring a marriage fully legitimate. While church leaders insisted on the necessity of a wedding ceremony, they also enforced rules that prohibited church weddings from taking place at certain times in the church year. The medieval church forbade weddings during Lent up to and including Easter Sunday, and during Advent up to and including Christmas Day. The Lutheran church did not allow weddings during Advent or Lent.[36] In the Church of England, over 140 days of the year were officially not available for wedding ceremonies, because these days fell in liturgical seasons where weddings were prohibited due to the need to focus on devotional matters. These seasons included Lent, Advent, and the period between the Sunday before Ascension Day and the Sunday after Pentecost. However, wealthier couples who did not want to wait could purchase a special license to allow them to marry even within these prohibited periods.[37]

In the Catholic Church both before and after the Reformation, the marriage ritual was a sacrament. A full Catholic wedding ritual involved a clear transition from secular to sacred space, since the first part of the ceremony took place at the church door. Weddings did not, however, need to take place with a congregation present, during a regular worship service. This ritual at the entranceway to the sacred space of the church building included the priest's formal declaration of the couple's intent to marry (and a moment to allow for any objections), the reciprocal vows, and the gift of a ring to the bride. Only after these rituals had been completed did the priest, the couple, and their accompanying family and friends move from the church

ed. Karin Maag and John Witvliet (Notre Dame, IN: University of Notre Dame Press, 2004), 243-78, esp. 266-67.

[36]Susan Karant-Nunn, *The Reformation of Ritual: An Interpretation of Early Modern Germany* (London: Routledge, 1997), 17.

[37]David Cressy, *Birth, Marriage, and Death: Ritual, Religion, and the Life-Cycle in Tudor and Stuart England* (Oxford: Oxford University Press, 1997), 298-99.

door to stand before the altar. At that point, the priest celebrated a
Mass, with the wedding couple kneeling on the steps leading to the
altar. After the Mass and the blessing, the husband was to receive the
kiss of peace from the priest and pass it to his bride.[38] Many couples,
however, dispensed with the wedding Mass, and only participated in
the rituals at the church door.[39]

Lutheran wedding services brought the couple into the church
from the very start. Because marriage was not a sacrament, Luther
left it up to local political authorities to prescribe how the wedding
ceremony should be conducted, though he did offer advice and models for a wedding liturgy, including the exchange of vows and the
prayers of the pastor. Lutheran political leaders came up with various
rules governing church weddings—some insisted that weddings
should only take place during a regular worship service, usually after
the sermon, so that the whole congregation could serve as witnesses
to the promises being made. However, other civil authorities did not
allow weddings to take place during Sunday worship, as the accompanying celebrations were seen as being incompatible with the Sabbath. In these territories, couples had to hold their church weddings
on a weekday instead.[40] Regardless of the day on which the marriage
occurred, the emphasis on the need to have one's wedding ceremony
take place in the sacred space of the church was a constant, both to
underline the solemnity of the vows and to ensure community over-
sight. For instance, the ordinances from Saxony in 1557 declare,

> And because some [people] get themselves married at home in
> their houses, courts, even under the sky and not in their church,
> from which all manner of impropriety follows, from now on
> except when necessary the marriage and giving together or

---

[38]Cressy, *Birth, Marriage, and Death,* 336-38.
[39]Karant-Nunn, *Reformation of Ritual,* 9.
[40]Karant-Nunn, *Reformation of Ritual,* 16-17.

blessing of the bride and the groom shall take place nowhere other than in the church before the Christian community, and with the prior knowledge of both parties' parents, guardians, or next of kin.[41]

Clearly even by the 1550s, the popular understanding that a wedding need not involve a trip to the church still prevailed among some families in Saxony.

In Reformed areas, though marriage was not considered a sacrament, couples were to exchange vows in church in the presence of the congregation during a regular worship service for the wedding to be legitimate. Couples had to notify the pastor in advance that they intended to marry, so that the names of the prospective husband and wife could be announced from the pulpit in the preceding weeks (the banns), so that anyone who knew of reasons why the marriage should not take place could inform the religious authorities. The usual period of time between the initial proclamation of the banns and the actual wedding was between three and six weeks. The wedding liturgy itself was brief, laying out the respective duties of husbands and wives according to Scripture. The pastor called on the congregation to fulfill a key role in the liturgy: not only to speak up if there was any impediment to the marriage but also to serve as witnesses to the vows.[42] In the process, the Reformed decisively moved the marriage liturgy from a private ceremony involving family and friends to a public one engaging the entire worshiping community.

FUNERAL SERVICES AND BURIALS

Both before and after the Reformation, the church building continued to play a key role in the final ritual of everyone's life—namely, their funeral. Catholic funeral practices involved processions, torches,

---

[41]Quoted in Karant-Nunn, *Reformation of Ritual*, 17.
[42]"The Form of Marriage" in Sprott and Leishman, *The Book of Common Order*, 129-34.

bell-ringing, and funeral and memorial Masses. Indeed, in areas where Catholics and Protestants were in conflict, as in France for instance, elaborate funeral rituals became the hallmark of a genuine Catholic funeral, whereas Huguenot funerals were largely devoid of liturgy. In fact, the distinction was so strong that any Catholic wishing for a simple funeral in the decades after 1560 risked being accused of being a covert heretic.[43]

Reformed church leaders wanted to make a clear distinction between what they perceived as superstitious Catholic funeral rites and their own practices. Yet in most instances even these attempts at reconfiguring the rites surrounding the dead still involved the church space. In the officially Reformed Dutch Republic, for instance, the Dutch Reformed clergy condemned all superstitious practices associated with pre-Reformation funerals, and in fact, the church leadership disassociated itself completely from burial rites. However, in spite of these strictures, the deceased members of Reformed families continued to be buried under the floors of the churches, just as their Catholic forebears had been. This seemingly odd clash between ordinance and practice stemmed from the fact that the church buildings in which the Reformed congregations worshiped were not the property of the church leadership but of the civic community. Thus burials in the church building were permissible, and even encouraged in some places as a fundraising venture, since people had to pay for the interment and the burial plot itself.[44]

The Reformed clergy's discomfort with the idea of burials within the church building transcended national boundaries. For instance, the Scottish *Form of Prayers*, originally written in Geneva in 1556, set out the following practices: "The corpse is reverently brought to the

---

[43]Penny Roberts, "Contesting Sacred Space: Burial Disputes in Sixteenth-Century France," in *The Place of the Dead: Death and Remembrance in Late Medieval and Early Modern Europe*, ed. Bruce Gordon and Peter Marshall (Cambridge: Cambridge University Press, 2000), 131-48, esp. 137-38.

[44]Spicer, *Calvinist Churches*, 152-54.

grave, accompanied with the Congregation; without any further ceremonies: which being buried the minister goeth to the Church, if it be not far off, and maketh some comfortable exhortation to the people, touching death and resurrection."[45] Thus although the Scottish reformers jettisoned gravesite ceremonies, they still included pastoral teaching in church as part of the funeral ritual. The Scottish *First Book of Discipline* of 1560 did however include a statement clarifying that the place of burial was not to be in the church building itself:

> In respect of diverse inconveniences we think it neither seemly that the Kirk appointed to preaching and ministration of the Sacraments shall be made a place of burial, but that some other secret and convenient place, lying in the most free aire, be appointed for that use, which place ought to be walled and fenced about, and kept for that use onely.[46]

This measure was echoed by the French Reformed Church: in 1596, the provincial synod of Bas Languedoc in the southeast of France noted that burials were not to be permitted "in the temples where the Word of God was preached and the holy sacraments were administered."[47] Both the Scottish and French Reformed ordinances seemed based as much on hygienic as on theological grounds, but their implementation ran into difficulties because of persistent demands from laypeople to continue their traditional practice of burying deceased family members under the church floor. Indeed, worshipers' conviction that the church building was sacred space did not cease at the time of their deaths. In many locations, medieval burial practices had favored burials in the church itself, either as close as possible to the center of holiness (namely, the high altar) or in a space

---

[45]Quoted in Gordon Raeburn, "The Changing Face of Scottish Burial Practices," *Reformation & Renaissance Review* 11, no. 2 (2009): 181-201, esp. 182.

[46]Quoted in Raeburn, "Changing Face," 183.

[47]Quoted in Spicer, "The Huguenots and Marks of Honor," 241.

families understood as theirs: occupied and claimed both by the living who stood or knelt or sat for worship in that spot and by their dead under the floor. These practices did not suddenly disappear with the coming of the Reformation. Indeed, contemporary evidence suggests that laypeople with sufficient funds took one of two possible approaches to fulfill their desire to have their dead relatives buried in the church building, in spite of the ordinances to the contrary. The first was to go ahead and carry out such a burial and pay any fines resulting from the offense. Some French Reformed communities in the seventeenth century, struggling to raise funds to cover their expenses, even sold the right for a burial in church to families who could afford the cost.[48] The second, a creative compromise that took root especially in Scotland, was to pay for the construction of what were known as "burial aisles." These were add-ons to the sides of existing church buildings, sometimes topped with a gallery with seating for the living members of family or clan in question. Deceased family members could be buried in the floor underneath. Because these burial aisles were add-ons to the original church building, church leaders were willing to consider these spaces as outside the bounds of the church proper.[49] Both of these options, however, required money, either for fines or for construction costs, and hence were only available to those with enough funds to do so.

The practice of burial in the church floor was particularly challenging in areas where there were confessional tensions, as in the northwestern German lands. In the prince-bishopric of Münster in the late sixteenth and early seventeenth centuries, Catholics, Lutherans, Reformed believers, and a small number of Anabaptists lived side by side. Because the territory was officially Catholic, Catholic clergy felt strongly that the purity of their sacred spaces ought to be maintained, including ensuring that these spaces were not

---

[48]Spicer, "The Huguenots and Marks of Honor," 241.
[49]Raeburn, "Changing Face," 184-88.

contaminated by the presence of heresy. Yet Protestants who lived in these same areas continued to want to be part of the community both in life and in death, and they insisted on their right to be buried in the parish churchyard or church building itself. In most instances, these families prevailed, and their loved ones were duly buried alongside their Catholic neighbors.[50] Similar conflicts surfaced in France. Some members of prominent Huguenot families, whose ancestors were buried in the floor of the (Catholic) parish church, still wanted to be buried alongside these ancestors, even though the current family members were Protestant. By and large, the Huguenot authorities did not object to having their members buried in a Catholic church, so long as no Catholic rituals took place during the funeral. Other Catholics, however, objected strenuously to the presence of any heretic, alive or dead, in their worship space. Both in these churches and in Catholic graveyards, deceased Huguenots who managed to be buried were in great danger of being dug up again and having their bodies dumped in trash heaps.[51]

CONCLUSION

Worship in church shaped the religious life of early modern Christians. Week by week, they gathered to pray, to hear God's Word, and to participate in the sacraments, but also to come together to mark key moments in a person's life, such as their marriage or their burial. Across the board, religious and political authorities expected congregations to be reverent, attentive, and engaged in public worship. Evidence suggests, however, that the atmosphere in places of worship could be significantly more lively and contentious than the authorities would have wanted. Although laypeople largely recognized that churches were sacred spaces, these spaces were not

---

[50]David Luebke, "Confessions of the Dead: Interpreting Burial Practice in the Late Reformation" *Archiv für Reformationsgeschichte* 101 (2010): 55-78.

[51]Roberts, "Contesting Sacred Space," 131-32.

hermetically sealed off from the rest of the world, and conflicts or tensions that festered in everyday life crossed the threshold into churches along with the worshipers.

FOR FURTHER READING

Dymond, David. "God's Disputed Acre." *Journal of Ecclesiastical History* 50, no. 3 (1999): 464-97.

Gordon, Bruce and Peter Marshall, eds. *The Place of the Dead: Death and Remembrance in Late Medieval and Early Modern Europe.* Cambridge: Cambridge University Press, 2000.

Graham, Michael. "Conflict and Sacred Space in Reformation-Era Scotland." *Albion* 33, no. 3 (2001): 371-87.

Hahn, Philip. "Sensing Sacred Space: Ulm Minster, the Reformation, and Parishioners' Sensory Perception, c. 1470 to 1640." *Archiv für Reformationsgeschichte* 105 (2014): 55-91.

Karant-Nunn, Susan. *The Reformation of Ritual: An Interpretation of Early Modern Germany.* London: Routledge, 1997.

Marsh, Christopher. "Sacred Space in England, 1560–1640: the View from the Pew." *Journal of Ecclesiastical History* 53, no. 2 (2002): 286-311.

Raeburn, Gordon. "The Changing Face of Scottish Burial Practices." *Reformation and Renaissance Review* 11, no. 2 (2009): 181-201.

Spicer, Andrew. *Calvinist Churches in Early Modern Europe.* Manchester: Manchester University Press, 2007.

Spicer, Andrew, ed. *Lutheran Churches in Early Modern Europe.* Farnham: Ashgate, 2012.

Spierling, Karen, Erik de Boer, and R. Ward Holder, eds. *Emancipating Calvin: Culture and Confessional Identity in Francophone Reformed Communities.* Leiden: Brill, 2018.

THREE

PREACHING

Faith commeth by hearing the word preached, then I reason thus:
No preaching, no faith; no faith, no Christ; no Christ, no eternall
life. . . . If we will have heaven, we must have Christ. If we will have
Christ, we must have faith. If we will have faith, we must have the
word preached. Thus I conclude that preaching generally, and for
the most part, is of absolute necessity unto eternall life.

ARTHUR DENT, THE PLAINE MANS PATHWAY TO HEAVEN (1625)

OF ALL THE VARIOUS ASPECTS of Reformation-era worship, the
one for which most evidence survives is preaching. Although there
are crucial differences between an orally preached sermon and a
written text, historians are fortunate in the abundance of early
modern sermons that have come down to the present day in written form. These stem from a wide range of geographical and confessional contexts, including Lutheran funeral sermons and postils, Anglican sermons (especially those preached and later
published in London), extensive collections of sermons by leading
reformers, including Heinrich Bullinger in Zurich and John

Arthur Dent, *The Plaine Mans Pathway to Heaven* (London: George Latham, 1625), 336-37.

Calvin in Geneva, and a vast trove of late medieval and early modern Catholic sermons.

Preaching as a feature of communal worship definitely predated the Reformation, in spite of the persistent Protestant misperception that pre-Reformation Christians never or very rarely heard sermons or that the sermons that were preached were not based on Scripture and not in the people's own language.[1] Yet the Reformation's emphasis on the centrality of Scripture and its exposition in worship meant that preaching took on a greater role as the Reformation took hold. Indeed, in many Reformed areas, the word for sermon became the word used to refer to attending worship. So Huguenots in France and the Dutch Reformed both said they were going to the sermon when they meant they were going to church for worship. For these early modern Christians, the sermon was an integral part of worship, because through the sermon, the Word of God was taught and expounded to the people. As a result, preaching lay at the heart of the worship experience. Indeed, as we have seen in the previous chapter, newly built Reformed churches often reoriented the church building away from the traditional cross-shaped Catholic architecture focused on the high altar to a more circular structure oriented around the pulpit. Thus in this instance, even the layout of church interiors could and did reflect the Reformed communities' worship priorities.

Yet simply stating that preaching became an increasingly important feature of worship for early modern Christians is not enough. Other questions must be considered: How did pastors select the sources for their sermons? Did they preach from Scripture or use

---

[1] See for instance Stephen Lawson's presentation on the Reformation and preaching at the 2017 Ligonier ministries conference, "The Preached Word and Reformation," Ligonier Ministries, 2017, www.ligonier.org/learn/conferences/next-500-years-2017-national-conference /preached-word-and-reformation. For a more balanced assessment, see Bruce Gordon, "Teaching the Church: Protestant Latin Bibles and Their Readers," in *The People's Book: The Reformation and the Bible*, ed. Jennifer Powell McNutt and David Lauber (Downers Grove, IL: IVP Academic, 2017), 13-32.

other sources as well? If they preached from Scripture, how did they select their texts? Did they preach from a lectionary, or independently pick and choose scriptural passages, or preach consecutively through books of the Bible? What approaches did they take in their sermons: exhortation, polemic, admonition, doctrinal instruction, encouragement, or all of the above? How did clergy learn to preach, and how were they vetted? What about preachers who were not ordained? Did the choice of language (Latin versus vernacular) and the venue (Sunday services, weekday services, worship in a school or university context) make a difference in terms of the form and content of the sermon preached? From the other side of the pulpit, how were sermons received? What qualities did people seem to want in a preacher, and what did they look for in a sermon?

↜

In 1553, the Reformed pastor Guillaume Farel preached a sermon in Geneva, just as the conflict between John Calvin and his supporters on the one side and the native Genevans known as the "enfants de Genève" on the other was reaching its peak. Although Farel had been among the first to bring the message of the Reformation to Geneva, he had been expelled from the city in 1538, and had subsequently served as pastor in the neighboring city and territory of Neuchâtel. Neuchâtel and Geneva are only about eighty miles away from each other, and Farel had several close friends among the pastors of Geneva, so he traveled to the city on a regular basis. Farel preached at the Wednesday-morning service in Geneva on November 1, 1553, and then went home to Neuchâtel. The following day, a delegation of Genevan young people appeared before the Genevan Small Council (the core group of magistrates), complaining that Farel had insulted them and verbally attacked them in his sermon. They claimed that Farel had called them atheists. On Saturday, November 11, Farel returned to Geneva and was asked by the magistrates not to preach until the matter had been investigated. On the 13th, two further groups appeared before the magistrates: first a delegation of pastors, headed by Calvin, and then a number of Genevans who had been in attendance at the sermon in question. The pastors highlighted Farel's long and distinguished service to the cause of the Reformation, while the inhabitants stated that they had not been offended but rather edified by Farel's sermon. Crucially, no one in the later groups refuted the earlier accusation that Farel had called people atheists in his sermon. In the end, the magistrates came down firmly on Farel's side, deciding that there was no case to answer. The Genevan city leaders noted in their minutes that he was their honored former pastor and that they would pay his travel expenses back to Neuchâtel. As a further mark of their esteem, the magistrates ordered that Farel be escorted by a Genevan herald on his way home to Neuchâtel.[2]

This vignette highlights several important aspects of Reformation preaching practice. First, sermons were often pointed discourses that could and did cause sharp reactions among those listening. Farel, like many of his colleagues, regularly preached in a prophetic mode, warning and admonishing congregations about beliefs and behaviors that fell short of God's commands. Second, in Geneva as in other areas with state churches, political authorities kept a close watch on what was preached and intervened when they felt sermons were too harsh or otherwise presented risks to public order. Finally, Reformation-era sermons were discussed, debated, argued over, and enjoyed both in church and outside church. In this instance, the divergent responses to Farel's sermon testify both to his congregation's close attention to what he was saying and to the incendiary effects sermons could have when speaking into political and social tensions at the time.

---

[2]See the English translation of the original primary-source document for this controversy in Karin Maag, ed., *Lifting Hearts to the Lord: Worship with John Calvin in Sixteenth-Century Geneva* (Grand Rapids, MI: Eerdmans, 2016), 61-62.

↜

On June 23, 1532, less than a year after the battle of Kappel between Swiss Catholics and Protestants, in which the Zurich reformer Huldrych Zwingli was killed, Pastor Leo Jud preached a fiery sermon in Zurich. In it, he vehemently and explicitly condemned the civil authorities of the city for not doing enough to defend the Reformed faith and for cozying up to Zurich's Catholic opponents. Four days later, the city magistrates called the pastors of Zurich together to remind them of their obligations to maintain peace and harmony in the city via their sermons. The city leaders then gave a point-by-point rebuttal of the main critiques voiced by Pastor Jud in his sermon. The councilors also reiterated the need for pastors to bring any concerns over morals or weakening of the Reformed faith directly to the city government rather than voice their grievances from the pulpit, "so as to maintain Christian discipline and honor."[3]

In this instance, as in the case of Farel's sermon, Jud's preaching was pointedly directed at a current-day situation. Here too the authorities took the matter seriously and invested time in crafting a response. In both situations, the sermons carried weight given that they were one of the leading forms of public discourse in the community. Unlike in the Genevan case, however, the Zurich civil authorities decided that Jud's sermon did in fact contravene the city's expectations as to its content and tone, and worked to remind pastors of their duty to ensure that their sermons contributed to public order rather than undermine it.

---

[3]For more on the sermon by Leo Jud and its aftermath, see Pamela Biel, *Doorkeepers at the House of Righteousness: Heinrich Bullinger and the Zurich Clergy 1535–1575* (Bern: Peter Lang, 1991), 93-98. For the text of the magistrates' response to Jud's sermon, see Emil Egli, *Aktensammlung zur Geschichte der Zürcher Reformation* (Nieuwkoop: De Graaf, 1973), 805-8.

↜

A third vignette: in 1561, Nicolas Le More wrote to the Genevan pastors from Guyenne in southwestern France, where he had recently been installed as pastor following his abbreviated studies at the Genevan Academy. He was pressed into service due to the rapid growth of Reformed congregations in France and the corresponding need for pastors. He wrote,

> First of all, the people here have received me very badly, partly because of my insufficiency, partly because (they say) I am too young, and it is impossible for them to believe that I am learned, and therefore, the word of God is not being respected as it should be. Whatever the case, everyone is criticizing my sermons, going so far as to say that I had held Anabaptist views, and that I had said that only the children of God should hold the goods of this world and should make good and legitimate use of them, and that all others were thieves and swindlers. . . . Another problem I am aware of is that I speak too quickly, and therefore, apart from the fact that I am in an area where they struggle to understand French, they cannot gain much from what I have to say.[4]

In this instance, a young pastor was failing to gain his parishioners' support, largely because his congregation evaluated his sermons and found them both hard to understand and doctrinally questionable. It is worth pointing out that Le More also noted later in the letter that the local people actually preferred a different man as their pastor, a local doctor who had been serving in the role of a pastor prior to Le More's arrival. Here we see some of the realities of a pastor's preaching life

---

[4]Letter from Nicolas Le More to the church of Geneva, November 1, 1561, published in the *Bulletin de la société de l'histoire du protestantisme français* 46 (1897): 466-68 (translation mine). Le More did manage to survive this first difficult period in ministry and continued to serve as a pastor and a chaplain up to his death in 1572.

clashing with our assumptions that pastors spoke and the people simply listened. In this community at least, the laypeople were active agents in their church life, who laid claim to fairly sophisticated theological knowledge to distinguish between Reformed and Anabaptist positions. Le More was so discouraged at the poor response to his sermons that he begged the Genevan pastors to let him return to Geneva and continue his studies instead.

∽

All three of these vignettes illustrate the complexities surrounding the practice of preaching in the Reformation era. On the one hand, preachers saw themselves as proclaimers and interpreters of God's Word. Their sermons were meant to teach, admonish, console, and warn. On the other hand, their hearers also had their own ideas about what constituted an appropriate sermon, and they pushed back when they felt their preachers were not teaching true doctrine or were taking undue advantage of the pulpit's near monopoly of authorized public discourse.

This chapter will look in depth at the practice of preaching in the Reformation era, across confessional groups and in a wide range of locations. The vast array of primary sources and recent scholarly research on preaching in the early modern world provides a treasure trove of examples to illustrate how sermons served as one of the primary means to shape both belief and communal worship in the early modern context. At the same time, we will explore how the practice of preaching sheds light on congregations' and individuals' responses to the messages they heard from the pulpit.

PREACHING BEFORE THE REFORMATION

In confessionally oriented works intended for a Protestant readership, some authors persistently repeat the notion that, prior to the Reformation, sermons were few and far between and not rooted in

Scripture.[5] In many instances, these authors are trying to build a strong contrast between the pre-Reformation and post-Reformation era, yet in the process they are distorting the historical record. Catholics attending worship prior to the Reformation definitely heard homilies and sermons, both in the Prone during Sunday Mass and during the special preaching seasons of Advent and Lent. The Prone was the vernacular part of the liturgy of the Mass, usually inserted after the offertory. It included bidding prayers with congregational responses, announcements regarding the life of the church and the parish, and instruction from the priest on the key teachings of the faith and morals. In the German lands, many cities by the fifteenth century had funded positions for preachers, whose responsibilities included giving a sermon every Sunday and feast day. One such well-known late medieval preacher was Johann Geiler von Kaysersberg, who was employed as the city preacher in Strasbourg beginning in 1478, about forty years before Luther's Reformation got underway. His contract stipulated that apart from his four weeks of vacation every year, he had to preach every Sunday and feast day of the year and every day during Lent. In case of illness, he had to notify the cathedral dean and find a qualified replacement.[6] Even in the rural areas of the Holy Roman Empire, medieval Catholic inhabitants increasingly expected their clergy to preach. For instance, villagers in Kraftshof in Bavaria made an agreement with the priest in the larger town of Poppenreuth in 1431, mandating the priest to supply a chaplain "who is a good speaker and can preach well, who will hear confessions and can administer all of the sacraments as is required of

---

[5]See for instance Steven Key, "Luther on Preaching," in *The Sixteenth-Century Reformation of the Church*, ed. David Engelsma (Jenison, MI: Reformed Free Publishing Association, 2007), 88-95.
[6]Larissa Taylor, *Soldiers of Christ: Preaching in Late Medieval and Reformation France* (New York: Oxford University Press, 1992), 21.

any priest."[7] In medieval France, surviving evidence also indicates that preaching was a regular occurrence, though more often carried out by a preaching expert (often a member of a Catholic religious order such as the Dominicans or Franciscans) hired by the local community.[8] Here, too, sermons were keyed to the lectionary and followed the pattern of the liturgical seasons. The prime seasons for preaching were Lent and Advent.[9]

Many of these sermons were collected together in volumes known as postils, intended for wider use by pastors. The sermons in these volumes followed the medieval lectionary—in other words, each sermon was keyed to the relevant biblical passage that was assigned to that Sunday. Some of the volumes of postils contained complete texts of sermons that then could be adapted or simply read from the pulpit, whereas others provided outlines that the preacher could then fill in.[10]

As for the themes or approaches of these late medieval sermons, these varied widely, from exhortations to repentance and moral reform to instruction in doctrine and piety.[11] These thematic sermons represented one stream in fifteenth- and sixteenth-century Catholic preaching. Other currents included more thoroughly exegetical sermons, such as those preached by Bishop John Fisher in England from the late 1400s up to the early years of the English Reformation.[12] Another leading influence on Catholic preaching both before and after the Reformation was the great Dutch humanist scholar Desiderius Erasmus, who called for sermons to make greater use of rhetoric in helping the faithful turn to God's mercy.[13] Although Erasmus never

---

[7]John Frymire, *The Primacy of the Postils: Catholics, Protestants, and the Dissemination of Ideas in Early Modern Germany* (Leiden: Brill, 2010), 19.

[8]Taylor, *Soldiers of Christ*, 20.

[9]Taylor, *Soldiers of Christ*, 20-21.

[10]Frymire, *Primacy*, xiii, 1.

[11]Thomas Worcester, "Catholic Sermons," in *Preachers and People in the Reformations and Early Modern Period*, ed. Larissa Taylor (Leiden: Brill, 2001), 3-33, esp. 4-9.

[12]Worcester, "Catholic Sermons," 11-13.

[13]Worcester, "Catholic Sermons," 14-15.

turned away from his Catholic faith, his 1516 Greek New Testament
and his deep interest in making Scripture more accessible to Christians at all levels of society helped inspire reformers to highlight the
central importance of preaching God's Word.[14]

REFORMATION-ERA PREACHING

Hence the Reformation did not introduce preaching into worship for
the first time, since medieval Christians had been used to hearing a
considerable number of sermons of different types in a wide variety
of settings. Instead, it would be more accurate to say that reformers
took over previous Catholic preaching practices, adapting or refram-
ing the medieval approaches to preaching to better suit their theological and liturgical aims.

As John Frymire points out, Luther's critique of Catholic preaching, although voiced as a claim that Catholics never heard sermons, in
fact centers on Luther's theological intent: sermons were to preach
justification by faith. Since in the German Reformer's estimation
Catholic sermons failed to do so, it was as if Catholics never heard
sermons at all.[15] For Luther, preaching was the most important and
regular way congregations encountered and came to understand the
Word of God.[16] Yet although many of Luther's sermons survive, he
did not write any homiletical treatise, leaving to Philipp Melanchthon the task of providing guidance for Lutheran preachers. Melanchthon's reflections on how to preach appear in a sequence of four
relatively short texts, all of which emphasize the importance of sermons as sources of doctrinal instruction and moral exhortation.[17]

---

[14]For more on Erasmus and his impact on the Reformation, see Christine Christ-von Wedel,
Erasmus of Rotterdam: Advocate of a New Christianity (Toronto: University of Toronto
Press, 2013).

[15]Frymire, *Primacy*, 23.

[16]Frymire, *Primacy*, 27.

[17]Max Engammare, *Prêcher au XVIe siècle: la forme du sermon réformé en Suisse (1520–1550)*
(Geneva: Labor et Fides, 2018), 40-53.

Melanchthon warned preachers about the dangers of allegorical interpretations of Scripture, though he did allow for careful use of this approach in preaching. He also summarized the aim of sermons as a means to move souls to fear God, to grow in faith and hope, and to love their neighbor.[18]

Few sources survive that provide information on the Anabaptists' theology of preaching, but contemporary testimony indicates that preaching for Anabaptist communities was much less about doctrinal instruction and much more about moral exhortation. The Word of God was front and center, and the preacher's role was to apply the Word to the lives of his hearers. In some Anabaptist circles, the preacher was known as the *Diener des Wortes* (servant of the Word) or the *Vermahner* (exhorter). Some Anabaptist communities also emphasized the involvement of the worshiping community in the sermon, offering opportunities for others to speak in turn at the end of the sermon to testify to the truth of the message or, in cases of disagreement, to put forward their interpretation instead.[19]

Among the Reformed, preaching that was faithful to Scripture was one of the marks of the true church, along with the proper administration of the sacraments of baptism and Communion and—for some— church discipline. As such, sermons received a great deal of attention. The most common interpretive method especially in the first decades was to read and analyze the text in its historical context but also lay out its contemporary application. By and large, Reformed leaders urged pastors to avoid allegorical interpretations and instead focus on the literal meaning of the text.[20] For John Calvin, sermons were the best and most effective way to bring congregations into the school of Christ.

---

[18]Engammare, *Prêcher au XVIe siècle*, 46.

[19]Alvin Beachy, "Theology and Practice of Anabaptist Worship," *Mennonite Quarterly Review* 40, no. 3 (1966): 163-78. See also John Oyer, "Early Forms of Anabaptist *Zeugnis* after Sermons," *Mennonite Quarterly Review* 72, no. 3 (1998): 449-54.

[20]James Thomas Ford, "Preaching in the Reformed Tradition," in Taylor, *Preachers and People*, 69.

Sermons were therefore not only supposed to teach the faithful what the Bible meant (hence a great deal of attention was given to explaining the meaning of words and the context of a passage) but also to teach them how to live out their faith. Calvin described the preacher as a shepherd, chasing off the wolves and feeding the sheep.[21] Sermons were meant to teach congregations the fundamental doctrines of the Christian faith, have them recognize the false teachings of rival confessional groups, but also to get them to live out these doctrines in their daily lives.[22] Later Reformed preachers continued in the same vein, many of them shaped by the influential homiletical treatise published by Andreas Hyperius in 1553, *De formandis concionibus sacris*. Hyperius stated that in his sermon, a pastor was to teach, exhort, admonish, and comfort his hearers. In France, Reformed writers of homiletical works advocated clarity, calm, and restraint in preaching. They recommended avoiding too many learned quotations or linguistic comments on scriptural passages, because educated members of the congregation might well already know that information and be bored, whereas those without as much education would simply be lost.[23]

In the Church of England, preaching became an increasingly important part of pastors' responsibilities, as noted in the official documents of the Church of England, including the Book of Common Prayer and the Thirty-Nine Articles (1571), which described the visible church as "a congregation of faithful men, in the which the pure word of God is preached, and the sacraments be duly ministered."[24] The theological importance of preaching was particularly strongly

[21]Ford, "Preaching in the Reformed Tradition," 65-88, esp. 67.

[22]Ford, "Preaching in the Reformed Tradition," 72.

[23]Françoise Chevalier, *Prêcher sous l'Edit de Nantes: la prédication réformée au XVIIe siècle en France* (Geneva: Labor et Fides, 1994), 52-56.

[24]Eric Josef Carlson, "The Boring of the Ear: Shaping the Pastoral Vision of Preaching in England, 1540–1640" in Taylor, *Preachers and People*, 249-96, esp. 260-61. For more on preaching in England, with a particular focus on the two-way communication between preacher and congregation, see Arnold Hunt, *The Art of Hearing: English Preachers and Their Audiences, 1590–1640* (Cambridge: Cambridge University Press, 2011).

expressed among those who supported further Reformation in the English church. To them, preaching became the best and most effective way to bring individuals and congregations to a deep awareness of their sinful state and their need for genuine repentance.[25] Thus many of the pastors who subscribed to the central importance of preaching did so by working hard to instill in their hearers a strong sense of their sinful misery. The imagery pastors used to describe their own role was that of a doctor lancing a sore: they had to go deep to get all the poison out, and had to hurt in order to heal.[26] Yet this focus on preaching about human depravity could backfire, as individuals and congregations became either highly anxious about their salvation, or frustrated by the constant emphasis on their sins. By the end of Elizabeth I's reign, popular pressure had encouraged a significant portion of English clergy to downplay preaching in favor of a greater attention to liturgy, prayers, and sacraments.[27]

Meanwhile, Catholic preaching continued to take place, shaped both by the official statements on preaching as issued by the Council of Trent and by the practice of preaching, especially as cultivated by new or revitalized religious orders, including the Jesuits. The Council of Trent concentrated mainly on ensuring that regular preaching took place in each diocese, and had less to say about the theological content or approach that these sermons should take. In its decrees issued in 1546, the council made preaching one of the key responsibilities of bishops:

> But seeing that the preaching of the Gospel is no less necessary
> to the Christian commonwealth than the reading thereof; and
> whereas this is the principal duty of bishops; the same holy
> Synod hath resolved and decreed, that all bishops, archbishops,

---

[25]Carlson, "Boring of the Ear," 250.
[26]Carlson, "Boring of the Ear," 265.
[27]Christopher Haigh, "The Taming of Reformation: Preachers, Pastors and Parishioners in Elizabethan and Early Stuart England," *History* 285 (2000): 572-88.

primates, and all other prelates of the churches be bound personally—if they be not lawfully hindered—to preach the holy Gospel of Jesus Christ.[28]

For their part, Catholic preachers like François de Sales deployed their oratorical skills in sermons designed to strengthen Catholics in their faith and win over wavering Protestants. De Sales stressed the importance of preaching from Scripture, although he preferred to concentrate on short passages or single phrases rather than preach sequentially through entire books of the Bible. Indeed, he noted that preachers could get their points across more effectively when their hearers were not distracted by trying to keep track of longer passages of Scripture.[29]

Across the confessional spectrum, therefore, church leaders stressed the importance of preaching as a means to convey the teachings of Scripture to congregations, but not simply for informational purposes. Sermons were meant to teach, but also to warn, exhort, and impel hearers to amend their lives. Polemical sermons continued to be preached from the first years of the Reformation onward, not surprisingly since one of the most effective ways for pastors to reinforce the beliefs of their own congregations was to highlight the significant differences between their own confessional views and those held by their opponents. Reformed pastors in France, for instance, regularly emphasized three main themes in sermons directed against their Catholic adversaries. These included attacks on the Catholic doctrine of transubstantiation, the role of the pope, and the Catholic emphasis on good works as part of what human beings could do to contribute to their salvation.[30] Polemical preaching also surfaced within confessional groups, as in the Lutheran German territories

---

[28]Decrees of the Council of Trent, session 5 (June 17, 1546), second decree, chap. 2, www.the counciloftrent.com/ch5.htm. See also Worcester, "Catholic Sermons," 18-20.

[29]Worcester, "Catholic Sermons," 24-26

[30]Chevalier, *Prêcher sous l'Edit de Nantes*, 200-201.

after Luther's death, when divisions deepened between hard-line and more moderate Lutherans. For instance, following the unresolved Weimar disputation of 1560 between the two sides, preachers in Saxony from both ends of the theological spectrum used their sermons to target each other's positions on salvation, baptismal regeneration, and the freedom or bondage of the human will.[31]

APPROACHES TO SCRIPTURE

Although their aims were similar, early modern preachers differed in their approach to selecting Bible passages as the basis for their sermons. The use of a lectionary to assign passages of Scripture to read Sunday by Sunday continued to be a key feature of several Protestant church liturgies following the Reformation. In particular, Lutheran and Anglican churches retained the lectionary, and as a result their sermons followed suit, tied to the passages (known as pericopes) assigned to each Sunday and feast day. Like medieval Catholics before them, Lutherans gathered these lectionary sermons together in published collections known as postils. Luther openly stated that preachers who wanted to should feel free to preach sequentially through entire books of the Bible but noted that most Lutheran pastors did not have enough training or confidence to do so. For these preachers, the postils could provide outlines, or a model, or even an entire sermon to explain the Scripture readings of the day. The postils also offered orthodox interpretations of Scripture, effectively countering the interpretations offered by radical groups who caused Luther such concern.[32]

A fascinating reflection on the enduring influence of these pericopes and postils from the medieval period right through the mid-sixteenth century in the German lands comes from the Reformed preacher Balthasar Cop. Cop served as one of the pastors in

---

[31]Patrick Ferry, "Confessionalization and Popular Preaching: Sermons Against Synergism in Reformation Saxony," *Sixteenth Century Journal* 28, no. 4 (1997): 1143-66.

[32]Frymire, *Primacy*, 34.

Neustadt under Duke Johann Casimir and later in the Palatinate under the Elector Frederick IV. In 1591, Cop published a *Hauskirchen Postill*, or "Postils for house churches" (meaning household worship). Although he favored the *lectio continua* approach to preaching championed by Reformed pastors in Geneva and in the Swiss lands, he admitted that the local population in the Palatinate was used to lectionary preaching and resisted other approaches to expounding Scripture. He noted that sequential preaching on books of the Bible happened during weekday services, but in the end, he bowed to the common local practice for Sunday sermons. Although the title of his work suggests that the book was intended for use in household worship, he did indicate in the preface that Reformed preachers might also use his postils in preparing their Sunday sermons.[33]

Although Cop ended up giving a measure of support to the local practice of lectionary-based sermons, his preference clearly continued to be for preaching that went through individual books of the Bible chapter by chapter and verse by verse. This type of expository preaching was pioneered in Zurich by Zwingli. When Zwingli was named as the people's priest at the Grossmünster in Zurich in 1519, his responsibilities included preaching to the inhabitants on a regular basis. In January of that year, he began preaching sequentially through the Gospel of Matthew. By 1525, he had preached through most of the New Testament and began turning to the Old Testament, starting with the Psalms.[34] The approach Zwingli modeled then spread to other Reformed areas, including the other Swiss cities, Geneva, and eventually Reformed communities elsewhere in Europe, including in Scotland, France, the Netherlands, and Hungary.

Although many Reformed pastors, especially in the first few decades, did adopt the sequential preaching model, they also would

---

[33]Frymire, *Primacy*, 226-31.

[34]Hughes Oliphant Old, *The Reading and Preaching of the Scriptures in the Worship of the Christian Church*, vol. 4, *The Age of Reformation* (Grand Rapids, MI: Eerdmans, 2002), 46.

interrupt the sequence if necessary, including for the quarterly celebrations of the Lord's Supper or on the major feast days of the Christian year, especially Easter Sunday. In some instances, Reformed preachers mixed and matched their approach to selecting passages of Scripture. In the 1520s, the Basel reformer Johannes Oecolampadius, for instance, appears to have preached some of his sermons based on the lectionary in use in the German Lutheran churches, while also offering a sequential series of sermons on the Gospel of Mark, but also independently selecting Scripture passages as the basis of his sermons at other times.[35] Indeed, Basel offers an example of a Reformed city that still preserved elements of lectionary-based preaching well into the mid-sixteenth century.[36]

THE PRACTICE OF PREACHING

The length of a sermon could vary considerably, depending both on the context in which it was preached (Sunday service, weekday service, special occasion, etc.) and on the pastor's own approach. There are indications in several sources that congregations (not surprisingly) preferred shorter sermons. Some preachers were conscious of the need to avoid going on too long. Geiler von Kaysersberg, for instance, was adamant that sermons should last no more than an hour, to the point of even stopping abruptly once the hour was up, whether or not he had reached the natural end of his sermon.[37] In many Protestant communities, Sunday sermons usually lasted one hour, while weekday sermons would be shorter, at around half an hour.[38] By the

---

[35]Engammare, *Prêcher au XVIe siècle*, 71-72.

[36]Engammare, *Prêcher au XVIe siècle*, 78.

[37]Taylor, *Soldiers of Christ*, 69.

[38]These are the estimated times for Strasbourg (René Bornert, *La Réforme protestante du culte à Strasbourg au XVIe siècle* [Leiden: Brill, 1981], 516-17) and for Geneva (Max Engammare, *On Time, Punctuality, and Discipline in Early Modern Calvinism*, trans. Karin Maag [Cambridge: Cambridge University Press, 2010], 65-77). Across the confessional spectrum, the length of time devoted to preaching could vary from ten minutes for a homily to two or three hours for a sermon preached during a special service of fasting and repentance.

end of the sixteenth century and into the seventeenth century, civil authorities in several areas put pressure on pastors to reduce the length of their sermons. For instance, in 1578, the ecclesiastical ordinances for Lutheran Württemberg ordered the following:

> On Sundays and feast-days, sermons should last not more than three-quarters of an hour, and at most should not go beyond an hour so that the people will not be annoyed by the frequent and lengthy overrunning, because the understanding of the common man cannot cope with all this at one time in a cheerful fashion. Instead, one should handle him like one handles the sick, whom one feeds often, but in small portions at any one time.[39]

The political authorities' pragmatic awareness of congregations' relatively short attention span was undoubtedly appreciated by the local population. Although sermons preached during Sunday worship services have garnered considerable attention, preaching could and did take place at other times as well. In Reformed areas, any gathering for communal worship necessarily called for a sermon, so that weekday services also served as a regular venue for preaching. Other occasions for sermons that occurred outside of regularly scheduled worship times included funerals, installations of new government leaders, and sermons preached for military troops about to go into battle.[40]

Considerable evidence survives for funeral sermons, largely because many of these were subsequently published, often paid for by the surviving family members and as a mark of honor to the deceased. Some clergy also published collections of model funeral sermons for use by other pastors. Protestant theology radically reshaped traditional Catholic teachings on the afterlife, rejecting purgatory and

---

[39]Engammare, *On Time*, 76.
[40]For the installation sermons and the military sermons, see Engammare, *Prêcher au XVIe siècle*, 110-17.

therefore also putting an end to requiem Masses and prayers for the dead. Luther's sermons preached at the funerals of the Electors of Saxony helped to launch the practice in Lutheran areas. Lutheran funeral sermons included theological reflections on the selected biblical text, designed to provide comfort to the bereaved, but also to remind hearers of their own mortality, their need to repent, and the importance of putting their trust in Christ.[41] By and large, Reformed areas downplayed funeral rituals including sermons, at least until the last years of the sixteenth century. One exception was once again the Swiss city of Basel, which held funeral services with sermons from the first years of the Reformation onward, perhaps due to influence from neighboring Lutheran territories. The collection of model funeral sermons in outline form published in Latin by Basel pastor Johannes Brandmüller in 1572 therefore sheds light on the city's unique practice. Although these sermons were intended as aids to other pastors rather than being full sermons preached at actual funerals, they do reiterate key theological themes that also emerged in Lutheran funeral sermons. These include the brevity of life, the need to prepare for death, and the prospect of the joys of heaven. Brandmüller also offered counsel on how to deal with the fear of death and how to respond to the death of a loved one.[42]

Although sermons preached in communal worship services for the laity were in the vernacular (including in Catholic contexts), Latin sermons did still continue. Catholics and Protestant preachers alike gave sermons in Latin in university worship services and at princely and royal courts. Catholic clergy also preached in Latin in monasteries, at church councils, and in the presence of the pope.[43]

---

[41]For more on Lutheran funeral sermons, see Irene Dingel, "'True Faith, Christian Living, and a Blessed Death': Sixteenth-Century Funeral Sermons as Evangelical Proclamation," *Lutheran Quarterly* 27, no. 4 (2013): 399-420.

[42]Amy Nelson Burnett, "'To Oblige My Brethren': the Reformed Funeral Sermons of Johannes Brandmüller," *Sixteenth Century Journal* 36, no. 1 (2005): 37-54.

[43]Taylor, *Soldiers of Christ*, 56.

How to Prepare Preachers

The need for trained clergy, especially in the face of competition from other confessional groups, concentrated the minds of church leaders across the board. For instance, the Council of Trent ordered each diocese to set up a seminary to train priests. This training, however, focused more on how to celebrate the sacraments and on the care of souls.[44] The attention given to preaching was left in the hands of bishops, who varied in the amount of attention they paid to training clergy in this practice. One helpful example comes from the archdiocese of Milan, where Archbishop Carlo Borromeo set out clear expectations for his clergy regarding how to preach. In the 1570s in particular, the diocesan clergy were meant to get together regularly once a month by district to conduct diocesan business but also to hear a sermon delivered by one of their members in turn. This sermon was then assessed by diocesan leaders in Milan. Research on both the regulations and the practice suggests that expectations for clergy without much formal education were fairly minimal: an acceptable sermon could consist of a vernacular paraphrase of a Scripture reading followed by a brief interpretation tying the themes of the passage to the importance of the sacraments of confession and Communion.[45]

Because preaching became one of the most important parts of Protestant worship services, especially in Reformed areas, the focus on sermons as the main vector for the transmission of faith to congregations meant that pastors needed to learn how to carry out this important task. The need for homiletical training was particularly acute in the first years of the Reformation, before formal centers of training and seminaries could be set up. Zurich developed one of the possible approaches to providing that training for pastors who were

---

[44]Kathleen Comerford, "The Influence of the Jesuits on the Curriculum of the Diocesan Seminary of Fiesole, 1636–1646," *Catholic Historical Review* 84, no. 4 (1998): 662-80.

[45]See Benjamin Westervelt, "The Prodigal Son at Santa Justina: The Homily in the Borromean Reform of Pastoral Preaching," *Sixteenth Century Journal* 32, no. 1 (2001): 109-26.

already holding posts in the new Reformed setup—namely, the *Prophezei*. Established in 1525, the *Prophezei* was originally intended as a continuing-education gathering, held five days a week in Zurich and bringing together pastors from across the city and countryside. Participants listened to an exegetical analysis of a given biblical passage provided by colleagues who were experts in Greek and Hebrew, followed by a sermon in the vernacular on the same passage. Similar gatherings of pastors to deepen their understanding of Scripture, share their insights, and develop their exegetical abilities took place in Strasbourg, in the French-speaking Swiss lands, and in Geneva beginning in the 1530s.[46] Reformed exiles and students who spent time in Geneva then brought these practices to their home countries, so that the practice spread to France, the Netherlands, Scotland, and England, with greater or lesser staying power depending on local circumstances. The Puritan wing of the English church took up the practice in their "prophesyings" beginning in the 1560s.[47] Although laypeople could and did attend these various forms of in-depth Bible study,[48] the prime targets were those who had to preach as part of their duties. This form of regular continuing education for pastors helped them develop their exegetical skills and learn how to transmit their understanding of the biblical text more effectively to their congregations in their sermons.

Alongside this training for those already in the pulpit, church leaders also focused on the need to provide adequate preparation for incoming pastors. In the decades following the Reformation, many confessional groups made plans to set the training of their future pastors on a firmer footing by creating or restructuring centers of higher education to provide the necessary preparation. In Reformed areas,

---

[46]For more on the practice in Geneva and elsewhere, see Erik de Boer, *The Genevan School of the Prophets: The congrégations of the Company of Pastors and Their Influence in 16th Century Europe* (Geneva: Droz, 2012).

[47]De Boer, *Genevan School*, 243-64.

[48]De Boer, *Genevan School*, 25, 49, 59-62.

Zurich, Bern, Lausanne, and Geneva all created academies for higher study by 1560, where future pastors could gain the skills they needed, including training in Greek, Hebrew, Biblical exegesis, and regular preaching practice.[49] Other areas followed suit, either adapting an already-existing university or establishing a new institution. Because preaching was such a central part of a pastor's responsibilities, candidates for ministry were regularly asked to preach a trial sermon at their ordination examination. Those who failed to convince the examiners about their preaching abilities, whether due to weaknesses in their scriptural or doctrinal knowledge or flaws in their delivery, were unlikely to be considered for ordination. Instead, depending on what the problem was, they would be sent back for further study or further preaching practice. In France, the Huguenot church order specified that future pastors who had satisfied the examination committee still had to preach three sermons over the course of three Sundays before their future congregation. This practice allowed congregations to get a sense of their incoming pastor's abilities and to register any concerns over the candidate's doctrine or preaching abilities.[50] The fact that the congregation's assessment of sermon delivery was the yardstick for their evaluation of the candidate shows yet again how central a role preaching played in Reformation worship. Indeed, the surviving testimonies from the pulpit and from the pew shed light on the expectations that shaped this core feature of worship in the early modern era.

RESPONSES TO PREACHING

By far the biggest complaint on the part of pastors and civil authorities regarding people's response to sermons during worship was their

---

[49]For more on the subject of preaching practice, see the recent article by Theodore G. Van Raalte, "On the Consistory Bench: Practice Preaching of the *Proposans* and *Proponenten* in the Reformed Churches of the Sixteenth and Seventeenth Centuries," *Mid-America Journal of Theology* 28 (2017): 43-66.

[50]Chevalier, *Prêcher sous l'Edit de Nantes*, 40-41.

lack of attentiveness. Leaders regularly complained about people talking to each other during the sermon, falling asleep, or otherwise not paying attention. The pastors were particularly sensitive to noise that might prevent their parishioners from hearing the sermon. Thus the kirk session records from Perth on March 6, 1587, ordered that infants being brought for baptism should remain outside the church building until the time of the sacrament, following the sermon, "for avoiding of tumults of the incoming of the people with them to bring them and also for the crying of the infant and bairn which make din in the time of the preaching so that others in coming thereto are stopped from hearing."[51] Pastors did not want their sermons drowned out by the noise of howling infants.

At times, the disturbances during sermon time had other, more significant root causes. In Geneva during the first years after Calvin's return from Strasbourg in 1542, the consistory regularly admonished people about "muttering" during the sermon. In this instance, their behavior had nothing to do with any complaining they might have been voicing about what they were hearing. Instead, these Genevans were simply using the sermon time to engage in their standard Catholic devotional practices—namely, reciting prayers and psalms in an undertone. Not surprisingly, the consistory insisted that these practices cease, not only to ensure that the person concentrated on the sermon, but also to prevent any distraction of those sitting nearby.[52] Others clearly disliked the sermons because of their length, or their tone, or both. The Genevan Jaques Simond fell asleep in Saint Gervais church in 1557, during a sermon preached by pastor Reymond Chauvet. His neighbor nudged him awake, a process to which Simond strongly objected. He then noisily left the church building

---

[51]*The Perth Kirk Session Books 1577–1590*, ed. Margo Todd (Woodbridge, UK: Boydell, 2012), 360 (wording modernized).

[52]Thomas Lambert, "Cette loi ne durera guère: Inertie religieuse et espoirs catholiques à Genève au temps de la Réforme," *Bulletin de la Société d'Histoire et d'Archéologie de Genève* 23, no. 24 (1994): 5-24, esp. 16-17.

while the sermon was still going on. When subsequently admonished by the consistory, Simond stated that after Chauvet had been preaching already for ninety minutes, Simond's leg hurt, and he needed to relieve himself. Beyond the specifics of this episode, Simond also complained that Chauvet's tone in his sermons was harsh and angry and that the pastor verbally attacked him for his continued Catholic sympathies.[53] In this instance, Pastor Chauvet could justifiably complain that Simond disrupted the sermon first by falling asleep and then by walking out of church while Chauvet was still preaching. Simond, however, also seemingly had grounds for complaint both due to the length of the sermon (well over the previously noted hour limit for Genevan sermons) and over the pastor's hostile tone.

Church leaders clearly expected that congregations would listen attentively to the sermons, but they also invested a great deal of energy in making sure that congregations retained the core of the message, even several days after a given sermon had been preached. In Geneva, for instance, in the first decade after the Reformation had been formally accepted in 1536, the consistory at its Friday meetings regularly asked those appearing before it to recall who had been preaching the previous Sunday, and what the sermon topic had been. Those who said they could not tell what the topic was because they failed to hear the sermon due to deafness were told to sit closer to the pulpit. Those who simply could not remember were told to go back and listen more closely the next time. Impressively, a number of Genevans were able to recall the basic ideas that the pastor had been trying to convey.

In spite of the numerous complaints of church leaders and the cases of disruptive churchgoers, there were clearly people in every congregation who valued preaching. Indeed, the records of church visitations (when committees of church leaders conducted inspections and asked for feedback from clergy and parishioners alike)

---

[53]Lambert, "Cette loi ne durera guère," 21.

provide strong evidence of congregations' desire for good and frequent sermons. In the Lutheran duchy of Württemberg, church visitors in the 1590s heard regular complaints from parishioners about infrequent or insufficient sermons. In many instances, these complaints came from smaller filial churches in areas with a shortage of pastors, such that the people only heard a sermon once a fortnight or once a month. The fact that laypeople protested these arrangements signals their desire to have more regular opportunities to hear the Word preached.[54] In the village of Rifferswil outside Zurich, parishioners complained about the preaching practices of their pastor Johann Ammann, who berated his congregation from the pulpit, calling them thieves and murderers in his sermons. In response, the congregation members lodged a formal complaint with the civil authorities in Zurich, accusing their pastor of slander.[55] Other complaints about pastors' preaching in Zurich's countryside included pastors whose voices were too soft, so that their sermons could not be heard, or whose accents were too thick for their congregations to understand what they were saying from the pulpit.[56] The congregation of Winterthur outside Zurich made a particularly detailed complaint about their pastor Hans Zart in 1553, noting that his preaching was very poor. He had apparently preached 150 sermons on Genesis but had only managed to get to chapter 5, and he had spent a whole year preaching on the second chapter of Ephesians. Not surprisingly,

---

[54]Bruce Tolley, *Pastors & Parishioners in Württemberg During the Late Reformation 1581–1621* (Stanford: Stanford University Press, 1995), 82-85.

[55]Bruce Gordon, "Preaching and the Reform of the Clergy in the Swiss Reformation," in *The Reformation of the Parishes: The Ministry and the Reformation in Town and Country*, ed. Andrew Pettegree (Manchester: Manchester University Press, 1993), 63-84, esp. 75. The civil authorities decided in favor of the congregation and fined Pastor Ammann.

[56]Bruce Gordon, *Clerical Discipline and the Rural Reformation: The Synod in Zürich, 1532–1580* (Bern: Peter Lang, 1992), 258 (Oswald Renner—thick accent and too soft-spoken), 266 (Gregor Seebach—too soft a voice), 272 (Ulrich Tubbrunner—too rapid and incomprehensible preaching pace).

this minute approach to Scripture was not what his congregation expected to hear in their pastor's sermons.[57]

CONCLUSION

The early modern practice of preaching in worship services was a common feature across confessional groups, even though the approach to Scripture and the themes addressed varied. Church leaders made a concerted effort to make sure their clergy had access to training or model sermons or other resources to help them take up this core responsibility. Although on the face of it the sermon or homily seems to be one of the least participative aspects of worship, with the preacher preaching and the people listening, evidence from early modern records suggests that the audience was not passive. Indeed, the religious authorities' emphasis on the importance of sermons as one of the principal ways for individuals and congregations to be shaped by the Word of God could bear fruit these leaders did not necessarily expect or want. Laypeople could assert their right to respond to the sermon and even weigh its theological merits, as in the case of the French parishioners of Nicolas Le More. While clergy might hope that congregations would take the sermon's message to heart, the preachers only had control of one part of the process— namely, the proclamation. The reception in the ears and hearts of their hearers was an entirely different matter.

FOR FURTHER READING

DeBoer, Erik. *The Genevan School of the Prophets: The Congregations of the Company of Pastors and Their Influence in 16th Century Europe.* Geneva: Droz, 2012.

Dingel, Irene. "'True Faith, Christian Living, and a Blessed Death': Sixteenth-Century Funeral Sermons as Evangelical Proclamation," *Lutheran Quarterly* 27, no. 4 (2013): 399-420.

---

[57] Gordon, *Clerical Discipline,* 277.

Engammare, Max. *On Time, Punctuality, and Discipline in Early Modern Calvinism*. Cambridge: Cambridge University Press, 2010.

Frymire, John. *The Primacy of the Postils: Catholics, Protestants, and the Dissemination of Ideas in Early Modern Germany*. Leiden: Brill, 2010.

Gordon, Bruce. *Clerical Discipline and the Rural Reformation: The Synod in Zürich, 1532–1580*. Bern: Peter Lang, 1992.

Hunt, Arnold. *The Art of Hearing: English Preachers and Their Audiences, 1590–1640*. Cambridge: Cambridge University Press, 2011.

Taylor, Larissa, ed. *Preachers and People in the Reformations and Early Modern Period*. Leiden: Brill, 2001.

Taylor, Larissa. *Soldiers of Christ: Preaching in Late Medieval and Reformation France*. Oxford: Oxford University Press, 1992.

Four

Prayer

Therefore brethren, I beseech you, even for the tender mercies of God,
let us no longer be negligent in this behalf; but as a people willing to
receive at God's hand such good things as in the common prayer of the
Church are craved, let us join ourselves together in the place of common
prayer, and, with one voice and one heart, beg of our heavenly Father
all those things which he knoweth to be necessary for us.

JOHN JEWEL, "OF COMMON PRAYER AND SACRAMENTS,"
IN CERTAIN SERMONS OR HOMILIES (1563)

THE ENGLISH AUTHOR OF THIS 1563 SERMON on the importance
of public prayer in the language of the people set his plea in historical
context, highlighting the crucial role of communal prayer in the Old
and New Testaments and in the life of the early church. His emphasis on the powerful effect of uniting hearts and souls in prayer was
echoed in the teachings and in the practice of sixteenth-century worship. Whether as part of a regular Sunday or weekday church service,
or at times of calamity or victory, public prayer was one of the most

"An Homily, wherein is declared, that Common Prayer and Sacraments ought to be ministered in a tongue that is understood of the hearers," in *Certain Sermons or Homilies, Appointed to Be Read in Churches* (London: printed for the Prayerbook and Homily Society,
1852), 327.

important aspects of early modern worship. Adoration, petition, confession, thanksgiving, and intercession all featured in these public prayers. Prayer in communal worship is of course only one aspect of a much broader topic, and the borderlines between individual and public devotions are not hard and fast. However, this chapter will focus primarily on prayer in a public setting, reserving a more in-depth discussion of private and family devotions to the chapter on worship outside church.

↩

The years 1570 and 1571 were very difficult ones in the Swiss city of Zurich and its rural hinterland. A cold winter and spring in 1570 led to a bad harvest that summer, further damaged by flooding in June. The winter of 1570–1571 was bitter: it was so cold and snowy that the lake of Zurich froze solid, and snow still lay on the streets in April. The winter grain rotted and Zurich's vineyards were destroyed. People died of the cold, of hunger, and of disease. Because of the persistent bad weather, the price of grain kept rising, doubling in price compared to a normal year. Heinrich Bullinger, the *antistes*, or senior pastor of Zurich, called on the city authorities to do more to alleviate the growing want. At the same time, he offered a theological and pastoral response to the crisis, stating that the sequence of natural disasters was a just punishment from God for the sins of the people and proposing special prayer services of repentance and turning to God for mercy. The magistrates agreed, and beginning in September 1571, they gave orders that the whole population in the city and in the countryside should assemble in church on Tuesday mornings from six to seven in summer and seven to eight in winter for an hourlong worship service of preaching and prayer, ending up with a specially composed prayer to implore God's mercy and forgiveness and turn away divine wrath. The bells were to be rung just like on Sundays, and no one was to work or open up their shops during the time of the service.[1] Zurich was otherwise quite conservative in terms of liturgical developments, and rarely went beyond its original set of prayers developed for its worship services in 1535.[2] Yet this vignette shows that in times of calamity, religious and civil authorities agreed that special prayers were needed. Indeed, the practice of gathering for special prayer services of repentance and petition could provide a pastorally and psychologically astute response to traumatic circumstances, especially in the context of early modern perceptions that disasters came from God's hand in response to human sin.

᠆᠊

In August 1546, a woman named Françoise Pollier, widow of Jean Lullin, was called before the Genevan Consistory because of her persistent refusal to receive the bread and wine in the quarterly celebrations of the Lord's Supper. As was often the case in the first decade after the formal start of the Genevan Reformation, during her appearance before the consistory she was asked to recite her prayers. The Genevan Consistory's expectation was always the same: people were to be able to recite the Lord's Prayer, the Apostles' Creed, and the Ten Commandments, all in the vernacular. These three texts were the framework for doctrinal instruction in the Genevan Catechism. Furthermore, the Lord's Prayer was recited at least once at every Genevan worship service. One would expect, therefore, that by 1546, Françoise Pollier had heard the prayer multiple times and would have internalized it. And yet when asked, she could not recite the entire prayer. Other Genevans had also ground to a halt in the middle of the prayer before the consistory, due to nervousness, ignorance, or unwillingness to comply. In Madame Pollier's case, however, the problem was not that she had failed to

---

[1]Hans Ulrich Bächtold, "Gegen den Hunger beten: Heinrich Bullinger, Zürich, und die Einführung des Gemeinen Gebetes im Jahre 1571," in *Vom Beten, vom Verketzern, vom Predigen. Beiträge zum Zeitalter Heinrich Bullingers und Rudolf Gwalters*, ed. Hans Ulrich Bächtold, Rainer Henrich, and Kurt Jacob Ruetschi (Zug, Switzerland: Achius, 1999), 9-43.
[2]Bächtold, "Gegen den Hunger beten," 9.

memorize the prayer she heard so often in worship, but that she understood only too well what the prayer meant, and that her personal circumstances prevented her from fulfilling the consistory's request. She said the prayer up to the phrase "And forgive us our sins, as we forgive those who sin against us." Here she stopped. Her brother had been killed, and she could not forgive the perpetrators. She said that she prayed that our Lord would forgive her better than she was able to forgive.[3] In this instance, an early modern believer was paying close attention and putting great weight on the words of the Lord's Prayer, which she regularly heard in church. Indeed, this vignette offers a strong counterweight to the worries of those at the time and subsequently who felt that repetition of the Lord's Prayer in communal worship services risked turning it into a quasi-magical or thoughtlessly parroted utterance.

↩

In both these instances, prayer was taken very seriously, both by the authorities who advocated it and by the people who participated in it. Yet the practice of prayer in public worship also gave rise to a number of controversies and debates. In what language should public prayers be voiced, in Latin or in the vernacular? As different confessional groups grew and asserted their own theological identities, were all forms of prayer equally acceptable or were some forms of devotion prohibited? On what grounds? Were church leaders meant to use set forms of prayer and have the congregation voice set responses, or was extemporaneous prayer the only truly genuine form of public devotion? What was the appropriate attitude and posture for the clergy and people at prayer? This chapter will investigate these issues in the broader context of the various early modern theologies of prayer and

---

[3] *Registres du consistoire de Genève au temps de Calvin*, ed. Thomas Lambert, Isabella Watt, and Wallace McDonald (Geneva: Droz, 2001), 2:267.

public prayer as taught to the laity and as practiced in Sunday, week-day, and special-occasion worship services.

THEOLOGIES OF PRAYER

Late medieval theologies of prayer varied depending on the theologian in question. From a lay perspective, however, prayer in the late medi-eval era was understood as a dialogue between the person or commu-nity praying and the holy or divine recipient of the prayer, in most in-stances a saint, the Virgin Mary, or God, whether prayed to as Father, Son, or Holy Spirit.[4] The core prayers all medieval Catholics were to know were the Pater Noster (the Lord's Prayer) and the Ave Maria (the Hail Mary).[5] Those who prayed voiced silently or aloud their ado-ration, confession, petitions for themselves, prayers of intercession for others, and prayers of thanksgiving. The purpose of prayer was both to bring petitions to God, whether directly or through the mediation of a saint or the Virgin Mary, but also to experience the nearness and tender care of God.[6]

From a Protestant perspective, Martin Luther articulated his the-ology of prayer in a number of works, most notably in his 1522 *Bet-büchlein*, or little book of prayer. In it he concentrated on the Lord's Prayer, the Ten Commandments, and the Apostles' Creed, not so much to teach doctrine (that was the purpose of the catechisms) but to use these three texts as springboards for teaching laypeople how to pray. Luther saw prayer as people's response to God, not as the first move from human beings reaching out to God. He therefore strongly

---

[4]See Virginia Reinburg's helpful definition of prayer in "Notes on John Bossy, 'Prayers,'" *Transactions of the Royal Historical Society*, Sixth Series 1 (1991): 148-50.

[5]The full text of the Hail Mary is "Hail Mary, full of grace, the Lord is with thee. Blessed art thou among women, and blessed is the fruit of thy womb, Jesus. Holy Mary, mother of God, pray for us sinners now and at the hour of our death, Amen."

[6]See Margot Fassler's analysis in "Psalms and Prayers in Daily Devotion: A Fifteenth-Century Devotional Anthology from the Diocese of Rheims: Beinecke 757," in *Worship in Medieval and Early Modern Europe: Change and Continuity in Religious Practice*, ed. Karin Maag and John Witvliet (Notre Dame, IN: University of Notre Dame Press, 2004), 15-40, esp. 34.

condemned any practices that turned prayer into a meritorious work that contributed to one's salvation. For Luther, prayer was grounded in human need that responded to God in trust.[7] His *Betbüchlein* also included Psalm texts and the Ave Maria. This last item may seem like a surprising inclusion, but Luther used the text (omitting its last petition) as a model of a prayer directed to God, in which Mary is simply a model believer. In the early years of the Reformation, Luther's unwillingness to reject the text outright allowed those who were struggling with the transition to Protestant worship to still find familiar points of reference, even if Luther interpreted the prayer very differently than in a medieval Catholic context.[8] Luther's theology of prayer called for people to pray with confident trust to God, not turning to the unreliable help of saints, and not trying to make prayer into a meritorious work.[9]

Anabaptist leaders left little evidence of their theology of prayer, although in "A Short, Simple Confession" sent to the Reformed authorities in Zurich in the 1580s, the anonymous author(s) highlighted the important role of the Holy Spirit as the source of prayer: "He also teaches us to pray fervently, for in the prophets he is called a Spirit of grace and prayer. He ignites the believing hearts with the fire of God's love, enlightens and strengthens what is dull and weak, warms and heats up what is cold and frozen before God, and consoles those who grieve over and regret their sins."[10] Among the Anabaptists, the practice of prayer in common worship varied considerably, from silent praying done by all present, to prayers said aloud and led by the

[7]Mary Jane Haemig, "Jehoshaphat and His Prayer Among Sixteenth-Century Lutherans," *Church History* 73, no. 3 (2004): 522-35, esp. 522-24.

[8]Michael Beyer, "Martin Luthers Betbüchlein," *Lutherjahrbuch* 74 (2007): 29-50, esp. 42-44.

[9]Timothy Wengert, "Luther on Prayer in the Large Catechism," in *The Pastoral Luther: Essays on Martin Luther's Practical Theology* (Grand Rapids, MI: Eerdmans, 2009), 179.

[10]"A Short, Simple Confession" (1588), in *Later Writings of the Swiss Anabaptists, 1529–1592,* ed. C. Arnold Snyder (Kitchener, ON: Pandora, 2017), 309.

worship leader. For instance, Balthasar Hubmaier described his practice in his congregation as follows:

> I have admonished the people to pray faithfully and without ceasing. Also in all my preaching I recited with the people loudly and kneeling a public confession, the Lord's Prayer, and a Psalm. I have also again restored the ringing of the bells, evening and morning and midday, when it was earlier done away by other preachers and for the people. I have indicated the ninth hour of prayer.[11]

Hubmaier's depiction of communal prayer in Anabaptist worship services echoed the practices of other reformers, which may well have been Hubmaier's intent in his writing, to lessen suspicions among other Christian groups that Anabaptists prayed and worshiped in anomalous ways.

Like other reformers, John Calvin emphasized the importance of prayer, both in private and in public worship. He underscored prayer's role in sanctifying believers and in increasing both their trust in God and their thankfulness. He urged the faithful to pray to God with reverence, focus, humility, and trust.[12] For Calvin, the starting point of prayer was God's gracious and loving invitation to believers to pray to him. These prayers were to be made in faith to God the Father through the intercession and mediation of Jesus Christ alone, and with the guidance, instruction, and support of the Holy Spirit. Prayers were to be shaped by the words of Scripture. Indeed, Calvin repeatedly advocated using scriptural texts, especially the Psalms, as models for prayer. Most importantly, Calvin stressed that believers should pray from the heart: "For there are many who cry out enough, but it is nothing more than a

---

[11]See Kenneth Davis, *Anabaptism and Asceticism: A Study in Intellectual Origins* (Eugene, OR: Wipf & Stock, 1998), 175.

[12]John Aloisi, "'The Chief Exercise of Faith': John Calvin and the Practice of Prayer," *Detroit Baptist Seminary Journal* 19 (2014): 3-21.

voice sounding in the air. All this is of no use unless the heart is touched. For if we desire that God hears us and answers our prayers, it is necessary that the heart speaks and is burning with a strong desire to pray to him and praise him."[13] Thus Calvin vehemently rejected both prideful and hypocritical prayers.

In the Church of England, corporate prayer was a crucial means of responding to God. In times of danger ultimately caused by generalized sinful behavior, prayers of contrition and acknowledgment of sin by the whole congregation could play a role in averting God's wrath. Conversely, prayers of thanksgiving offered by the body of the faithful were entirely appropriate and even necessary to acknowledge God's saving acts.[14] The liturgies for morning prayer and evening prayer included in the Book of Common Prayer from 1549 onward served as both devotional and teaching tools, connecting worshipers more firmly both to God and to their neighbors. Ashley Cocksworth's in-depth study of the theology that underpins Evensong shows how the service of prayers, psalms, and other readings from Scripture was carefully structured to move worshipers from a genuine awareness of their own sin and need for God to an assurance of divine forgiveness and confidence in praying for others.[15]

Across the confessional spectrum, the similarities between the various theologies of prayer stand out, especially when it came to public prayer. The following overview of the practices of communal prayer in worship services shows both the commonalities and the distinctives that emerged as each confessional group sought to

---

[13]From a fragment of a sermon by Calvin on Acts 2:46-47, quoted in I. John Hesselink, "John Calvin on Prayer," introduction to John Calvin, *On Prayer: Conversation with God* (Louisville: Westminster John Knox, 2006), 1-31, esp. 23.

[14]Natalie Mears, "Special Nationwide Worship and the Book of Common Prayer in England, Wales and Ireland, 1533–1642," in *Worship and the Parish Church in Early Modern Britain*, ed. Natalie Mears and Alec Ryrie (Farnham, UK: Ashgate, 2013), 43-45.

[15]Ashley Cocksworth, "Being Moved in Sundry Places: Evensong, Transformation and the Theology of Prayer," *Theology* 115, no. 5 (2012): 350-56.

shape this key component of worship and teach its practice effectively to the population.

Special Prayers

Although both Catholic and Protestant churches adopted formal liturgies that shaped the practice of prayer in their regular worship services, occasions of national or general celebration or calamity could lead to a proclamation of special prayers to mark the occasion. For example, in England, Henry VIII commissioned his archbishop Thomas Cranmer to prepare a special set of prayers and litanies to support his military campaign in France. Under his successor Edward VI, special prayers were offered at various times, including during the wars against Scotland beginning in 1548 and the epidemic of sweating sickness beginning in 1551. Subsequent occasions for special prayers under later monarchs included wars, plagues and other epidemics, royal pregnancies and births, and plots against the ruler (and subsequent prayers of thanksgiving when the plots were defeated).[16] A 1628 prayer for the English fleet sent to provide military aid to the Huguenots besieged by the king of France at La Rochelle offers an example of a surviving single-page special prayer to be used in corporate worship:

> And whereas now, for the reliefe of some of our distressed brethren, our Gracious Sovereigne thy beloved servant, is moved, out of zeale to thy house, and compassion of the Members of thy Mysticall Body, to send foorth a Fleete to Sea for their reliefe, wee are humble and earnest suiters to thy Divine Majesty, that thou wilt mercifully bee pleased to accept of this endeavour, as a Sacrifice offered to thy selfe. And to blesse this Navie, and all that serve in it, that they may effect that, about which they are sent, and then returne with safetie, to the

---

[16]Mears, "Special Nationwide Worship," 31-57, esp. 35-37.

honour of thy Name the comfort of our gracious King
CHARLES, the refreshing and encouragement of all those
that wish well to the happinesse and prosperitie of the Reformed Churches.[17]

This example of a special prayer to be read out in worship across
England effectively links political objectives and a theological perspective. If taken to heart, this prayer and others like it could contribute to shaping England's Protestant identity. Churches in other
countries adopted similar approaches in times of calamity, as seen
in the first vignette at the start of this chapter, and in Scotland in
November 1587, when plague threatened Edinburgh, Leith, and
other communities. The kirk session of Perth took the opportunity to plan a series of services of prayer and fasting, calling on
inhabitants to join

> in prayer to God that it would please him to remove the plague
> of the pest from the towns of Edinburgh, Leith etc and to pre-
> serve us therefrom as also to preserve us from the pest of the
> soul which is papistic ignorance maintained presently by the
> Jesuits and papists new come in, who press to bring men under
> the thralldom of idolatry and ignorance and from the true
> knowledge of Christ our savior revealed to us in his word and to
> embrace their superstition, rites and ceremonies from the
> which the lord preserve us.[18]

In this instance, the Perth kirk session drew parallels between the
dangers of the physical plague and the spiritual plague caused by what
the church leaders saw as the contagion of the Jesuits' teaching. They
made effective use of the opportunity of special communal prayers to

---

[17]John Craig, "Bodies at Prayer in Early Modern England" in Mears and Ryrie, *Worship and the Parish Church*, 177.

[18]*The Perth Kirk Session Books 1577–1590*, ed. Margo Todd (Woodbridge, UK: Boydell, 2012), 381 (spelling modernized).

both highlight a specific natural danger and alert their congregations to the equally deadly spiritual menace in their environment.

POSTURES OF PRAYER

All church leaders in the early modern period agreed that prayer was an integral part of corporate acts of worship. The appropriate posture for prayer, however, was subject to debate. Should one stand, sit, or kneel? Early medieval Catholic prayer practices of standing with one's arms raised transitioned to kneeling and joining one's hands in prayer by the twelfth century.[19] Although the notion that Catholics prayed in church on their knees, while Protestants sat or stood for prayers was prevalent, even in the Reformation era, the reality was in fact somewhat different. In England, the Book of Common Prayer of 1549 enjoined the clergy and parishioners to kneel for morning and evening prayer and for the confession of sins, though these injunctions were dropped in the 1552 and 1559 editions.[20] The Reformed rejected any kneeling for prayer or devotion in front of images or altars or relics. However, kneeling during the public prayers at worship in Geneva was the common practice throughout the sixteenth century, as evidenced by the testimony of a Catholic witness in the 1550s: "As soon as they come into church, each person chooses a spot and sits down, as in a school, and there they wait until the preacher goes into the pulpit. As soon as the preacher appears, they all kneel down except for him. He stands with his head uncovered and his hands folded together to pray."[21] The kneeling in question may well have been more of a leaning forward to rest one's knees on the bench in front rather than a full kneel on the

---

[19]Christian Grosse, "Y a-t-il une raison réformée des gestes de pieté? Usages controversés de l'agenouillement (xvie- XVIIIe siècle)," in *Les protestants à l'époque moderne: une approche anthropologique*, ed. Olivier Christin and Yves Krumenacker (Rennes: Presses Universitaires de Rennes, 2017), 531-49, esp. 532.

[20]*The Book of Common Prayer 1549* (repr., New York: Church Kalendar Press, 1881), 6, 9, 219.

[21]*Passevent Parisien* (1556) in *Lifting Hearts to the Lord: Worship with John Calvin in Sixteenth-Century Geneva*, ed. Karin Maag (Grand Rapids, MI: Eerdmans, 2016), 63.

ground, since in 1584 Pastor Charles Perrot was reprimanded by the city government for having wanted people to do the full kneel during the public prayers. The magistrates pointed out that to do the full kneel was awkward, especially for women, as there was not enough space between the benches.[22]

Beyond kneeling, when engaged in prayer during public worship, should one raise one's eyes to heaven or close them? Were verbal ejaculations or groans appropriate or important in corporate prayer? In the English context, the use of groans or even tears in public prayers was particularly prevalent among the godly, who understood these signs as evidence of the power of the Holy Spirit at work in the person praying. In some instances, as in the prayer services held in Mildenhall in 1584, the noise of tears and groans during prayer was so loud that it could be heard clear across the street.[23]

In England, the Book of Common Prayer did not mandate the practice of closing one's eyes during public prayer. Instead, it seems to have developed as a result of concern among the godly about visual distractions. Closing one's eyes during prayer was thus a way of focusing one's attention during prayer. This practice only made sense, however, if either the wording of the set prayers was so well-known as to be memorized or if the pastor led extemporaneous prayer to which the congregation listened in silence.[24]

How Were People Taught to Pray?

Because prayer was such an important feature of both public and private devotion, religious leaders invested considerable energy in making sure their people knew how to pray. This instruction was conveyed in different ways, often through books (primers, books of

---

[22]Grosse, "Y a-t-il une raison réformée des gestes de pieté?," 539.

[23]Craig, "Bodies at Prayer," 182.

[24]Craig, "Bodies at Prayer," 184–90.

hours, prayer books, and catechisms) but also through oral teaching and the use of mnemonic devotional objects, such as rosaries.

In the late medieval world, repetition of the Pater Noster and the Ave Maria was encouraged at every turn, whether as a devotional practice centering on the use of rosary beads or as part of a penance or at the start or end of a sequence of other prayers.[25] The practice of using rosaries to recite sets of the Lord's Prayer and the Hail Mary and reflect on key moments of the life, death, and resurrection of Christ and the life of the Virgin Mary grew increasingly popular in Europe by the later fifteenth century. The portability of rosaries and their flexible use as devotional aids meant that they bridged the gap between private and public prayer. Faithful Catholics could and did pray their rosaries together whether at home or at church.[26]

A second way to teach the practice of prayer was through the use of texts. Primers and books of hours were bestsellers in the late medieval world. In general, these works provided a range of prayers and texts from Scripture. Primers usually taught the basic prayers: the Pater Noster and the Ave Maria. Books of Hours ranged from very simple to very ornate works, which included litanies, psalms, liturgies (including the liturgy for the dead), prayers in Latin and in the vernacular, images, and religious calendars noting the feast days of the church. Although in the early Middle Ages books of hours were expensive, their price dropped over time, and these items became generally affordable once they became available in print.[27] When used in corporate worship, a book of hours offered its owner devotional texts that could be read in an undertone while attending Mass.

---

[25]R. N. Swanson, "Prayer and Participation in Late Medieval England," in *Elite and Popular Religion: Papers Read at the 2004 Summer Meeting and the 2005 Winter Meeting of the Ecclesiastical History Society*, ed. Kate Cooper and Jeremy Gregory (Woodbridge, UK: Boydell, 2006), 130-38.

[26]Frank Senn, *The People's Work: A Social History of the Liturgy* (Minneapolis: Fortress, 2006), 245-46.

[27]See Eamon Duffy, "Elite and Popular Religion: The Book of Hours and Lay Piety in the Later Middle Ages," in Cooper and Gregory, *Elite and Popular Religion*, 140-61, esp. 141-49.

These books helped shape medieval prayer life, and indeed in many instances they were the only books a family might own.[28]

The Reformation did not sound the death knell for prayer books. In fact, many mainline Protestant groups adopted the practice to encourage prayer both at home and at church. Lutherans produced numerous prayer books that included prayers for all sorts of situations, from the daily round of work and rest to prayers in times of danger (pregnancy and childbirth, war, threat of death, personal despair, etc.). These prayer books offered biblical models and scriptural texts in crafting these prayers. For instance, the prayer of King Jehoshaphat in 2 Chronicles 20 appeared in numerous Lutheran prayer books as a model prayer for those facing persecution or despair.[29]

Among the Reformed, the practice of providing prayers as examples for use by the laity also continued. In Zurich, Leo Jud's *Shorter Catechism* (1538) provided prayers for before and after meals, when rising in the morning and before going to sleep.[30] Calvin's 1541/1542 Genevan Catechism, for instance, included a series of model prayers to be used at various moments during the day, from getting up in the morning, to meal times, to preparation for school or work, to going to bed at night.[31]

The other main way to teach people how to pray and help them understand the meaning of the prayers recited in worship (especially the Lord's Prayer) was to do so through catechetical instruction. Most Protestant catechisms focused on three main texts: the Ten Commandments, the Apostles' Creed, and the Lord's Prayer. Reformers focused considerable attention on teaching the words and the meaning

---

[28]Virginia Reinburg, "Oral Rites: Prayer and Talk in Early Modern France," in *Spoken Word and Social Practice: Orality in Europe (1400–1700)*, ed. Thomas Cohen and Lesley Twomey (Leiden: Brill, 2015), 375–92, esp. 376–77.

[29]Haemig, "Jehoshaphat and His Prayer," 525–29.

[30]David Priestly, trans., "Leo Jud: The Shorter Catechism," *Zwingliana* 44 (2017): 199–267.

[31]For the text of these prayers, see Maag, *Lifting Hearts to the Lord*, 85–88.

of the Lord's Prayer to their people.[32] In several Anabaptist communities, for instance, there is evidence of the use of catechisms to teach the words and significance of the Lord's Prayer to new believers prior to their baptism.[33] In the Genevan countryside in the 1560s, the diary of pastor Charles Perrot shows him patiently devoting parts of his catechetical instruction to working with the small children of his congregation to get them to learn how to say properly the words of the Lord's Prayer.[34]

These various practices illustrate how creative religious leaders were in teaching and implementing the practice of public prayer in worship. However, a number of key differences in the practice of public prayer among early modern European worshipers persisted and gave rise to considerable debate in the period.

CONFLICTS OVER THE LANGUAGE OF PRAYER

For medieval and early modern Catholics, the bulk of the liturgy and prayers during Mass were in Latin. Even though the prayers were in Latin, that did not mean that congregations were cut off from communal prayer, since they did have access to texts that explained the ritual of the Mass, including the prayers uttered by the priest. For instance, *The Lay Folks' Mass Book*, originally written and used in France from 1150 onward, crossed the English Channel and was available in English by the fourteenth century.[35] This work explained in the vernacular what was happening at various points during the Mass, and also provided guidance on what the laity were meant to do at various points during the service. Its approach offers a window

---

[32]See for instance the section on the Lord's Prayer in Leo Jud's catechism in Priestly, "Leo Jud: The Shorter Catechism," 243-53, 261-62.

[33]Russel Snyder-Penner, "The Ten Commandments, the Lord's Prayer, and the Apostles' Creed as Early Anabaptist Texts," *Mennonite Quarterly Review* 68, no. 3 (1994): 318-35.

[34]"Managing a Country Parish: A Country Pastor's Advice to His Successor" (1567), in Maag, *Lifting Hearts to the Lord*, 69.

[35]Ramie Targoff, *Common Prayer: The Language of Public Devotion in Early Modern England* (Chicago: University of Chicago Press, 2001), 20-22, and n. 22.

into how laypeople could still actively participate in prayer alongside the priest, even if they knew no Latin:

> When the priest goes to his book,
> His private prayers for to look,
> Kneel thou down and say then this,
> That next in black written is:
> It will thy prayer much amend,
> If thou will hold up both thy hands,
> To God with good devotion,
> When thou sayest this orison
> *God receive thy service.*[36]

This extract focused on the prayers said by the priest prior to the consecration of the bread and wine. According to *The Lay Folks' Mass Book*, the laity in attendance had an important assistive role to play in asking God to bless the ritual action of their priest as he prayed in Latin.

The use of Latin in communal worship, especially in the prayers, did not disappear completely in the churches that grew out of the Reformation. Because early modern schooling beyond the basic level took place in Latin, worship services held in schools, academies, and universities continued to be in Latin in many places, including in Lutheran and Anglican contexts. In 1523, in his preface to his German vernacular liturgy, Martin Luther continued to support the practice of public worship in Latin alongside the vernacular. As he noted,

> It is not now my intention to abrogate or to change this service [the Latin liturgy of 1523]. It shall not be affected in the form which we have followed so far; but we shall continue to use it when or where we are pleased or prompted to do so. For in no

---

[36]Targoff, *Common Prayer*, 21.

wise would I want to discontinue the service in the Latin language, because the young are my chief concern.[37]

Evidence for the continued use of Latin in worship in educational contexts also includes the 1560 Latin translation of the Book of Common Prayer, intended for use in English universities and in Ireland, especially in Gaelic-speaking areas.[38] Thus for some early modern Christians, the practice of worshiping and praying in Latin persisted alongside the move to worship in the vernacular.

For many Reformation-era congregations, however, one of the main changes in communal worship was the wholesale shift from Latin to the vernacular in the liturgy, including the prayers. Some church leaders objected to this change, including in England, where conservative Catholic voices spoke out against using English rather than the traditional Latin for prayers. The main argument advanced by Bishop Stephen Gardiner during the reign of Edward VI, and John Christopherson, the dean of Norwich Cathedral and later bishop of Chichester in the reign of Mary I, was that vernacular prayers led by the clergy actually distracted laypeople from their devotions. As Christopherson stated,

> It is much better for them not to understand the common service of the church, because when they hear others praying in a loud voice, in the language that they understand, they are letted from prayer themselves, and so come they to such a slackness and negligence in praying, that at length, as we have well seen in these late days, in manner pray not at all.[39]

---

[37]Martin Luther, "The German Mass and Order of Service," in *Luther's Works*, vol. 53, *Liturgy and Hymns*, ed. Ulrich S. Leopold (Philadelphia: Fortress, 1965), 62-63.

[38]Senn, *People's Work*, 145. See also Francis Proctor, *A History of the Book of Common Prayer, with a Rationale of Its Offices* (Cambridge: MacMillan, 1861), 61.

[39]See Targoff, *Common Prayer*, 14-15.

In other words, Christopherson and those who shared his perspective argued for the continuation of prayers in Latin led by the clergy, as these would not distract the laity from their own devotions, and would allow the priest to continue his prayer offered on behalf of all the faithful.

In contrast, most Protestant church leaders stressed the importance of prayer in the vernacular, which could be understood and taken to heart by the people. Indeed, the reformers consistently emphasized the didactic function of prayer, meant to model for believers how to pray and what to pray for. Hence prayers led by the pastors had to be in the people's own language, and had to be said clearly and distinctly out loud.[40] As the twenty-first sermon in the 1563 *Certain Prayers and Homilies, appointed to be read in churches* noted,

> And therefore, whilst our minister is in rehearsing the prayer, that is made in the name of us all, we must give diligent ear to the words spoken by him, and in heart beg at God's hand those things that he beggeth in words. And to signify that we do so, we say, Amen, at the end of the prayer that he maketh in the name of us all. And this thing can we not do for edification, unless we understand what is spoken. Therefore it is required of necessity, that the common prayer be had in a tongue that the hearers do understand.[41]

Hence public prayers had to be in the language of the people, so that they could understand and assent to what was being prayed in their names.

In England, the transition from the 1549 to the 1552 Book of Common Prayer accentuated not only the importance of the laity's understanding of the prayers but also their active participation. Where the 1549 Book of Common Prayer tended to use "I" and "my" in prayer

---

[40]Targoff, *Common Prayer*, 22-23.
[41]"An Homily, wherein is declared," 330.

litanies involving spoken congregational responses, the 1552 edition changed these to "we" and "our," thus drawing the congregation further into the act of responsorial prayer.[42]

STRUGGLES OVER PROHIBITED PRAYERS

Because prayer was the most direct way for human beings to connect to the divine, whether in individual or collective prayer, religious authorities were keen to ensure that only the right prayers were offered, in the right language, at the right time. Within a mindset that stressed communal confessional unity, anything else could result in trouble, both for the individual who erred and for the faith community as a whole. Hence in Reformed Geneva, the consistory was quick to admonish those who prayed the right prayer but in the wrong language (the Lord's Prayer in Latin rather than in the vernacular) or who prayed the wrong prayer (the Ave Maria was a particular concern especially in the first decade of the Reformation). The consistory also investigated people who prayed the wrong prayer in the wrong context, as in the case of Aima Griosa, a widow accused of kneeling down and saying "Requiescant in pace, amen" over the tomb of her late husband. Two other women had joined her in her prayers, and also sprinkled handfuls of dirt in lieu of holy water, according to the consistory's charges. The consistory admonished them, and told them to attend public worship more regularly and desist from all superstition and idolatry.[43]

Indeed, many reformers were quick to condemn prayers for the dead as part of the entire economy of prayers, rituals, memorial Masses and chantries, and other practices that buttressed the doctrine of purgatory and enriched the pre-Reformation church. Praying specifically for the deceased person (as opposed to prayers for

---

[42]Targoff, Common Prayer, 28-29.
[43]The widow was using the final prayer of the Latin funeral Mass: "May they rest in peace, Amen." As we will see in the chapter on worship practices outside church, liturgical or para-liturgical acts surrounding burials were particularly controversial. Registres du consistoire de Genève, 4:15, 20.

comfort for their bereaved relatives) would imply lack of confidence in God's gift of salvation through Jesus Christ, and would revive the specter of a works-based theology.[44] A good example of the theological reasoning directed at a lay audience against prayer for the dead comes from the Church of England's sermons on prayer in *Certain sermons or homilies, appointed to be read in the churches* published in 1563, during the early part of Queen Elizabeth's reign. The third section of "A Homily or Sermon Concerning Prayer" uses both scriptural references and quotations from early church fathers to dispose briskly of the issue of prayer for the dead. The sermon states, "As the Scripture teacheth us, let us think that the soul of man, passing out of the body, goeth straightways either to heaven, or else to hell, whereof the one needeth no prayer, and the other is without redemption. The only purgatory wherein we must trust to be saved, is the death and blood of Christ."[45] In other words, one should turn to Christ for salvation in this life, and should not pray for the deceased, for the dead are destined either for heaven (in which case they have no need of prayers) or for hell (in which case prayer will not help).

It is worth noting that the prohibition on prayers for the dead was not universal among Protestant leaders, nor did it apply to all possible circumstances in which such prayers might be offered. For instance, both Huldrych Zwingli in Zurich and Martin Luther in Wittenberg in the early years of the Reformation left the door open for private prayer for the deceased, in which the surviving friend or relative would ask God to have mercy on them. Indeed, Zwingli framed his advice in the context of his awareness of how hard it was to move people away from their traditional concern for the welfare of someone's soul after death, noting, "I don't condemn anyone with a concern for the dead

---

[44]Ian Hazlett, "Was Bucer an 'Aérian'? The Question of Praying for the Dead," *Reformation and Renaissance Review* 4, no. 2 (2002): 135-51, esp. 135-39.

[45]"An Homily or Sermon concerning Prayer," in *Certain Sermons or Homilies*, 310.

invoking God to be merciful to them."[46] For his part, the Strasbourg
reformer Martin Bucer went a bit further, allowing for prayers of
thanksgiving in remembrance of those who have died, even in the context of public worship and funeral services, as well as in private prayer.[47]

In England under Edward VI, the authorities moved to get rid of
all forms of liturgical prayer previously in use during Catholic worship. Once the Book of Common Prayer was put into use in 1549,
there were to be no possible rivals or reminders of previous Catholic
forms of prayer. The sermons included in the collection of *Certain
Sermons, or Homilies appointed to be read in Churches* strenuously rejected any prayer directed to saints, or angels. God the Father, Jesus
Christ (humanity's mediator before the face of God), and the Holy
Spirit were the only acceptable recipients of prayer.[48] The 1549 *Act
for the abolishing and putting away of divers books and images* directed
at bishops made it crystal clear that nothing associated with the previous forms of common prayer was to be retained:

> [We] straightly . . . command and charge you, that immediately
> upon the receipt hereof, you do command the dean and preben-
> daries of the cathedral church, the parson, vicar or curate and
> church wardens of every parish, within your diocese, to bring
> and deliver unto you or your deputy—all antiphoners, missals,
> grails, processionals, manuals, legends, pies, portasses, journals,
> and ordinals, after the use of Sarum, Lincoln, York, or any
> other private use, and all other books of service, the keeping
> whereof should be a let to the usage of the said book of common
> prayers, and that you take the same books into your hands—
> and them so deface and abolish that they never after may serve

---

[46]Hazlett, "Was Bucer an 'Aérian'?," 144-45.
[47]Hazlett, "Was Bucer an 'Aérian'?," 145-50.
[48]"An Homily or Sermon concerning Prayer," 297-303.

either to any such use, as they were provided for, or be at any time a let to that godly and uniform order.[49]

The purposeful destruction of rival liturgical texts was meant to prevent clergy and people from maintaining or reverting to the use of the wrong prayers in the eyes of the new Protestant leadership. In some cases, however, texts that could be used as the basis for prayers (such as calendars indicating the feast days of various saints) were preserved, but altered or amended, adding in the names of Protestant heroes and martyrs, and scoring out the names of Catholic saints. For instance, one or more early modern owners of a surviving manuscript book of hours from the late fifteenth century for use in England added in the names of Thomas Cranmer, Hugh Latimer, and Thomas Ridley along with the dates of their executions under Queen Mary, and crossed out the feast day of Thomas à Becket, one of England's most famous medieval saints.[50] This survival of a pre-Reformation Catholic aid to prayer and devotion shows how difficult it was for the authorities to eliminate everything that could serve to support Catholic prayer life. At the same time, the reworking of the text is evidence of creative appropriation of sacred time to fit within the new Protestant perspective. Protestant printers also began printing fully Protestant calendars, to accompany Psalters, collections of prayers, or devotional works. These calendars focused on highlighting biblical events, such as the people of Israel's crossing of the Jordan or the conversion of Paul. They also included the major christological feast days of the liturgical year. These calendars also included current-day or recent events, such as the birth and death dates of various reformers and the dates of accession of key monarchs.[51]

---

[49]Targoff, *Common Prayer*, 25.

[50]Gania Barlow, "Protestant Martyrs Added to a Book of Hours in English Ownership," *Notes and Queries* 58, no. 2 (2011): 208-10.

[51]Max Engammare, "The Growth and Decline of Huguenot Calendars," in *On Time, Punctuality, and Discipline in Early Modern Calvinism*, trans. Karin Maag (Cambridge: Cambridge University Press, 2010), 125-91.

Although these Protestant calendars did not build direct connections between the highlighted dates and specific prayers, they did offer a competing product that could encourage thankful remembrance in prayer and fit within a Protestant worldview.

CONFLICTS OVER SET VERSUS EXTEMPORANEOUS PRAYER

One of the enduring debates in Reformed churches following the Reformation was over the words used in prayer in corporate worship. One of the most difficult aspects of the debate over set prayers versus extemporaneous prayers had to do with the prayer that Jesus taught his disciples in the Gospels—namely, the Lord's Prayer. Was this prayer meant to be prayed in worship services and, if so, under what circumstances and how frequently? For some among the Reformed, the prayer could too quickly become ritualistic, particularly if it was repeated more than once during the same worship service.[52] In 1549, when the Genevan magistrates requested that the pastors make greater use of the Lord's Prayer in public worship, Calvin strongly objected, stating, "As for the Pater, we say it twice on Sundays twice at each service and also during the catechism [service], and to do otherwise would be an incantation and a magic charm, just as in the past people used to say In principio erat verbum."[53]

Thus debates raged over whether it was best to use a set form for prayer, or whether extemporaneous prayer was the only true and valid way of leading congregations in worship. The controversy was particularly acute in England, where those who sought further reform in the Church of England strongly objected to the use of the Book of Common Prayer. To them, its set prayers and responses, and the repetition of prayers from worship service to worship service, were too reminiscent of

---

[52]Judith Maltby, "'Extravagencies and Impertinences': Set Forms, Conceived and Extempore Prayer in Revolutionary England" in Mears and Ryrie, *Worship and the Parish Church*, 224.

[53]See Robert Kingdon and Thomas Lambert, *Reforming Geneva: Discipline, Faith and Anger in Calvin's Geneva* (Geneva: Droz, 2012), 41. The Latin phrase means "In the beginning was the Word," from the start of the Gospel of John.

the Latin Mass, even though the prayers were said in English. Instead of the Book of Common Prayer, these supporters of further reformation advocated extemporaneous, unrehearsed prayer uttered by the clergy through the inspiration of the Holy Spirit.[54]

For their part, their opponents who supported the continuing use of the Book of Common Prayer and set prayers in public worship critiqued extemporaneous prayer on several grounds. For instance, in a sermon preached in Chelmsford in 1632 to his fellow clergy at their quarter sessions meeting, the Essex priest John Browning chose as his text Ecclesiastes 5:2: "Be not rash with thy mouth, and let not thine heart be hasty to utter anything before God: for God is in Heaven, and thou upon earth, therefore let thy words be few."[55] In his sermon, Browning highlighted the historic roots of set prayer in communal worship from the time of the early church onward and condemned extemporaneous prayer in church services. He rhetorically asked, "How many idle words, irreverent, unmannerly, ridiculous, if not blasphemous passages fall from many, in their suddenly conceived prayers?"[56] Not surprisingly in the light of his chosen text, one of Browning's main concerns about extemporaneous prayer in public worship was its inordinate length, in contrast to the much shorter set prayers. Indeed, Browning set out nine reasons why using shorter set prayers in public worship was the right approach, both theologically and practically:

1. That the weakest devotion of the meanest Christian may not be oppressed.

2. That the people might have space and place to joyne with the Priest, and give their assent to their owne prayers.

---

[54]See Maltby, "Set Forms," 221-43.

[55]John Browning, "Of the Duties, Nature, and Lawes of Publike Prayer: A Sermon Preached in Chelmsford at a Quarter-Sessions, 1632," in *Publike-Prayer and the Fasts of the Church: Six Sermons, or Tractates* (London: Richard Badger, 1636), 65-97.

[56]Browning, "Of the Duties," 85 (emphasis original).

3. That by their often responds, the mind of the people may be kept from wandering.

4. That their devotion (thus) might be the more excited and stirred up.

5. That their attention (thus) might be kept waking, by their often responds, which were expected from them.

6. That hereby they might shew their confidence in God's mercy by CHRIST's merits, as contrary to the Heathen practice, *Mat. 6.7.*

7. That by such means the Priest also might in such spaces be both eased, and refreshed in the time of prayer.

8. That there might be a space for meditation.

9. But especially that our *Saviour's* command might be observed, who hath thus, both by his precept and example, commanded.[57]

Browning's strong defense of set prayers provides a window into the challenges faced by clergy who had to find ways to lead in communal prayer and hold their congregation's attention in the process. His commonsense observation that people are more likely to pay attention and not let their minds wander if they are active participants in the process through their responses in set prayers argues for pedagogical insight on the part of those advocating for set prayer.

Yet the Puritan wing of the English church managed to get the Book of Common Prayer banned during the period of the Commonwealth (1649–1660), and a *Directory for Public Worship* was authorized already in 1645. This new work called for pastors to pray extemporaneously, but ran into a number of difficulties. Some clergy worried that they lacked the inspiration to lead their congregation in prayer without a form of words to turn to. Some instead substituted prayers of their own that they wrote out in advance, thus not using the Book of Common Prayer and presumably not repeating the same prayer

---

[57]Browning, "Of the Duties," 90-91 (emphasis original).

week by week, but hardly adopting the genuine notion of extemporaneous prayer. This halfway house was known as "conceived prayers."[58]

The *Directory for Public Worship* entrusted the entire task of public prayer during worship services to the pastor: he was to pray and the people were to listen in reverent silence. Ironically, therefore, even though the critics of the Book of Common Prayer condemned it for being too formulaic, it had at least allowed laypeople to participate actively in public prayer by voicing the responses in bidding prayers and litanies. The extemporaneous prayers of the clergy as mandated by the *Directory for Public Worship* encouraged the clergy to speak, but kept the laity silent.[59]

CONCLUSION

These debates over the practice of prayer in early modern churches highlight how important prayer was as a key component of worship. Although there was broad agreement that prayer linked people to God and to each other, controversies over how to pray, in what language, and in what form divided confessional groups from each other and even created internal dissent. The deep divisions that emerged over what was meant to bring the worshiping community together before the face of God are somewhat ironic. Yet the stakes were high: because public prayer opened a conduit between God and his worshiping people, it had to be done right.

FOR FURTHER READING

Cressy, David. *Birth, Marriage, and Death: Ritual, Religion, and the Life-Cycle in Tudor and Stuart England.* Oxford: Oxford University Press, 1997.

Haemig, Mary Jane. "Jehoshaphat and His Prayer Among Sixteenth-Century Lutherans." *Church History* 73/3 (2004): 522-35.

---

[58]Maltby, "Set Forms," 237-38.
[59]Craig, "Bodies at Prayer," 173-96, esp. 183-84.

Mears, Natalie and Alec Ryrie, eds. *Worship and the Parish Church in Early Modern Britain*. Farnham: Ashgate, 2013.

Senn, Frank. *The People's Work: A Social History of the Liturgy*. Minneapolis: Fortress Press, 2006.

Targoff, Ramie. *Common Prayer: The Language of Public Devotion in Early Modern England*. Chicago: University of Chicago Press, 2001.

FIVE

BAPTISM

---

*In Christ—indeed in our baptism, since we are baptized into
Christ—we have the forgiveness of sins without ceasing. So even if
you fall and sin out of weakness—as happens, alas, too much and
too often, without ceasing—then run and crawl to your baptism,
in which all of your sins are forgiven and washed away; draw
comfort, lift yourself up again; and believe that in baptism you
were washed not only from one sin but from all your sins.*

MARTIN LUTHER,
"SERMON ON THE DAY OF CHRIST'S EPIPHANY" (1546)

OF ALL THE TEACHINGS OF JESUS, the command to baptize seems
among the most straightforward. The Scriptures offer both the account of Jesus' own baptism and his command in Matthew 28:19-20
to "go and make disciples of all nations, baptizing them in the name of
the Father and of the Son and of the Holy Spirit, and teaching them
to obey everything I have commanded you." At first glance, it would
seem that there would be few points of divergence among Christians
regarding this facet of worship. And yet, even today, questions and

---

See *Acts*, ed. Esther Chung-Kim and Todd R. Hains, Reformation Commentary on Scripture, New Testament VI (Downers Grove: IVP Academic, 2014), 266-67.

debates abound. The use of water for baptism seems clear. But should one immerse the candidates or sprinkle water on them? Should one baptize infants or simply dedicate them, waiting to baptize them until they are old enough to testify to their faith on their own behalf? If baptizing infants, is the practice of having godparents or sponsors make promises in the child's name important, or should parents alone make these promises? Should religious instruction of the candidate (or of the parents in the case of an infant) precede baptism? Does baptism make someone into a full member of his or her faith community, or is there another step or ritual or sacrament that needs to occur at a later date? Can the ritual of baptism be done with only the family of the baptismal candidate present, or should baptism only be celebrated with the whole congregation in attendance? Is emergency baptism ever valid? If baptism is such an important starting point for a Christian's life, what theological and pastoral responses are there for families whose child dies before he or she can be baptized?

These are not new questions. In fact, church leaders in the Reformation era wrestled with these same issues, coming up with a range of possible responses. Although their liturgical practices and theologies of baptism differed, Reformation-era Roman Catholics, Lutherans, Reformed Christians, and Anabaptists all held to the same core practice when it came to baptism: a person was baptized with water in the name of the Father, Son, and Holy Spirit.

Beyond these points of agreement, however, were divergences of practice rooted both in theology and in differing liturgical traditions. By examining how baptism was celebrated across the confessional spectrum in the Reformation era, we can better understand how this pivotal sacrament was enacted in early modern worship and gain new insights into the roots of contemporary debates over baptism in worship. To start, let us consider some occasions when the celebration of a baptism caused controversy.

Disputes over the Practice of Baptism

For the vast majority of early modern Christians, their first encounter with communal worship occurred when they received the sacrament of baptism, even though the practice of infant baptism meant that they would have no later recollection of the event. Given the general agreement across Christian denominations as to the importance of a trinitarian baptism done with water, one might be forgiven for thinking that surely this aspect of worship practice would be relatively trouble-free in the Reformation era. However, as the following accounts show, the practice of baptism could bring closely held theological perspectives and deeply rooted social practices into tension. The resulting conflicts shed light on how Reformation-era Christians understood the fundamental meaning of this sacrament.

In the early 1590s, a butcher brought his baby daughter for baptism in the German city of Dresden, one of the main cities in Saxony. Beginning in 1586, the new Elector of Saxony, Christian, had begun to implement further religious reforms in the Lutheran territory, pushing it in a more Calvinist direction. One of the hallmarks of a more Calvinist understanding of baptism was to reject any perceived remnants of Catholic practices in the sacrament, including the use of exorcisms.[1] Elector Christian thus banned the use of exorcisms in baptism in Saxony beginning on July 4, 1591. However, the butcher turned out to be a staunch proponent of the Lutheran ritual, and attended the baptism with his cleaver in hand, threatening to strike the pastor with the cleaver if the pastor tried to omit the exorcisms.[2] Here we have someone who had internalized the ritual of baptism to

---

[1] Exorcisms here refers to the rituals of prayer and anointing that were meant to deliver the baptismal candidate from the power of Satan.

[2] Bodo Nischan, "The Exorcism Controversy and Baptism in the Late Reformation," *Sixteenth Century Journal* 18 (1987): 31-52, esp. 36-39.

such an extent that he was prepared to use force to have one particular part of the rite retained for his daughter. In his eyes, the exorcism was not an indifferent matter or an optional aspect but was a core component of a fully valid baptism.

⸺

In the first two decades after Geneva formally accepted the Reformation in 1536, there were clear gaps between the pastors' understanding of what it meant to be truly Reformed and the population's perspective on this matter. Calvin and his colleagues were always worried about the possibilities of resurgent Catholic superstition, even in the baptismal ritual. By 1546, the Genevan pastors had established an edict promulgated by the Genevan city council, listing names that could not be given to Genevan children at baptism. Many of the names on the list were associated in the pastors' minds with Roman Catholicism, including the names of the three wise men (Melchior, Gaspard, and Balthasar) and the name Claude (and all variants thereof), because there was a shrine to St. Claude right outside Geneva in Catholic Savoy. The Genevans, however, tended to name the children after themselves, or after the infants' godparents, and in this first generation after the Reformation, all the adults had "Catholic" names, including Gaspard, or Balthasar, or Claude. So the following scenes occurred at Genevan baptisms on more than one occasion when the sponsor presented the child for baptism at the end of a sermon during a regular worship service. In August 1546, when the pastor asked for the name of the child, the sponsor replied "Claude." In response, the pastor baptized the baby "Abram." Uproar ensued, with the father (Ameyd Chappuis) eventually summoned to the consistory to explain himself, especially as it appeared that after the baptismal rite in church had been completed, the father took the baby home and had him rebaptized by a midwife, giving him the name Claude. In his interview with the consistory, Chappuis insisted that the church baptism had not been valid, because he had heard the pastor say that the baby was baptized "in the name of Abram" rather than in the name of the Father, Son, and Holy Spirit.[3] Here baptism became the ground of conflict within one confessional group, with the pastors' theological anxieties confronting the Genevans' desire to honor the godfather of their child in the naming ceremony during the baptism.

෴

In Amsterdam's French-speaking (Walloon) church on Sunday October 11, 1615, three infants were due to be baptized by pastor Thomas Maurois. However, in the interval between the prayers spoken by Pastor Maurois and the moment when the babies would be baptized, another pastor, Simon Goulart the younger, came forward and carried out the baptisms instead. At first glance, the problem here seems to be one of protocol and mixed signals between the pastors, but in fact the issue was a much deeper one. Goulart had been suspended from preaching and barred from the Lord's Supper in the previous month, due to an anti-predestinarian sermon he preached on September 15. Therefore, in the eyes of his consistory, he should not have had any role in any celebration of the sacraments, much less tried to usurp Pastor Maurois's role in the baptisms. Debate raged in the consistory and congregation as to whether the baptisms carried out by Goulart were in fact valid or whether they needed to be redone.[4] In this instance, a baptismal rite became the venue for a wider conflict over pastoral authority, church discipline, and the theology of election.

---

[3]Karen Spierling, *Infant Baptism in Reformation Geneva* (Aldershot, UK: Ashgate, 2005), 140-52.
[4]Karin Maag, "Called to Be a Pastor: Issues of Vocation in the Early Modern Period," *Sixteenth Century Journal* 35 (2004): 65-78, esp. 66-68. There is no evidence in the records that the baptisms were redone.

↜

These three accounts from different places and time periods share an important common feature: all three underscore the importance of baptismal rituals in defining the parameters of the community of faith. To understand better how the rites of baptism helped strengthen believers' identity, let us consider why and how baptisms were celebrated in the Reformation era.

WHY BAPTIZE?

Each competing confessional group in Reformation Europe articulated its own vision of baptism's purpose. At times, as in the case of the Zurich reformer Huldrych Zwingli and the Anabaptist leader Balthasar Hubmaier, these contrasting understandings of the sacrament were articulated in back-and-forth polemical tracts.[5] In most cases, the sources for theologies of baptism can be found in confessions, catechisms, liturgies, and minutes of church councils and synods, as well as in doctrinal works and sermons.

Roman Catholic baptismal theology held that the original sin that clings to infants presented for baptism is washed away by the waters of baptism and that the sacrament opens to them the way to heaven, setting them on the path of salvation.[6] In his *Summa Theologiae*, Thomas Aquinas upheld the necessity of infant baptism:

> Now children contract original sin from the sin of Adam; which is made clear by the fact that they are under the ban of death, which "passed upon all" on account of the sin of the first man, as the Apostle says in the same passage (Romans 5:12). Much more, therefore, can children receive grace through

---

[5]For more on Hubmaier and Zwingli's writings on baptism, see C. Arnold Snyder, "Swiss Anabaptism: The Beginnings, 1523–25," in *A Companion to Anabaptism and Spiritualism, 1521–1700*, ed. John Roth and James Stayer (Leiden: Brill, 2007), 45-81, esp. 69-72.

[6]J. V. Fesko, *Word, Water, and Spirit: A Reformed Perspective on Baptism* (Grand Rapids, MI: Reformation Heritage Books, 2010), 34-35.

Christ, so as to reign in eternal life. But our Lord himself said (John 3:5): "Unless a man be born again of water and the Holy Ghost, he cannot enter into the kingdom of God." Consequently it became necessary to baptize children, that, as in birth they incurred damnation through Adam so in a second birth they might obtain salvation through Christ. Moreover, it was fitting that children should receive baptism, in order that being reared from childhood in things pertaining to the Christian mode of life, they may the more easily persevere therein.[7]

Removing the power of Satan from the baptismal candidate was the important first step, carried out via exorcisms pronounced by the priest before the baptismal candidate ever entered the church. These exorcisms formed a crucial part of the Catholic prebaptism ritual from the third century onward.[8]

Luther's theology of baptism also focused on the sacrament's role in removing original sin, but he placed the central emphasis not on the water of baptism but on the role of God's Word in the sacrament.[9] The third question and answer on baptism in Luther's 1529 *Small Catechism* highlights this important feature:

> How can water do such great things? It is not the water indeed that does them, but the word of God which is in and with the water, and faith, which trusts such word of God in the water. For without the word of God the water is simple water and no baptism. But with the word of God it is a baptism, that is, a gracious water of life and a washing of regeneration in the Holy Ghost.[10]

---

[7]Thomas Aquinas, *Summa Theologiae*, trans. the Fathers of the English Dominican Province (London: Burns Oates, & Washbourne, 1920), III, Q. 68, art. 9.

[8]Nischan, "Exorcism Controversy," 31-52, esp. 32.

[9]Fesko, *Word, Water, and Spirit*, 55-56.

[10]Martin Luther, *Small Catechism* (1529), in *Triglot Concordia: The Symbolical Books of the Evangelical Lutheran Church: German-Latin-English* (St. Louis: Concordia Publishing House, 1921).

Baptism, according to Luther, "effects forgiveness of sins, delivers from death and the devil, and grants eternal salvation to all who believe."[11] In baptism, God acted to justify and save without regard for human deeds or merit.[12] Thus baptism was necessary for all believers, and infants who died unbaptized remained under the weight and penalty of original sin. It is worth pointing out that Lutheran theologians articulated a range of views on baptism's effect on salvation. For instance, Philipp Melanchthon in his *Loci communes* provided a more in-depth analysis of baptism as a sign pointing to the promises of God, adding, "You can be justified without a sign, provided you believe."[13]

For the Reformed, the sacrament of baptism itself was not properly salvific—instead, it was a sign and seal of the covenant between God and his people, marking the newly baptized as one of God's flock. Infants were thus to be baptized as a sign of their membership in the community of God's covenant people. In Zurich, for instance, responding to Anabaptist critiques, Zwingli argued that infants ought to be baptized, because they too were part of the household of God alongside their believing parents. As he noted, "The children of believers are as much within the church and as much among the sons of God as are their parents."[14] Just as circumcision had functioned as a sign of the covenant among the people of Israel, so baptism now served as a sign of the covenant for Christians.[15] As Calvin noted in his *Institutes of the Christian Religion*, "The children of believers are baptized not in order that they who were previously strangers to the church may then for the first time become children of God, but rather that, because by the blessing of the

---

[11]See *The Book of Concord*, ed. Theodore Tappert (Philadelphia: Fortress, 1959), 348.

[12]For more on Luther's baptismal theology, see Bryan Spinks, "Luther's Timely Theology of Unilateral Baptism," *Lutheran Quarterly* 1 (1995): 23-45.

[13]Philipp Melanchthon, *Loci communes theologici*, in *Melanchthon and Bucer*, ed. Wilhelm Pauck (Philadelphia: Westminster, 1969), 134.

[14]Huldrych Zwingli, "Refutation Against the Tricks of the Catabaptists" (1527), in *Selected Works of Huldreich Zwingli*, ed. Samuel Macauley Jackson (Philadelphia: Longmans, Green, 1901), 142.

[15]Spierling, *Infant Baptism in Reformation Geneva*, 34-35.

promise they already belonged to the body of Christ, they are received into the church with this solemn sign."[16]

In early modern England, the theology of baptism articulated during the reign of Edward VI shifted from a position closer to the Lutheran perspective to a more Reformed view, as evidenced in the baptismal liturgies included in the 1549 and 1552 Book of Common Prayer. The 1549 liturgy of baptism was largely modeled on German baptismal liturgies as used in Strasbourg, Nuremberg, and Wittenberg. The English rite of 1549 included a translation of Luther's baptismal prayer known as the Flood Prayer, because of its references to Noah and his family in the ark surviving the great flood, and to the people of Israel safely crossing the Red Sea while the pursuing Egyptians drowned. The prayer includes the following statement: "that by this wholesome laver [washing] of regeneration, whatsoever sin in them may be washed clean away; that they, being delivered from thy wrath may be received into the ark of Christ's Church, and so saved from perishing."[17] Thus in 1549, the liturgy of the Church of England understood baptism as a washing away of original sin. But by 1552, the second Book of Common Prayer simplified the baptismal liturgy and took the sacrament in a more Reformed direction, shortening the Flood Prayer and taking out any references in the prayer to the waters of baptism washing away original sin. In the 1552 liturgy, the prayer before the baptism itself included the following petition: "Regard, we beseech thee, the supplications of thy congregation, and grant that all thy servants which shall be baptized in this water, may receive the fullness of thy grace, and ever remain in the number of thy faithful and elect children."[18] The emphasis on the baptismal ritual as a sign of the child's status as one of the elect echoed Calvin's views.

---

[16]John Calvin, *Institutes of the Christian Religion*, ed. John T. McNeill, trans. Ford Lewis Battles (Philadelphia: Westminster, 1960), 4.15.22.

[17]*The Book of Common Prayer 1549* (repr., New York: Church Kalendar Press, 1881), 233.

[18]*The Second Prayer-Book of Edward VI, 1552* (London: Griffith, Farran, Browne, [n.d.]), 176.

By the reign of Elizabeth, the 1559 Book of Common Prayer followed the liturgy of the 1552 edition. By the later sixteenth century, therefore, the Anglican church followed Reformed theology regarding baptism, seeing the sacrament as the sign of adoption into the family of God, and as a seal of salvation.[19]

For their part, the Anabaptists felt that the Lutherans and Reformed had abdicated their stated desire to be faithful to Scripture, and had only gone partway to a genuine Reformation. The Anabaptists read Jesus' words in Matthew 28, and understood baptism as the sacrament that follows on from a decision taken by a believer old enough to testify to his or her own faith. In a way, the Anabaptists were reviving the early church practice of administering baptism to adult catechumens after a protracted process of religious instruction. To the Anabaptists, baptism was an outward witness of the inner conversion of the new believer from a life of sin to a life of repentance and following Christ.[20] In Balthasar Hubmaier's words, "[Baptism] is nothing else than a public confession and testimony of an inward faith and commitment."[21] For Hubmaier and his fellow Anabaptists, a valid baptism only took place when a person freely confessed his or her own faith and requested the sacrament. The Zurich Anabaptist leader Felix Manz reiterated and reinforced this perspective in his interpretation of Acts 10, regarding the baptism of Cornelius by Peter. Manz explained the purpose of baptism as follows:

> After the receiving of this teaching and the descent of the Holy
> Spirit, which was evidenced to those who had heard the word of

---

[19]See Will Coster, *Baptism and Spiritual Kinship in Early Modern England* (Aldershot, UK: Ashgate, 2002), 49-51.

[20]Hughes Oliphant Old, *The Shaping of the Reformed Baptismal Rite in the Sixteenth Century* (Grand Rapids, MI: Eerdmans, 1992), 84-99.

[21]See Jonathan Rainbow, "'Confessor Baptism': The Baptismal Doctrine of the Early Anabaptists," *American Baptist Quarterly* 8 (1989): 276-90, esp. 284.

Peter by the speaking in tongues, they were thereafter poured over with water, meaning that just as they were cleansed within by the coming of the Holy Spirit, so they were also poured over with water externally to signify for the inner cleansing and dying to sin.[22]

Manz emphasized the role of baptism as an external confirmation of an internal transformation that had already occurred.

WHO WAS BAPTIZED?

In early modern western Europe, Roman Catholics, Lutherans, and the Reformed and Anglicans primarily baptized infants. Baptisms of adult converts from other faiths were rare in these churches in the sixteenth century, though in the fifteenth century, Catholic church and state pressures on Jews and Muslims in Spain had led to adult conversions and baptisms, many of these forced. Christian missionary work on other continents in the sixteenth century did lead to adult baptisms, sometimes en masse, though within a few generations, here too infant baptism became the norm. In Europe, the Anabaptists held a distinctly different position on who should be baptized. They held strictly to believer's baptism and refused to administer the sacrament to infants, since these could not testify to their own faith prior to receiving the sacrament. This view separated them from the rest of society, and placed them in danger from fellow Christians because Anabaptist adult baptism, at least in the first generations, seemed to imply a rejection of their own infant baptism. Rebaptism had been a crime already under Roman law at the time of the Donatists in the early church.[23]

---

[22] Quoted in Abraham Friesen, "Acts 10: The Baptism of Cornelius as Interpreted by Thomas Müntzer and Felix Manz," *Mennonite Quarterly Review* 64, no. 1 (1990): 5-22.

[23] See Glenn Sunshine, *A Brief Introduction to the Reformation* (Louisville: Westminster John Knox, 2017), 45.

WHO COULD BAPTIZE?

For Catholics, Lutherans, Anglicans, and Reformed churches in the early modern era, a valid baptism normally was administered by an ordained member of the clergy. Catholics before and after the Reformation left room for emergency baptisms by a layperson (usually a midwife) in cases when a baby was in imminent danger of death and there was no time to bring the infant to church for the sacrament. Given the high rates of infant mortality at or shortly after birth, the issue of emergency baptisms touched many families directly. In Elizabethan England, for instance, estimates are that 2 percent of all children born had died by the end of the first day of life, and 5 percent by the end of their first week.[24] Midwives were taught the trinitarian baptismal formula and were ordered to have clean water to hand in the birthing room in case of need. Lutherans also authorized midwives to perform emergency baptisms in case of need. Both Lutheran clergy and church ordinances underscored this important obligation as a key part of midwives' duties. Indeed, in Joachimstal during the Thirty Years' War, when the formerly Lutheran community was in Catholic hands, Lutheran midwives successfully retained the right to baptize infants in Lutheran households, in spite of the petition of the Catholic cantor to do so in their stead.[25] In the Church of England in the sixteenth century, emergency baptisms by midwives persisted, but by the seventeenth century the prevalent practice was to call a pastor to come to the home to administer the sacrament if a baptism needed to be performed in a hurry.[26] For their part, the Reformed insisted that the only valid baptism was one done in church by an ordained pastor and worked to eliminate the practice of emergency

---

[24]David Cressy, *Birth, Marriage, and Death: Ritual, Religion, and the Life-Cycle in Tudor and Stuart England* (Oxford: Oxford University Press, 1997), 117.

[25]Christopher Brown, "Early Modern Midwives and the Lutheran Doctrine of Vocation," *Journal of Lutheran Ethics* 4, no. 2 (2004): www.elca.org/JLE/Articles/783.

[26]Cressy, *Birth, Marriage, and Death,* 117-23.

baptisms carried out by laypeople, especially by midwives. As Calvin noted in his *Institutes of the Christian Religion,*

> It is also here pertinent to observe, that it is improper for private individuals to take upon themselves the administration of baptism; for it, as well as the dispensation of the Supper, is part of the ministerial office. For Christ did not give command to any men or women whatever to baptize, but to those whom he had appointed apostles.[27]

In contrast, Anabaptists, especially in the first years of their communities, held that believers could baptize each other upon request—clergy were not necessary for the rite to be valid. In 1525, for instance, the young Zurich patrician Conrad Grebel, a layman, baptized Jörg Blaurock at the latter's request. Other baptisms followed among the gathered group, though it is unclear whether Grebel or Blaurock did the baptizing.[28]

Across the board, the Roman Catholic Church, Lutheran, Anglican, and Reformed churches held that baptism was a sacrament that could only be administered once in one's lifetime. Anabaptists also held to this view, though it seemed to outsiders that adult converts to Anabaptism were in fact being baptized for a second time. However, because they rejected the validity of infant baptism, adults who joined the Anabaptist movement felt the believers' baptism they received upon conversion was the first and only real administration of the sacrament. The Catholic Church did recognize that in some instances it might be impossible to discover whether a child had in fact been baptized by a midwife. Thus the church developed the concept of a conditional baptism, which only took effect if the sacrament had

---

[27]Calvin, *Institutes* 4.15.20.
[28]Paul Brand, "'They Had Said Nothing About Rebaptism': The Surprising Birth of Swiss Anabaptism," *German History* 22, no. 2 (2004): 155-80, esp. 160.

not previously been carried out on the child.[29] The Church of England also developed a short ritual in cases where there was uncertainty over the validity of an emergency baptism.[30] Yet even these conditional baptisms did not alter the fact that baptism was a once-only sacrament, mutually recognized as valid across confessional groups. In other words, someone who converted from Roman Catholicism to the Reformed faith would not be rebaptized, nor would someone whose faith journey went in the opposite direction.

WHEN AND WHERE COULD A BAPTISM TAKE PLACE?

The Catholic emphasis on baptism as necessary for salvation meant that the church urged parents not to delay in bringing their infants for baptism. In general, the practice was to have the baby baptized within eight days of birth.[31] A regular (nonemergency) Catholic baptism was to take place in church, beginning at the threshold with the exorcism rituals, and then moving to the font for the actual baptism. The font was located close to the main (western) entrance to the church. Thus the baptismal ritual visibly marked the entrance of the newly baptized into the Christian community.[32] As noted above, because baptism was necessary for salvation, the Catholic Church admitted the practice of emergency baptisms. An emergency baptism properly administered was fully valid and would not be repeated, since to repeat a baptism was to reject the salvific power of the first baptism.

Luther's understanding of the effectiveness of baptism resting in the power of the Word of God meant that baptisms were normally to be celebrated in church, led by a pastor, and in the presence of the

---

[29]See Paul Turner, "On Conditional Baptism," *Worship* 91 (2017): 4-11, esp. 4-6.

[30]*The Book of Common Prayer: The Texts of 1549, 1559, and 1662*, ed. Brian Cummings (Oxford: Oxford University Press, 2011), 56 (1549), 150 (1559), 419 (1662).

[31]Old, *Shaping*, 25.

[32]Malcolm Lovibond, "In the Triune Name: Some Aspects of Baptismal Practice in Early Reformed Churches," *Reformation and Renaissance Review* 7 (2005): 320-21.

congregation. One of the main pieces of evidence pointing to the importance of baptism as a congregational ritual was the shift in the location of the baptismal font, from its original location near the church door to its Reformation relocation in the center of the church, in the midst of the congregation.[33]

For its part, the Anglican Book of Common Prayer noted that baptisms should normally be celebrated on the closest Sunday or holy day following the birth. Baptisms were to take place in church during a regular worship service, so that congregation members could bear witness to the receiving of the baptized into the body of the faithful and bring to mind their own baptisms.[34] The baptismal fonts in English churches remained by the church doors, in the same location as before the Reformation. Vigorous debates later surfaced in the English church between Anglicans and Puritans over whether the sacrament ought to be celebrated by the entrance doors or close to the pulpit and whether the font should be used or replaced by a basin, a receptacle less laden with Catholic symbolism.[35]

Although baptisms in England after the Reformation were usually meant to take place in church, the Book of Common Prayer did allow for private baptism at home in case of need, and even provided instructions on how to carry out such a baptism correctly. Children who received this emergency baptism and subsequently lived were to be brought to church by their family so that the priest could confirm that the baptismal ritual had correctly been carried out. This verification also involved many of the same prayers and readings as a regular in-church baptism.[36]

As noted above, for the Reformed, the only valid baptism was one that took place in church during a regular worship service, although

---

[33]Frank Senn, *Christian Liturgy: Catholic and Evangelical* (Minneapolis: Fortress, 1997), 292.

[34]Cummings, *The Book of Common Prayer* (1549), 46, 52-53.

[35]Lovibond, "In the Triune Name," 335-36. See also Coster, *Baptism and Spiritual Kinship*, 57-64.

[36]Cummings, *The Book of Common Prayer* (1549), 52-56.

some families, especially in the higher levels of society, pushed hard for baptisms at home to protect their children from cold and disease.[37] Across the board, Reformed pastors moved the location of the sacrament from the church doors to the center of the church, usually near the pulpit.[38] Private baptisms at home or at church were not acceptable, as the baptism had to take place in the context of the preaching of the Word and in the presence of the congregation. Emergency baptisms were invalid, and midwives in Geneva who displayed any tendency to perform emergency baptisms could expect to be called before the Genevan Consistory to be reprimanded. The Genevan pastors also strenuously rejected any attempt to bring babies who had seemingly died to the chapel of Notre Dame de Grace, outside Geneva, where traditionally such babies were miraculously revived long enough to receive baptism.[39] The fact that at least one Genevan family attempted to have their infant revived long enough to receive baptism in 1542 points once again to the gap between the official and popular understanding of the sacrament. The pastors held to the Reformed doctrine of baptism as the nonsalvific seal of the covenant while the family faced with a dying child wanted to ensure that their little boy did not die unbaptized.[40]

For Anabaptists, the location of the baptism was not an issue given that most of the Anabaptist worship gatherings in the sixteenth century took place in private homes or outdoors. The timing of baptisms depended both on the availability of someone to do the baptizing and on the presence of individuals seeking baptism. Since Anabaptists rejected infant baptism, there was no urgency or rush to have one's child baptized. In fact, some Anabaptist parents challenged the norms and

[37]Graeme Murdock, *Calvinism on the Frontier, 1600–1660: International Calvinism and the Reformed Church in Hungary and Transylvania* (Oxford: Clarendon, 2000), 156-58.
[38]Lovibond, "In the Triune Name," 323-32.
[39]Spierling, *Infant Baptism in Reformation Geneva*, 79-81.
[40]*Registers of the Consistory of Geneva in the Time of Calvin*, ed. Robert Kingdon, Thomas Lambert, and Isabella Watt (Grand Rapids, MI: Eerdmans, 2000), 81-82.

beliefs of their surrounding communities by refusing to have an emergency baptism, even if their child was in danger of death. For instance, in 1534 in Saxony, the wife of Valentin Schade gave birth to twins. The first child survived the birth, but the second twin was born dead. A few days after her delivery, both the mother and the surviving twin sickened and died. Valentin Schade had several opportunities between the birth and death of the first twin to have the infant baptized (the midwife who assisted at the birth and pushed for baptism was Schade's aunt), but refused on the grounds of his Anabaptist beliefs.[41] This Anabaptist father had internalized the teachings of his faith to such an extent that he was not anxious about having his child die unbaptized. This account underscores how dramatically a theology of baptism could shape individual practice.

Who Attended and Made the Promises?

In Catholic, Lutheran, Anglican, and Reformed areas, the makeup of those attending baptisms was fairly consistent. Apart from the baby, the godparents or sponsors (often including the midwife) formed the core of the group. The mother was absent, recovering from the birth. Church leaders increasingly insisted that the father of the baby should be present, even though customary pre-Reformation practice was to have him excused on the grounds that baptism emphasized spiritual kinship rather than the physical relations that had led to the birth of the child. In other words, the presence of the father might contaminate the purity of the sacrament.[42]

The presence of godparents was crucial, as they were the ones who spoke the promises on behalf of the infant receiving baptism. They were also the ones charged with the spiritual upbringing of their godchildren, ensuring that the children learned their prayers and the

---

[41] Kat Hill, *Baptism, Brotherhood, and Belief in Reformation Germany: Anabaptism and Lutheranism 1525–1585* (Oxford: Oxford University Press, 2015), 98-99.

[42] Spierling, *Infant Baptism in Reformation Geneva*, 91-92.

basics of their faith. The practice of having godparents present infants for baptism has its roots in the medieval period and derives from the earlier practice of having sponsors present adult candidates for baptism in the early church. Over time, the practice of having godparents became both a religious obligation and a social tie, knitting individuals and families together in bonds of spiritual kinship. Indeed, on the basis of this spiritual kinship, the medieval Catholic Church put strict rules in place barring marriages between godparents, between godparents and parents, or between godparents and their godchild.[43] Luther retained the practice of having godparents make vows in the child's name at baptism, and the Lutheran church put a great deal of emphasis on the godparents' role in the faith formation of their godchild.[44] Similarly in the Anglican church, the godparents spoke the vows on behalf of their godchild, forsaking the devil, assenting to the articles of the Apostles' Creed, and requesting baptism. In the 1552 Book of Common Prayer, the baptism concluded with an exhortation from the priest directed to the godparents, reminding them of their solemn obligation to teach their godchildren the fundamentals of the faith and ensure that they "heare sermons."[45] In Reformed areas, the practice of having godparents present the child at baptism was retained, albeit without any extensive theological discussion as to the significance of their role. In some locations, as in Geneva, for instance, there were clear tensions between the religious authorities' emphasis on recruiting confessionally orthodox godparents and the population's desire to use godparent selection as part of traditional kinship and network-building processes.[46]

In Anabaptist baptisms, neither parents nor godparents were part of the ceremony. Surviving sources are not consistent when it

---

[43]Spierling, *Infant Baptism in Reformation Geneva*, 108-12.
[44]Spierling, *Infant Baptism in Reformation Geneva*, 106.
[45]Cummings, *The Book of Common Prayer* (1549), 56.
[46]Spierling, *Infant Baptism in Reformation Geneva*, 111-12.

comes to the presence of other Anabaptist believers as witnesses to the sacrament. Given that many baptisms took place during a worship gathering, the presence of others can certainly be inferred. By the end of the sixteenth century, as some Anabaptist communities became more settled, the evidence suggests that congregational members did play a key role in baptisms, as in Strasbourg in 1557, for instance. There, when two men came to request baptism, the congregation's leaders presented the men to the congregation, asking them to testify to the men's upright lives and worthiness to receive baptism.[47]

WHERE WERE THE MOTHERS?

When considering attendance at baptism, the common feature in Roman Catholic, Lutheran, Anglican, and Reformed baptisms was not so much who was present as who was absent—namely, the mother. In all four instances, mothers were not expected to attend the baptism of their child, as they were still recovering from the birth. For Reformed mothers, there were no other specific rituals or worship practices to denote their return into the body of the faithful following their confinement.

In Catholic, Lutheran, and Anglican areas, however, the mothers had a separate ceremony to look forward to, known in French as the *relevailles*, in German as the *Kirchgang*, and in English as "churching." There was no strong theological impetus for this ritual. In fact, already in the Middle Ages, the Catholic Church had officially declared that women who had given birth were not in any way unclean and could, if they chose, immediately reintegrate their worshiping community after giving birth. However, already by the twelfth century

---

[47]Claus-Peter Clasen, *Anabaptism: A Social History, 1525–1618; Switzerland, Austria, Moravia, South and Central Germany* (Ithaca, NY: Cornell University Press, 1972), 105.

there was strong popular pressure for a special ritual for new mothers, and this practice persisted, even after the Reformation.[48]

In the Catholic ritual, the mother's female friends and the midwife accompanied her to church six weeks after the birth. There she was met by the priest at the entrance to the church and blessed with prayers and holy water. She was then led to the altar for more prayers. In some German locations, the new mother then circled the altar up to three times with her female companions, before being blessed again. In return for the blessing and in thanksgiving, the mother would give an offering.[49] The Lutheran ritual retained many of these elements, including the mother coming to church with her female friends and relations, kneeling at the altar, and prayers and blessings being spoken by the pastor. However, crucially this ritual now took place during a regular worship service rather than at a separate time.[50] The Church of England also retained the pre-Reformation rite of churching in the Book of Common Prayer but by 1549 had shifted the focus away from purifying the new mother toward providing her and her companions with the opportunity to give thanks within a ritual setting.[51] Although Puritans objected to the churching rite as a remnant of Jewish practice and tensions grew over whether women coming for churching should wear a veil, the practice of churching continued up to the English Civil War, and resumed at the restoration of the English monarchy in 1660 with the accession of Charles II.[52]

---

[48]Susan Karant-Nunn, *The Reformation of Ritual: An Interpretation of Early Modern Germany* (London: Routledge, 1997), 75-76.

[49]Karant-Nunn, *Reformation of Ritual*, 76-77.

[50]Karant-Nunn, *Reformation of Ritual*, 78-81.

[51]Cummings, *The Book of Common Prayer* (1549), 91-92. See also David Cressy, "Purification, Thanksgiving, and the Churching of Women in Post-Reformation England," *Past and Present* 141 (1993): 106-46, esp. 119-20.

[52]Cressy, "Purification, Thanksgiving," 132-44.

WHAT HAPPENED DURING THE BAPTISM?

The Catholic baptismal liturgies prior to the Reformation varied somewhat according to the diocesan ritual they followed. The ritual of Breslau, for instance, was not identical to the ritual of Cologne.[53] But even though the wording was not identical, the main elements of the liturgy remained the same and were maintained in the Catholic Church after the Reformation. Most of the liturgy took place in Latin, though the questions posed to the sponsors or godparents regarding intent to seek baptism and the name of the child were in the vernacular.[54] The baptismal liturgy began with a series of exorcisms involving both words and gestures (blowing on the child, touching her ears and nose with spittle) to free the infant from the power of Satan. The priest also read from Matthew 19:13-15 and recited the Lord's Prayer and the Apostles' Creed. After the exorcisms, reading, and prayers, the child was brought to the font. There the sponsors answered questions on the child's behalf, renouncing Satan. The priest then anointed the child with holy oil, before asking the sponsors to testify to the candidate's faith in Christ and confirming the child's desire to seek baptism. The infant was then undressed, and immersed three times with the words of baptism being said during the immersions. The infant was then anointed with holy oil, dressed in a white baptismal garment, and given a lighted candle.[55]

The Lutheran version of the baptismal rite also evolved over time. Luther's first baptismal liturgy in German, published in 1523, was a direct translation of the Catholic Latin liturgy. It omitted a few of the exorcisms at the beginning, and introduced a prayer based on

---

[53]See Old, *Shaping*, 4-5.

[54]Old, *Shaping*, 21-22.

[55]"Ritual of Bishop Henry of Breslau," in Kent Burreson, "Water Surrounded By God's Word: The Diocese of Breslau as a Window into the Transformation of Baptism from the Medieval Period to the Reformation," in *Worship in Medieval and Early Modern Europe: Change and Continuity in Religious Practice*, ed. Karin Maag and John Witvliet (Notre Dame, IN: University of Notre Dame Press, 2004), 204-9.

scriptural passages related to God's saving action in and through water, known as the Flood Prayer. By 1526, Luther's baptismal liturgy had been streamlined and simplified, retaining even fewer exorcisms and deleting a range of practices, including the priest blowing on the child, as well as the use of spittle and oil and the presentation of a lit candle.[56] Luther and Lutheran theologians after him considered the exorcism rituals to be adiaphora (matters indifferent) and thus optional, yet Luther himself referred to the exorcisms as powerful words that testified to the unbaptized infant's state of original sin and his or her desperate need of God's saving grace in baptism. The Lutheran baptismal liturgy was not uniform across all Lutheran areas. By and large, the northern and eastern Lutheran territories in the Holy Roman Empire followed the ritual laid out in Luther's 1526 rite. Lutheran areas in the south and west, however, tended to align their baptismal practices closer to the Reformed practices, including omitting the exorcisms entirely.[57]

The Anglican baptismal liturgy as laid out in the 1549 Book of Common Prayer and reiterated in the 1559 edition prepared at the start of Elizabeth's reign omitted the exorcisms entirely but retained the vestigial catechetical instructions via the questions posed to the godparents. The baptism service began with the priest leading those assembled in prayer, including an English translation of Luther's Flood Prayer. He then read from Mark's Gospel about Jesus receiving the children and gave a short address emphasizing God's loving willingness to receive the baptized into his kingdom. After everyone joined in a short prayer, the priest then reminded the godparents of their responsibilities and had them respond to his questions, as outlined above. After more prayer, the child was baptized (either by immersion or by sprinkling) and marked with the sign of the cross.

---

[56]Karant-Nunn, *Reformation of Ritual*, 50-52.
[57]Nischan, "Exorcism Controversy," 32-33.

Those present then joined in reciting the Lord's Prayer, followed by another prayer from the priest and his charge to the godparents.[58]

The Zurich baptismal ritual laid out by Huldrych Zwingli in 1525 was even simpler. There were no exorcisms, nor any catechetical questions based on the Apostles' Creed, nor any vows taken by the sponsors. Instead, the pastor began with an invocation based on Psalm 124:8, then asked the godparents to confirm their desire to have the child baptized. After prayers, the child was baptized with the words of Matthew 28, was clothed in a white gown, and received a blessing. Although the earlier Zurich baptismal liturgy prepared by Leo Jud had advocated baptismal immersion, Zwingli's ritual was silent about whether the pastor immersed the child or poured or sprinkled water on the infant.[59]

The Genevan baptismal liturgy as set out in the 1542 *Forme des prières* also avoided any exorcisms or other ceremonies condemned by Calvin as the product of human invention. Baptisms in Geneva could only take place during church services, after the sermon had been preached. Those bringing the baby to baptism would come forward, close to the pulpit. There the pastor confirmed the family's desire to seek baptism. The liturgy continued with an extensive explanatory statement from the pastor, giving the biblical grounds for infant baptism, followed by a communally recited prayer asking God to protect and instruct the child in faith, and by the Lord's Prayer. The pastor then reminded the congregation of the importance of their promises to help bring up the child in the faith. Everyone present then recited the Apostles' Creed and then listened to further instruction from the pastor on the importance of teaching both doctrines and morals to the child. The child was then named and baptized by having water poured on his or her head.[60]

---

[58]Cummings, *The Book of Common Prayer*, 46-52 (1549), 141-46 (1559).

[59]Old, *Shaping*, 63-64.

[60]Spierling, *Infant Baptism in Reformation Geneva*, 55-60. See also Old, *Shaping*, 171-76.

Compared to the situation for other confessional groups, information on Anabaptist baptism practices is scarce. Few of the Anabaptist
groups in the sixteenth century created written liturgies, so that most
of the information available on how baptisms took place in Anabaptist
circles comes from eyewitness accounts or participants' testimonies.
Furthermore, practices varied between different Anabaptist groups.
Some evidence has survived, however. In 1535 a group of Anabaptists
were interrogated in the Harz region of Saxony. They testified that
they knelt down and asked the leader for baptism, and then answered
questions about their faith and their desire to follow Christ and be obe-
dient to God, even to the point of death. The baptizer then used water
to draw a cross on their forehead and baptized them in the name of the
Trinity.[61] Other accounts of Anabaptist baptisms follow a similar pattern: kneeling, requesting baptism, confessing one's sins and testifying
to one's beliefs, and then receiving baptism, either by having water
poured on the head or by being marked on the head with water.[62]

FROM BAPTISM TO CONFIRMATION

In the early church, where the rite of baptism was administered primarily to adult converts at least in the early years, those seeking baptism
could be catechized prior to receiving the sacrament. At their baptism,
they could answer questions and testify to their faith by themselves, and
immediately receive Communion. As time went on, however, baptism
increasingly became a sacrament for infants, who could not testify to
their faith. Therefore, the gap between baptism and first Communion
widened, since the medieval church wanted youngsters to be catechized
and learn the basics of their faith before receiving Communion and to
confess their sins and be absolved before partaking in the sacrament for
the first time.[63] Furthermore, the medieval church developed the rite of

---

[61]Hill, *Baptism, Brotherhood, and Belief,* 98-135, esp. 129-30.
[62]Clasen, *Anabaptism,* 102-6.
[63]Karant-Nunn, *Reformation of Ritual,* 66.

confirmation, a sacrament celebrated by the bishop, who laid his hands on the confirmation candidates' heads, confirming their baptism and strengthening them in their faith.[64]

Among Protestants, the importance of catechesis before one's first Communion retained great importance, but confirmation, with its emphasis on the central sacramental role of the bishop, was more problematic. The Reformed rejected confirmation rituals, though they did still underscore the need for mastery of the basics of Christianity before a young person participated in the Lord's Supper for the first time.[65] Part of the theological challenge surrounding confirmation, both for Lutherans and for Anglicans who developed a confirmation rite, was over the relationship between baptism and confirmation. If confirmation was required, did that imply that the sacrament of baptism was in some way insufficient?[66]

Luther largely rejected confirmation rites, as he found no scriptural basis for them. Other reformers did however craft confirmation liturgies, including Philipp Melanchthon and the Strasbourg reformer Martin Bucer.[67] For Bucer, confirmation was not a sacrament, but was an important marker in the life of young Christians, when they publicly affirmed in church and in the presence of their families that they upheld the promises made at their baptism. One of the main drivers behind Bucer's support for confirmation was the need to answer the critiques of Anabaptists, who condemned the disjunction between infant baptism and the importance of having individual Christians profess their faith. As outlined in the church ordinances Bucer prepared

---

[64]Senn, *Christian Liturgy*, 194-95.

[65]For more on this topic, see the chapter on the Lord's Supper.

[66]For more on the relationship between baptism and confirmation in the German context, see Amy Nelson Burnett, "Confirmation and Christian Fellowship: Martin Bucer on Commitment to the Church," *Church History* 64, no. 2 (1995): 202-17. For an overview of the issues right up to the present day, see Drew Nathaniel Keane, "A Reconsideration of the Continued Practice of Confirmation in the Episcopal Church," *Anglican Theological Review* 100, no. 2 (2018): 245-66.

[67]Senn, *Christian Liturgy*, 292-93.

for the German principality of Hesse in 1539, one or more of the children answered questions on the Apostles' Creed. Each child then had to reply (in the affirmative) to the following question: "Do you believe and confess, and will you also commit yourself to the fellowship and obedience of the church of Christ?"[68] This profession of faith was then followed by the pastor or superintendent laying his hands on the head of each of the youngsters in turn, saying, "Receive the Holy Ghost, your protection against all that is wicked, strength and help toward all that is good, from the gracious hand of God the Father, Son, and Holy Ghost. Amen."[69]

In the Church of England, the Book of Common Prayer laid out both the confirmation liturgy and a preamble explaining why confirmation was both important and necessary. The two main reasons given included providing an opportunity for the young people (having been catechized) to testify to their faith and assume for themselves the promises made on their behalf at their baptism.[70] Confirmation also strengthened young people against the increasingly great danger of spiritual temptations at that age:

> That by imposition of hands and prayer they may receive strength and defense against all temptations to sin, and the assaults of the world and the devil; it is most meet to be ministered, when children come to that age, that partly by the frailty of their own flesh, partly by the assaults of the world and the devil, they begin to be in danger to fall into sin.[71]

Although the preamble was identical in the 1549 and 1552 Book of Common Prayer, the bishop's words said during the imposition of hands did change, moving from a two-part consecration and sign of the cross

---

[68]Burnett, "Confirmation and Christian Fellowship," 205.
[69]Karant-Nunn, *Reformation of Ritual*, 68.
[70]*The Book of Common Prayer 1549*, 244.
[71]*The Book of Common Prayer 1549*, 244.

on each young person to a shorter statement simply asking God to "defend this child with thy heavenly grace, that he may continue thine for ever, and daily increase in thy holy spirit more and more, until he come unto thy everlasting kingdom."[72] The shorter and more succinct 1552 confirmation liturgy highlighted concerns noted above about any liturgical words or practices that might suggest that the original baptism was somehow insufficient.

CONCLUSION

Although their theological emphases and ritual practices differed, the various churches' practice of baptism retained many common elements. The trinitarian formula and the use of water (whether via immersion, pouring, or sprinkling) remained central. Baptism marked each believer as a member of the household of faith. The continued emphasis on creedal statements offered by members of the baptismal party and on promises to teach the baptized about their faith (in the case of infants) highlights the common desire to see baptism as the first step in a life-long journey of ever-deepening faith. Through catechetical instruction, those who had been baptized as infants were to grow in their knowledge of their faith and claim it as their own before their first participation in the sacrament of Communion. The growing insistence in many Reformation churches that a baptism was only valid if celebrated in the presence of the congregation also attests to the central role of the Christian community as witnesses and teachers of the faith to the baptized. Crucially, those in attendance were also to recall their own baptisms during the celebration of the sacrament, thus binding all the members of the community ever closer to each other and to God. While baptism was a one-time sacrament that marked believers' entry into the Christian community, the regularly repeated sacrament of Communion was equally if not more important in fostering believers' ongoing life of faith.

---

[72]*The Second Prayer-Book of Edward VI*, 187.

FOR FURTHER READING

Burnett, Amy Nelson. "Confirmation and Christian Fellowship: Martin Bucer on Commitment to the Church." *Church History* 64, no. 2 (1995): 202-17.

Clasen, Claus-Peter. *Anabaptism: A Social History, 1525–1618: Switzerland, Austria, Moravia, South and Central Germany*. Ithaca, NY: Cornell University Press, 1972.

Cressy, David. "Purification, Thanksgiving and the Churching of Women in Post-Reformation England." *Past and Present* 141 (1993): 106-46.

Fesko, J. V. *Word, Water and Spirit: A Reformed Perspective on Baptism*. Grand Rapids, MI: Reformation Heritage Books, 2010.

Hill, Kat. *Baptism, Brotherhood, and Belief in Reformation Germany: Anabaptism and Lutheranism 1525–1585*. Oxford: Oxford University Press, 2015.

Lovibond, Malcolm. "In the Triune Name: Some Aspects of Baptismal Practice in Early Reformed Churches." *Reformation and Renaissance Review* 7 (2005): 318-36.

Maag, Karin, and John Witvliet, eds. *Worship in Medieval and Early Modern Europe*. Notre Dame, IN: University of Notre Dame Press, 2004.

Nischan, Bodo. "The Exorcism Controversy and Baptism in the Late Reformation." *Sixteenth Century Journal* 18 (1987): 31-52.

Old, H. O. *The Shaping of the Reformed Baptismal Rite in the Sixteenth Century*. Grand Rapids, MI: Eerdmans, 1992.

Senn, Frank. *Christian Liturgy: Catholic and Evangelical*. Minneapolis, MN: Fortress Press, 1997.

Spierling, Karen. *Infant Baptism in Reformation Geneva*. Aldershot: Ashgate, 2005.

Six

Communion

---

*Whenever this matter is discussed, when I have tried to say all,
I feel that I have as yet said little in proportion to its worth. And
although my mind can think beyond what my tongue can utter,
yet even my mind is conquered and overwhelmed by the greatness
of the thing. Therefore, nothing remains but to break forth in
wonder at this mystery.*

JOHN CALVIN, *INSTITUTES OF THE CHRISTIAN RELIGION*

IN 1542, A CONTROVERSY BROKE OUT among the pastors of Eisleben,
Martin Luther's hometown. At a Communion service, a certain
amount of consecrated wine was left in the chalice at the end of the
celebration and a deacon, who had not himself received Communion
that day, took it upon himself to drain the contents of the cup. Was
he guilty of mishandling the consecrated wine and treating it as if it
were any random beverage, as the Lutherans thought the Swiss Reformed might do from a memorialist position?[1] Or did his actions

---

John Calvin, *Institutes of the Christian Religion*, ed. John T. McNeill, trans. Ford Lewis Battles
(Philadelphia: Westminster, 1960), 4.17.7.

[1]Again, the term *Swiss Reformed* refers to the Protestant churches and communities who
belonged to the Swiss Confederation or its territories. Geneva did not join the Swiss Confederation until 1815, and so is not included in this term.

signify excessive Roman Catholic–inspired concern over how to dispose of the consecrated wine in a holy manner? Perturbed by the incident and divided over what to do with leftover consecrated wine, the clergy looked to their superintendent, Valentin Vigelius, who in turn wrote to Wittenberg for advice. In his response, Philipp Melanchthon did not find fault with the deacon, since the presence of Christ in the bread and the wine was rooted in the actual celebration of the sacrament. He particularly wanted to avoid any danger of returning to a Catholic veneration of the elements themselves. Once the liturgy was done, the elements could safely be consumed, but he recommended that for the sake of weak consciences, the leftover wine should be shared out among those who were the last to come forward to receive the sacrament, rather than being drunk up by someone who had not partaken of it. The controversy in Eisleben rolled on, however, eventually causing Martin Luther to intervene by writing letters on two occasions. In his first letter, Luther rebuked those who had strongly defended the deacon's actions and accused them of adopting a Zwinglian perspective. For Luther, the consecrated elements continued to be holy even after the celebration of the sacrament was done, and they needed to be handled with reverence. In his second letter, Luther worked to harmonize his and Melanchthon's perspectives, and therefore, like Melanchthon, Luther strongly recommended sharing out any remaining consecrated wine among those who had received the sacrament that day.[2]

Although the actions that set off this controversy may seem trivial at first glance, the ensuing interventions show how the practical aspects of Communion and its theological underpinnings were closely intertwined. The deacon's draining of the chalice caused debate and uncertainty precisely because behind his action lay very different understandings of the nature of the wine and the bread.

---

[2]Timothy Wengert, "Luther and Melanchthon on Consecrated Communion Wine (Eisleben 1542-43)," *Lutheran Quarterly* 15, no. 1 (2001): 24-42.

⌣

From the mid-1550s until the early seventeenth century, the magistrates of the German city of Wesel engaged in a fascinating cross-confessional experiment. The civic leadership ordered that all ten thousand inhabitants attend the same Communion services. This statement was startling and potentially problematic because Wesel was a confessionally divided city: it had a Lutheran majority, a Catholic minority, and a considerable number of Dutch Reformed refugees all living within its city walls. Yet to ensure religious peace, the authorities insisted that everyone, regardless of his or her confessional affiliations, was to attend the very same celebration of the sacrament. The quarterly Communion services were Lutheran in form: featuring altars, vestments, candles, the use of wafers rather than regular bread, and the elevation of the Communion elements at the moment of consecration. Not surprisingly, a number of the Reformed living in Wesel felt very uncomfortable with these practices and were unwilling to participate. To ensure religious peace and to continue to be able to stay in Wesel, the Reformed church leaders put pressure on Reformed laypeople to take part in these Communion services, but also negotiated a number of compromises with their hosts. These adjustments included allowing Reformed believers to choose whether to receive the elements directly in their mouths Lutheran-style or to receive the wafer in their hand, as was the practice in Reformed communities. Meanwhile, some of Wesel's Lutheran inhabitants were very perturbed about having to take Communion alongside these Calvinist refugees, and objected strongly to the presence and participation of those who did not believe in the physical presence of Christ in the bread and the wine. The civic authorities, however, continued to insist that everyone was to attend and participate. The surviving evidence suggests that Catholics also took part in these quarterly celebrations of Communion, including members of the Order of

St. John, although Catholics were authorized to receive only the bread if they wished, and were also granted permission to light candles in front of the images of saints in the city's churches and to sing hymns in Latin before the start of the worship service.[3]

Although the obligation to participate in these city-wide Communion services fell apart by the early seventeenth century, not least due to increasing confessionalization and the rising pressures of the Thirty Years' War, this example challenges and complicates any tidy mental scheme of separate and distinct Communion theologies and practices emerging from the Reformation era. This chapter will present contrasting views on and approaches to the sacrament, but this vignette reminds us that underlying these divisions was and remains a fundamental desire to have the sacrament serve as a bond of unity among Christians.

Theologies of the Sacrament

The medieval Catholic Church taught that the sacrament of the Eucharist could only be celebrated by a legitimately ordained priest. Valid ordination, rather than moral purity of the priest (or the lack thereof), was the key to determining whether the sacrament had truly been celebrated and ensuring that the miracle of transubstantiation had occurred. Medieval theologians debated at great length how and in what ways Christ was physically present in the bread and wine. By the late medieval period, the standard theological explanation was that the bread and wine were composed of both substance (their inner reality) and accidents (their outward appearance). The doctrine of transubstantiation taught that while the accidents remained unchanged (bread still looked and tasted like bread, and wine still looked and tasted like wine), the elements' substance had changed and become the substance of the body and blood of Christ. The

---

[3]Jesse Spohnholz, "Multiconfessional Celebration of the Eucharist in Sixteenth-Century Wesel," *Sixteenth Century Journal* 39, no. 3 (2008): 705-29.

opening creed of the Fourth Lateran Council in 1215 used the word *transubstantiation* but did not formally define it. Later theologians, including Thomas Aquinas, used Aristotelian categories to explain how miraculously, at the moment of consecration, the bread and wine became transformed in substance into the body and blood of Christ, all the while retaining the external reality of bread and wine.[4] At the Council of Trent (1545–1563), Catholic Church leaders worked to define the nature of the Mass, describing it as a "true and proper sacrifice," but not clarifying their definition of sacrifice in this context. Catholic theologians after Trent wrestled with how to explain the reality of the Mass as a sacrifice without ignoring or downplaying Christ's one-time sacrifice of himself on the cross.[5]

Martin Luther's theology of the sacrament evolved over time, starting with a traditional Catholic understanding of a two-way interaction: the prayers and the elements were offered to God and God's grace came down to the people. By 1520, in his "Sermon on the New Testament," Luther moved to a unidirectional perspective, in which God blessed the people with his presence in the sacrament. This gift of God precluded any notion of the sacrament as a sacrifice offered by human hands or as a meritorious human work. Luther also emphasized that the sacrament of Communion always and only had its effect when rooted in the preaching of the Word.[6] The most distinctive feature of Luther's eucharistic theology was his insistence on the bodily presence of Christ in the bread and the wine. Although he rejected the doctrine of transubstantiation due in part to the medieval critique against it, he still wanted to maintain the conviction that when Christ said "This is my body," he did not simply mean that the bread signified his body or the wine signified his blood. Luther

---

[4]Gary Macy, "The Medieval Inheritance" in *A Companion to the Eucharist in the Reformation,* ed. Lee Palmer Wandel (Leiden: Brill, 2014), 15-37, esp. 23-30.

[5]Robert Daly, "The Council of Trent" in Wandel, *Companion,* 159-82.

[6]Volker Leppin, "Martin Luther," in Wandel, *Companion,* 39-56, esp. 44.

stressed the importance of believing the words of Christ: the body
and blood of Christ were genuinely present in and with the bread and
the wine, just as Christ himself was both fully human and fully divine.[7] Later Lutheran theologians echoed Luther's approach: they
stressed the real presence of Christ in the sacrament, advocated frequent partaking of the sacrament, but also rejected private Masses
and Masses for the dead, which could be celebrated without a congregation's being present. The Lutheran Swedish church order of 1571
stated, for instance, "Therefore all masses in which the sacrament is
celebrated otherwise than in this manner such as *Missae privatae,
Missae pro defunctis, Missae votivae,* etc., shall be utterly set aside, and
a public mass shall be celebrated in the congregation where all so
many as are disposed shall approach this sacred and salutary supper."[8]
Thus the Lutheran approach to Communion stressed God's actions
and Christ's genuine, corporeal presence in a ritual that necessarily
involved both the preaching of the Word and the active participation
of at least some of the congregation.

For Zwingli and the Swiss Reformed, Communion was a sacrament since Christ had commanded his disciples to continue to celebrate it in his memory. Zwingli's eucharistic theology focused above
all on the words of Christ at the Last Supper: "Do this in remembrance of me." As a result, Zwingli saw the sacrament primarily as a
sacred commemoration of Christ's one-time sacrifice, and strongly
stood against any understanding of the sacrament that spoke of re-
enacting the sacrifice or that saw the elements of bread and wine as
containing the physical presence of Christ in any way. Both Zwingli
and his successor Heinrich Bullinger saw the bread and wine of
Communion as a sign that represented or signified the body and
blood of Christ. Unlike in Roman Catholic theology, the bread and

[7]Leppin, "Martin Luther," 46-47.
[8]In Eric Yelverton, *The Mass in Sweden: Its Development from the Latin Rite from 1531 to 1917*
(London: Harrison and Sons, 1920), 60.

wine themselves did not convey grace, and those who partook in the sacrament without having faith received no spiritual benefit. However, faith-filled participants in the sacrament did benefit from their participation, both in their closeness to God and to one another. For the Swiss Reformed, therefore, the sacrament was both an occasion for commemoration and a way to bind the members of the congregation to one another, overcoming divisions and hostilities. As Bullinger noted in his sermon on the Lord's Supper in his *Decades*,

> Therefore, as we are not void and without Christ before the supper, but are quickened by him and made his members or partners; so that in the very action of celebration of the supper the promise is renewed unto us, and we renew and continue that fellowship which we have in Christ by the body and blood of Christ spiritually, truly participating in his life and all good gifts through faith.[9]

This emphasis on Communion as the rite that renewed fellowship with Christ and with one another was a hallmark of the Swiss Reformed tradition.

Calvin's theology of the Lord's Supper echoed many of the insights of other reformers, though the Genevan reformer was particularly interested in finding a way to keep his view from sliding either toward memorialism or toward a literal and physical presence of Christ in the bread and the wine. Like the Swiss Reformed, Calvin understood the sacrament as both a visible sign and seal of God's promises in Christ. He also articulated several significant features that made his Communion theology distinctive, including the key role of the Holy Spirit in lifting up the hearts of believers during the liturgy to partake of Christ's body and blood spiritually in the bread and the

---

[9]Quoted in Carrie Euler, "Huldrych Zwingli and Heinrich Bullinger," in Wandel, *Companion*, 57-74, esp. 71.

wine.[10] Calvin's approach was taken up by the Reformed churches that spread out across Europe, including in France, in the Netherlands, and in Scotland, where John Knox offered his perspective on the Lord's Supper, in line with Calvin's views:

> In setting forth bread and wine to eat and drink, he [Jesus Christ] confirms and seals up to us his promise and communion (that is, that we shall be partakers with him in his kingdom); and he represents unto us, and makes plain to our senses, his heavenly gifts; and also gives unto us himself, to be received with faith, and not with mouth, nor yet by transfusion of substance; but so, through the virtue of the Holy Ghost, that we, being fed with his flesh, and refreshed with his blood, may be renewed both unto true godliness and to immortality.[11]

Knox's stress on Communion as both a visible sign and a genuine partaking of Christ's body and blood illustrates the rich complexity of Reformation-era thought on the sacrament.

Anabaptist understandings of the sacrament echoed the Swiss Reformed perspective in many ways, though with a few distinctive features. Like Zwingli, the Swiss Anabaptists strongly emphasized the central role of remembrance in their theology of the Lord's Supper. Across the board, Anabaptists shared a commitment to three key features of the sacrament: its importance as a meal that drew the community of believers together, its access only to those who were fully committed members of the faith community, and its example of sacrifice, to be emulated by those who partook of it.[12] The strongly communal aspect of the Lord's Supper among Anabaptists

---

[10]Nicholas Wolterstorff, "John Calvin," in Wandel, *Companion*, 97-113.

[11]John Knox, *A Summary, According to the Holy Scriptures, of the Sacrament of the Lord's Supper* (1550), in Bryan Spinks, *Do This in Remembrance of Me: The Eucharist from the Early Church to the Present Day* (London: SCM Press, 2013), 293.

[12]John Rempel, "Anabaptist Theologies of the Eucharist," in Wandel, *Companion*, 115-37, esp. 119.

is reflected in a section from "A Short, Simple Confession," a manuscript collection of Anabaptist texts originally penned in the last quarter of the sixteenth century. In the thirteenth article, "Whether the Lord's Supper is a simple and empty symbol," the anonymous writer highlights both Christ's sacrifice and the bonds of love and faith that unite all those who join in the Supper:

> Whoever has a true hunger and thirst for such a sacrifice and follows our Lord Christ in upright and Christian obedience and believes that he truly eats this bread and drinks this wine, he is also partaking of the true body of Christ and his true blood through faith. Likewise, whoever acknowledges those as his brothers, who partake of the Supper with him, who stand in the same faith as he does, against whom he carries no animosity [also partakes of the body of Christ]—for Christ's Supper is a physical coming together of Christian believers in love.[13]

Thus for Anabaptist communities, celebrations of the sacrament were above all occasions for the faithful to strengthen their bonds of love with one another and with God.

In the English church, eucharistic theology shifted from a traditional Catholic understanding during much of Henry VIII's reign and during the reign of his daughter Mary to a Reformed understanding during the reigns of Edward VI and Elizabeth. Henry VIII's Act of Six Articles of 1539 strongly reaffirmed the doctrine of transubstantiation. But under the leadership of Archbishop Thomas Cranmer, Anglican theological perspectives on Communion stressed the importance of the sacrament as a sacrifice of praise and thanksgiving and rejected the doctrine of a corporeal presence of Christ in the bread and the wine. Instead, Communion was a visible sign and

---

[13]"A Short, Simple Confession on the Thirteen Articles Which Were Debated in 1571 at Frankenthal in the Palatinate," in *Later Writings of the Swiss Anabaptists*, ed. C. Arnold Snyder (Kitchener, ON: Pandora, 2017), 424-25.

seal of God's love, confirming and strengthening believers' faith. Anglican theologians agreed that the sacrament conveyed spiritual benefits to those who partook in faith, but no spiritual grace touched those without faith, who only ate the physical bread and drank the physical wine.[14]

CONTROVERSIES

Each early modern confessional group outlined its own understanding of Communion both in positive terms and with an eye to opposing other perspectives. Hence Protestant theologians consistently rejected the Catholic doctrine of transubstantiation, and Lutheran and Reformed theologians clashed repeatedly from the 1529 Colloquy of Marburg onward over their divergent understandings as to how exactly and in what form Christ was present in the sacrament. The Swiss Reformed and Genevans managed to hammer out an agreement that laid out their eucharistic theology in the Consensus Tigurinus of 1549, largely in order to present a more united front against Lutheran pressure. It is ironic that the sacrament designed to bring the Christian community together around the Lord's Table was also the focal point of incendiary polemic on all sides. Yet a closer look at the practices surrounding the celebration of the sacrament helps to explain just why feelings ran so high. The presence of Christ, understood in divergent ways, was a hallmark of Communion. Hence any disagreement over the sacrament was not merely a difference of opinion but an attack on the sacred.

Divisions over the presence of Christ were also rooted in significant christological differences. In particular, the Lutherans stressed that Christ's human and divine natures continued to be closely united even after Christ's ascension to heaven. Though Christ was indeed seated at the right hand of God, he was also present both in his divine and

---

[14]James Turrell, "Anglican Theologies of the Eucharist," in Wandel, *Companion*, 139-58.

human nature in the church and in the world. This understanding is known as the doctrine of ubiquity. The Reformed, for their part, asserted that after his ascension, Christ's human body remained in heaven, seated at the right hand of God. They made clear distinctions between Christ's two natures and rejected the Lutheran doctrine of ubiquity, especially when it came to the physical presence of Christ in the elements of the consecrated bread and wine.[15]

PRACTICE OF THE SACRAMENT

Preparation. In many early modern churches, receiving the sacrament of Communion was a sacred high point in one's Christian life. Basic preparatory elements before receiving Communion included making sure that one's outward appearance was suitable for participation in the sacrament. In Lutheran Schleswig-Holstein, for instance, the government authorities laid out instructions as to what clothes needed to be worn to church "to honor the preaching of God's Word and the holy sacraments." Laypeople were warned not to turn up in shirtsleeves, but to make sure that they were wearing a jacket or at the very least a hood or a cloak.[16]

Beyond matters of apparel, the priority was to prepare oneself inwardly. In some churches, including among early modern Catholics and Anglicans, the accepted practice was to receive the sacrament while fasting, so that the elements of Communion would not be commingled with everyday food. For late medieval Catholics, preparing to receive the sacrament meant making one's general confession to a priest beforehand, in order to receive the sacrament with sins forgiven and the resulting penances accomplished. For his part, Luther advocated spiritual preparation for receiving the sacrament through prayer and reflection, but did not make prayer or fasting mandatory.

---

[15] See Leppin, "Martin Luther," 52.
[16] Matthias Range, "'Wandelabendmahl': Lutheran 'Walking Communion' and Its Expression in Material Culture," *Journal of Ecclesiastical History* 64, no. 4 (2013): 731-68, esp. 761.

In the introduction to his liturgy for the Latin Mass in 1523, he noted, "The best preparation is, as I have said, a soul moved and vexed by sins, death, temptations, and hungering and thirsting for healing and strength."[17]

Reformation-era churches went beyond recommendations for individuals to injunctions for clergy to make sure the congregations in their charge prepared in advance for the celebration of the sacrament. In the Church of England, the Book of Common Prayer enjoined the clergy to prepare the congregation the previous week, or at least a day before, with a sentence of warning about the dangers of coming to the sacrament without due forethought and about the importance of inward preparation. The pastor's words were "My duty is to exhort you to consider the dignity of the holy mystery and the great peril of the unworthy receiving thereof, and so to search and examine your own consciences, as you should come holy and clean to a most godly and heavenly feast."[18]

Among several Reformed churches, including in Geneva and in France, where Communion took place relatively infrequently, each celebration of the sacrament was preceded by a Sunday worship service of preparation one to two weeks beforehand. These preparatory services offered pastors the opportunity to preach on the need to prepare one's heart and one's life to receive the sacrament and to warn those whose lives were disordered or whose knowledge of the faith was shaky that they should not participate in the sacrament unless they remedied these problems.

From the perspective of church leaders, the most important feature of preparation was to ensure that those coming to partake in the sacrament were in fact worthy of receiving it. This winnowing of

---

[17]Martin Luther, "Formula of Mass and Communion for the Church at Wittenberg" (1523), in *Works of Martin Luther* (Philadelphia: Muhlenberg Press, 1932), 6:96.

[18]*The First Prayer-Book of Edward VI: Compared with the Successive Revisions of The Book of Common Prayer* (Oxford: J. Parker, 1877), 128.

worthy and unworthy could be done in different ways. In Reformed communities in France and in Scotland, admission to the Lord's Supper came by way of a token, usually made of lead, distributed in advance by the elders to those of the congregation whose behavior and knowledge of the faith met the church leaders' standards. Those who received such a token brought it with them to church on the Sunday when the Lord's Supper was to be celebrated and handed the token in to an elder before approaching the table.[19]

Whether churches used tokens, or gave the clergy the responsibility of vetting people's access to the sacrament, one of the key facets of preparation was catechesis. Those partaking in the sacrament were supposed to know the fundamentals of their faith. In some Lutheran areas, church orders laid out the details of this pre-Communion verification. Cologne's 1543 church order set out a liturgy for Saturday evening Vespers, known as the *Beichtgottesdienst*, or confessional service, to be attended by all those wanting to take the sacrament the next day. In the Vespers service, the pastor would preach on the significance of the Lord's Supper, and then examine the prospective communicants. The liturgy also included a time of individual confession and absolution.[20] In Geneva, this catechetical training took place week by week in Sunday-afternoon catechism services, intended primarily for the young and for servants. But before each quarterly celebration of the Lord's Supper, people were also supposed to show evidence that they could recite the Lord's Prayer, the Ten Commandments, and the Apostles' Creed, and could answer questions about the meaning of these texts. The account of Charles Perrot, who was pastor in the Genevan countryside in the 1560s, provides striking evidence of this practice:

---

[19]Raymond Mentzer, "Reformed Liturgical Practices," in Wandel, *Companion*, 231-50, esp. 236-41.

[20]Frank C. Senn, *The People's Work: A Social History of the Liturgy* (Minneapolis: Fortress, 2006), 352.

During the four or five Sundays before Easter I used to announce that everyone should turn up at the temple at the catechism hour, and that instead of holding a catechism class I
would question people individually, asking them to think carefully about the state of their faith. . . . I used to begin by getting one or more individuals from the row of men to recite the
Lord's Prayer, the Creed, or the Commandments, choosing
especially those who seemed the mostly likely to be ignorant.
And I would counsel all those who did not have too poor a
memory to learn the Commandments by heart, and I would
try to help them to do so before they came to the Lord's Supper. [Perrot then followed the same process with the women.]
Those who answered reasonably well were received at Communion, and those who genuinely had good intentions were
tolerated also. Those to whom all of this meant nothing were
warned that they must not present themselves in so ignorant a
state. However, the minister should not refuse to admit to
Communion anyone who presents himself, except those he has
earlier decided to report to the Consistory in the city. It should
be noted that in order to get people to answer properly (in the
interrogations) you have to put the question to them several
times over, and also to take care not to vary the wording from
one year to the next, if you can.[21]

This testimony provides invaluable evidence both of the Genevan
clergy's commitment to ensuring that their parishioners had internalized these key texts and teachings of the faith, and of the challenges in
achieving the desired objectives. The fact that Perrot recommended
not changing the wording of the questions from year to year strongly

---

[21]Charles Perrot, "Managing a Country Parish" (1567), in *Lifting Hearts to the Lord: Worship with
John Calvin in Sixteenth-Century Geneva*, ed. Karin Maag (Grand Rapids, MI: Eerdmans,
2016), 69-70.

implies that people had memorized answers to specific questions without necessarily understanding the content of their responses.

Preparation for one's first Communion. One specific instance of preparation for participation in the sacrament deserves further attention—namely, preparation and examination of those partaking in the sacrament for the very first time. In the Catholic Church, the age of first Communion from the time of the Fourth Lateran Council (1215) onward was set at twelve to fourteen years old, though it dropped closer to age seven by the time of the Council of Trent.[22] Luther insisted that young people needed to show evidence of their knowledge of the fundamentals of the faith before being able to receive the Eucharist for the first time, meaning that in practice, the age of first Communion was around fourteen.[23] Among the Reformed, the age at which a child was thought to be ready to participate in the sacrament was about the same. The 1564 ordinances from Reformed Neuchâtel, near Geneva, specified, for instance, that "fathers and mothers will take care to have their children, both boys and girls, taught in such a way that they will be ready to give an account of their faith starting at age twelve."[24]

Communion and church discipline. The vetting of those eligible to participate in the sacrament, whether via confession and absolution, by means of a physical token, or by oral examination of their morals and knowledge of the faith prior to the celebration of Communion, was thus an integral part of the process. Religious leaders across the confessional spectrum agreed that partaking in the sacrament without being right with God and one's neighbor was dangerous, both for the individual and for the other members of the

---

[22]Pierre Caspar, "Examen de soi-même, examen public, examen d'état: de l'admission à la Sainte-Cène aux certificats de fin d'études, XVIe—XIXe siècles," *Histoire de l'éducation* 94 (2002): 17-74, esp. 19. See also Richard DeMolen, "Childhood and the Sacraments in the Sixteenth Century," *Archiv für Reformationsgeschichte* 66 (1975): 49-71, esp. 52-56.

[23]DeMolen, "Childhood and the Sacraments," 60.

[24]Caspar, "Examen de soi-même," 23.

congregation, since God's wrath at the sacrilege could justifiably target the entire community. However, opinions were divided as to how best to ensure that those partaking in the sacrament were in the right spiritual condition to do so.

Those with the most stringent standards for access to the table were the Anabaptists. For these separatist and highly localized communities who regulated their own internal affairs without reference to state officials or church hierarchies, the central focus on having Communion be a meal for the gathered faithful meant that those who did not conform to the community's faith and moral standards were barred from participation. In fact, Anabaptist communities regulated access to the sacrament and to membership in the community as a whole by way of the ban. Those whose faith and behavior fell short of the community's standards were both barred from the Lord's Supper and from ordinary interactions with fellow Anabaptists until they repented. As the Swiss Anabaptist Thomas Meyer noted in his pre-1575 text, "Concerning the Ban,"

> I affirm this, that man makes himself partaker of others' sins against Scripture, in giving the Supper to them and having fellowship with those who should be banned and shunned according to Holy Scripture.
>
> Thus is indicated the first reason why evil should be separated from the devout and the believers; namely, because believers are to be a holy temple of God, a holy congregation of God, yes a pure body of Christ. In order to have fellowship with Christ your head, all godless and vile people should be removed and separated from the body and fellowship of Christ and his believers, so that the body of Christ, that is, his congregation, not have spots, wrinkles, or other such things, but rather be holy and blameless.[25]

---

[25] [Thomas Meyer], "Concerning the Christian Ban," in Snyder, *Later Writings of the Swiss Anabaptists*, 112.

The Anabaptists' high standards, which might at first glance make the movement too morally challenging for potential converts, actually worked in their favor by the early seventeenth century, when Reformed Swiss authorities complained repeatedly that the Anabaptists were attracting dedicated converts, specifically because of their stringent expectations regarding faith and behavior. These converts felt that the Reformed churches, in contrast, were too lax and made little effort to push members to live lives of deep Christian commitment.[26]

Luther's 1523 liturgy for the Latin Mass provided guidelines for the clergy's decisions as to which laypeople should be admitted to the sacrament. Luther advocated having those who wanted to partake indicate their intentions to the pastor in advance, so that he could ascertain both their knowledge of the faith and their way of life. However, Luther quickly added that the faith assessment did not have to be done every time: "But I think it will be sufficient if this questioning and investigation of him who seeks to be communicated is done once a year."[27] Although he left room at the table for those who repented from their sins, Luther also offered a list of those whose sinful behavior barred them from the sacrament: these included anyone who was a "fornicator, adulterer, drunkard, gamester, usurer, slanderer, or one made infamous by some manifest crime."[28] In a similar fashion, the 1571 Swedish Lutheran church order laid out a list of those who were barred from Communion, including strangers, the insane, children under eight or nine years of age, and notorious sinners who had not been reconciled to the church prior to the celebration.[29]

According to the Book of Common Prayer, the criteria for admission to the sacrament of Communion included both adequate knowledge of

---

[26]John Roth, "The Limits of Confessionalization: Social Discipline, the Ban, and Political Resistance Among Swiss Anabaptists, 1550–1700," *Mennonite Quarterly Review* 89, no. 4 (2015): 517-37, esp. 528-31.

[27]Luther, "Formula of Mass," 94.

[28]Luther, "Formula of Mass," 94.

[29]Senn, *The People's Work*, 191.

the faith and a moral lifestyle. Specifically, those wanting to receive the sacrament had to be able to recite the brief catechism included in the Book of Common Prayer. He or she could not be an "open and notorious evil liver" or someone who had "done any wrong to his neighbors by word or deed."[30] Clergy were also enjoined to prohibit anyone who exhibited signs of hatred or malice because of current quarrels from partaking in the sacrament. The prayer book made the clergy the gatekeepers for access to Communion, but the clergy themselves were aware of the twin dangers of too much rigor or too much laxity. If the rules were strictly enforced, too many laypeople either would suffer spiritual discouragement or would be confirmed in their spiritual laziness and make no attempt to amend their ways. The spiritually anxious could also turn away from the very remedy for their lack of spiritual confidence. If the clergy did not enforce the rules, then both sinful individuals and the community at large were in danger of punishment from God for their impious participation.[31]

In Geneva and in Reformed communities that followed the Genevan model, access to the Lord's Supper was regulated by the consistory, the body of pastors and elders also known in Scotland as the kirk session. In Geneva, the consistory met weekly except during the week prior to the quarterly Communion services, when the frequency of meetings rose to twice or three times in that week. The extra meetings were needed specifically because those who had previously been temporarily barred from the sacrament because of lack of knowledge of the fundamentals of their faith or failures in their moral or spiritual lives sought reconciliation and permission to approach the table once again. The consistory also intervened if someone decided on his or her own not to partake of the Supper at one of the celebrations—unilateral

---

[30]Christopher Haigh, "Communion and Community: Exclusion from Communion in Post-Reformation England," *Journal of Ecclesiastical History* 51, no. 4 (2000): 721-40, esp. 722.
[31]Haigh, "Communion and Community," 724-28.

decisions not to partake were signs of a problem that needed to be aired and could not be allowed to fester.

Frequency. Among late medieval Catholics, the general practice (and indeed the rule of the church from the time of the Fourth Lateran Council in 1215) was to receive the sacrament of Communion once a year, at Easter time. More frequent Communion was possible, but receiving the host more than three times a year would be quite unusual.[32] Although laypeople received the sacrament infrequently, the liturgy of the Mass was celebrated daily in many churches, and even several times a day at different altars within the same church, even without any laypeople present, since a Mass was fully valid when offered by an ordained celebrant with or without a congregation on hand. Memorial Masses were particularly important examples of private Masses: medieval Christians regularly gave money to ensure that Masses would be celebrated either in their own memory or in memory of a loved one. These memorial Masses, celebrated by chantry priests paid by the donations, were understood as particularly meritorious acts, that would help the souls of the remembered dead get through purgatory more swiftly.[33]

In Lutheran churches, the original practice was to celebrate Communion every Sunday. Thus, in theory at least, frequent Communion participation was possible. However, the popular pre-Reformation tradition of infrequent Communion participation persisted, so much so that in southern German Lutheran churches, the frequency of Communion celebrations shifted to once a month or bimonthly. Even then, some parishioners did not participate in the sacrament regularly and would leave the worship service after the sermon

---

[32] Amy Nelson Burnett, "The Social History of Communion and the Reformation of the Eucharist," *Past and Present* 211 (2011): 82.

[33] Although chantry priests were limited by canon law to saying one Mass a day, they served in other ways by participating in the liturgy of the hours and serving as assistants at other Masses. See Clive Burgess, "'For the Increase of Divine Service': Chantries in the Parish in Late Medieval Bristol," *Journal of Ecclesiastical History* 36, no. 1 (1985): 46-65.

and before the Communion liturgy got underway if they were not
intending to participate.[34]

Because the records detailing early modern Anabaptist worship
practices are so few and far between, the issue of frequency of Communion celebrations is hard to determine. However, surviving evidence
does suggest that the sacrament was not celebrated according to any
particular schedule, and was held rather infrequently, depending on the
ability of the Anabaptists in a given area to gather together. In 1528, for
instance, Catholic authorities interrogated a group of captured Anabaptists. Of the five people arrested and questioned, two had not received
Communion for two years, one had received the sacrament in both
kinds a year earlier, and one testified that a large group of Anabaptists
had held a celebration of the Lord's Supper on Maundy Thursday, just
a few weeks before his own arrest.[35] Indications from other communities suggest that the frequency of celebrations of the sacrament could
vary from once a year among the Hutterites, to each time the Anabaptist community gathered, in Zollikon near Zurich, for instance.[36]

Among the Reformed, the frequency of celebration of the Lord's Supper varied, although a quarterly celebration (at Easter, Pentecost, in early
September, and on the Sunday closest to Christmas Day) was quite common. Although Calvin stated on several occasions that more frequent
Communion would be preferable, the Genevan magistrates ruled in
favor of the quarterly Lord's Supper services, each with a Sunday of preparation beforehand. In Scotland, Communion services tended to take
place only once a year, generally around Easter. For their part, the Hungarian Reformed moved to slightly more frequent Communion services,
holding these six times a year, at Advent, Christmas, Ash Wednesday,

---

[34]Burnett, "Social History of Communion," 117.

[35]Michele Zelinsky Hanson, "Anabaptist Liturgical Practices," in Wandel, *Companion*,
251-72, esp. 266.

[36]Wally Kroeker, "The Element of Unity in the Anabaptist Practice of the Lord's Supper,"
Direction 12, no. 3 (1983): 29-38, esp. 34.

Easter, Ascension Day, and Pentecost.[37] The Hungarian Reformed practice of celebrating Communion services on days of the liturgical year such as Ash Wednesday that were not even recognized as key dates of the church calendar by other Reformed churches shows how divergent worship practices could be even within the same confessional group.

In the Church of England, the Book of Common Prayer stated that Communion was to be celebrated at least three times annually, including at Easter. While most churches seem to have kept to this schedule, difficulties could arise when congregations still stuck to their traditional once-a-year practice. In other words, there could well be significant differences between the number of times churches offered Communion and the number of times a given parishioner actually received the sacrament. Over time, the frequency of Communion celebrations increased, to four times a year, or even monthly in some churches.[38]

Altars or tables? In the consecrated medieval churches, altars (especially the high altar) were particularly sacred spaces. Indeed, the immediate area around the altars reflect this holy status as it was restricted space, reserved for the clergy and those authorized to help in the celebration of the ritual of the Mass. Laypeople were kept at a reverent distance from the high altar, usually gathering behind a screen that divided the nave from the choir where the high altar was located.[39]

In the Lutheran German lands, pre-Reformation altars, complete with candles, crucifixes, and altarpieces, continued in use for the celebrations of Communion, although the priest now faced the congregation. If need be, in cases where there was no room for a pastor to stand behind a preexisting fixed altar with an altarpiece, an additional freestanding altar could be set up in front of the old one.[40] Numerous Lutheran churches also commissioned new altarpieces to adorn their liturgical space,

---

[37]Mentzer, "Reformed Liturgical Practices," 235-36.
[38]Turrell, "Anglican Liturgical Practices," 273-91, esp. 281-82.
[39]Andrew Spicer, "Sites of the Eucharist," in Wandel, *Companion*, 323-62, esp. 323-31.
[40]Spicer, "Sites of the Eucharist," 337-39.

displaying images that articulated Lutheran theology in visible form, such as the contrast between the law and the gospel, or depictions of the Last Supper. Reformed believers in the German lands and elsewhere reacted strongly against the survival and ongoing adornment of these altars, charging the Lutherans with idolatry and with a desire to perpetuate the idea of the sacrament of Communion as a sacrifice offered to God by human hands. Instead, the Reformed favored plain and portable Communion tables, set up each time the sacrament was to be celebrated.[41] In some Reformed communities, however, the tables were either permanently set up in a location where they were not in the way (as in Geneva), or were in fact constructed of more durable and immovable materials, such as stone (as in the Reformed churches in the Pays de Vaud). To make sure no one confused them with pre-Reformation altars, these tables stood on pedestals and had an oval or polygonal shape.[42]

In the Church of England, the reconfiguration of space to have the Communion liturgy match the prevalent theological stance was a gradual process. Under Henry VIII, the liturgy of the Mass remained as it had been before the Reformation got underway. During the reign of his son Edward, tables set up in the center of the chancel replaced altars. The latter were supposed to be removed from churches beginning in 1549.[43] The replacement of altars with tables provided a visual illustration of the shift from understanding the sacrament as a reenacted sacrifice to a sacred meal. The 1552 Book of Common Prayer further underscored the difference between altars and Communion tables by ordering that the tables be positioned lengthways, whereas the altars had stood widthwise.[44]

[41]Bodo Nischan, "Becoming Protestants: Lutheran Altars or Reformed Communion Tables?," in *Worship in Medieval and Early Modern Europe: Change and Continuity in Religious Practice*, ed. Karin Maag and John Witvliet (Notre Dame, IN: University of Notre Dame Press, 2004), 92-111.

[42]Spicer, "Sites of the Eucharist," 348.

[43]Turrell, "Anglican Liturgical Practices," 273-77.

[44]Spicer, "Sites of the Eucharist," 350.

Figure 6.1. Lucas Cranach the Elder, Wittenberg Altarpiece, Stadtkirche, Wittenberg (1547)

The elements. Already before the Reformation, the question as to whether laypeople could or should receive both the bread and the wine at Communion had caused deep divisions. Indeed, this debate lay at the heart of the long-standing and eventually locally successful pressure of Jan Hus and his colleagues and supporters in Bohemia to allow Bohemian Christians to receive Communion in both kinds. The Catholic Church's position was that since Christ was fully present in both the bread and the wine, a communicant who only received the bread had still fully received Christ. The dangers of spillage of the consecrated wine, which according to Catholic theology changed its substance to become the blood of Christ upon consecration, also played a key role in the Catholic Church's reluctance to have the laity receive the cup.

Beginning in 1566, the Roman Catechism and the Roman missals stated that the hosts or Communion wafers could only be made of wheat, not oats or peas or other grains. The wheat had to be of finest quality, and the baking was done in special presses, often in monasteries and convents, accompanied by psalm-singing.[45] The wine could be either red or white, but white wine was preferred, because it stained less if dripped.[46] Because of their sacred character once they had been consecrated, the unconsumed hosts had to be preserved with honor. Therefore, late medieval and early modern Catholic churches began to set aside a chapel or a tabernacle or some other location in which to preserve and display the reserved consecrated hosts. These spaces could include Blessed Sacrament chapels, where candles were kept burning as a visible sign of the presence of Christ. Other ceremonies that grew up around the adoration of the consecrated hosts included the Forty Hours liturgy, in which relays of the faithful prayed in front of the displayed Blessed Sacrament for a total of forty hours, representing the amount of time elapsed between

---

[45]Senn, *The People's Work*, 173.
[46]Isabelle Brian, "Catholic Liturgies of the Eucharist in the Time of Reform," in Wandel, *Companion*, 185-203, esp. 187.

Christ's death on the cross and his resurrection. This ritual first appeared in Italy in the 1520s, and then spread northward to France.[47]

In England, the 1549 Book of Common Prayer had ordered churches to use wafers for Communion. Under Edward, the first and second editions of the Book of Common Prayer reworked the liturgy for Communion in significant ways. In the 1549 liturgy, the priest was not supposed to raise up the consecrated elements, and Communion could only be celebrated if there was at least one congregant present as well as the priest. Although wafers were still used, they were supposed to be free of any stamped images. The 1552 edition went further: regular yeast bread replaced the wafers. In 1559, the revised Book of Common Prayer had again called for yeast bread, but the royal injunctions of the same year prescribed the use of wafers. Over the next two decades, conflicts over what kind of bread to use caused controversy in the English church. Those who looked for further reform in the Church of England advocated the use of yeast bread, whereas traditionalists preferred the wafers. The controversy continued until 1604, when the royal injunctions of James I called for good-quality ordinary bread to be used.[48]

Communion practices. For lay Catholics, the key moment in the sacrament of the Eucharist was the elevation, when the priest lifted up in his hands the consecrated host and the consecrated cup. This elevation signaled that the miracle of transubstantiation had occurred. The visible cue was preceded by an audible one—namely, the ringing of bells. Thus laypeople would know when this holy moment had occurred, and would kneel and pray in the presence of Christ in the elements. Christians were meant to be reconciled to God and to their neighbor before partaking in the sacrament. This high bar helps

---

[47]Brian, "Catholic Liturgies," 192-97.

[48]Turrell, "Anglican Liturgical Practices," 280-81. See also Christopher Haigh, "'A Matter of Much Contention in the Realm': Parish Controversies over Communion Bread in Post-Reformation England," *History* 88 (2003): 393-404.

explain in part why both church leaders and congregations tended to emphasize the importance of a spiritual Communion via attentive presence at Mass, especially at the moments of elevation and consecration of the elements, as being spiritually equivalent to a physical partaking of the sacrament. Moments of spiritual Communion during the Mass could also include a time of special prayers said by laypeople when the priest partook of the bread and the wine, since he was partaking on behalf of all the faithful, and the period during which the pax-board circulated, first among the clergy and then among the congregation, as a sign of their spiritual union with each other and with God.[49]

The practice of distributing the bread and wine to congregations during the celebrations of the sacrament varied greatly, both between and among confessional groups. Communion practices in the late medieval Catholic Mass included having the congregation come forward in batches to kneel at the altar rail, then recite together a confession of sins before being absolved by the priest. A consecrated host was then placed by the priest in the mouth of each of the recipients. Each person was then given a measure of unconsecrated ablution wine, to make sure that no crumbs of the consecrated host remained in his or her mouth, but were all swallowed. Because so many people received the sacrament in the same time period in the Easter season, special Communion services were held separately from Masses, where clergy distributed the consecrated hosts to the people, following a general confession of faith and absolution. In some areas, by tradition, groups of people were meant to receive their Easter Communion on specific days. For example, in Zofingen in the northern Swiss lands, young people received Communion on

---

[49]Amy Nelson Burnett, "The Social History of Communion and the Reformation of the Eucharist," *Past and Present* 211 (2011): 77-119, esp. 82-84.

Maundy Thursday, whereas older congregation members partook of the sacrament on Easter Sunday.[50]

Luther's reworking of the Catholic Mass retained many aspects of the pre-Reformation practice. People still came forward to stand before the altar, knelt, and received the bread in their mouths from the hand of the pastor. In a clear break from Catholic practice, the faithful also now received the consecrated wine, sipping from the chalice proffered by the pastor.[51] Several early modern Lutheran church orders also followed Luther's instructions by having men and women line up to partake of the elements separately, generally with women coming up to the left side of the altar and the men to the right.[52] However, other Lutheran churches in the early modern era adopted different strategies for Communion. In Lübeck in 1531, for instance, the city's church order set out a pattern whereby one pastor would distribute the bread to everyone on the left side of the altar, and another pastor would share out the wine on the right-hand side, thus necessitating movement or walking between the two stations, usually by walking behind the altar. Even under these circumstances, however, the men still lined up and were served first. This *Wandelabendmahl,* or "walking Communion," proved to be an efficient way to distribute the bread and wine to larger groups. The single-person kneeling benches on both the left and right side of the altar allowed for each person to receive the bread and the wine on an individual basis even while lining up as part of a larger group.[53]

Among Anabaptists, celebrations of the Lord's Supper incorporated other key rituals apart from the sharing of the bread and the wine. The most important of these was the practice of footwashing. This ritual embodied many of the key Anabaptist teachings about

[50]Burnett, "Social History of Communion," 86-87.
[51]Burnett, "Social History of Communion," 103-4.
[52]Range, "'Wandelabendmahl,'" 733-35.
[53]Range, "'Wandelabendmahl,'" 735-60.

the sacrament of Communion: footwashing too recalled Jesus' actions at the Last Supper and bound members of the group to one another in love and service.[54]

In Reformed communities, there was little uniformity of practice when it came to ensuring that each member of the congregation who was eligible received his or her portion of bread and wine. In the Zwinglian church, the distribution took place while the congregation remained seated on their benches: the plates of ordinary household bread and the wooden cups holding wine went up and down the rows, passed from person to person. In most other Reformed churches, congregation members came forward to receive the bread and wine, but even then practices differed. In Geneva, France, and Hungary, people came forward to stand in small groups around the trestle tables that had been set up: first the men, then the women. The pastor gave each person a piece of the bread in his or her hand. The congregants then put the bread into their mouths, chewed, swallowed, and then received the cup of wine from which they sipped, before returning to their places. In the Reformed churches in the Netherlands and in Scotland, however, people came forward in groups, but in these countries, each church member actually took a seat at the table, passing the bread and wine from person to person beginning with the pastor at the center of the table.[55] In 1634, an English visitor to the Dutch Republic, Sir William Brereton, left an eyewitness account of Communion practices he saw in Leiden:

> We found them receiving the sacrament at a long table covered with a white cloth, placed lengthways in an aisle which stands over across the church: the men, I imagine had all received together at the same place; we only saw women receive sitting; in

[54]Timothy George, "Early Anabaptist Spirituality in the Low Countries," *Mennonite Quarterly Review* 62, no. 3 (1988): 257-75, esp. 270.

[55]Mentzer, "Reformed Liturgical Practices," 243-46.

the middle of whom, on the one side, was placed the minister, who after he had consecrated to bread and wine, did administer the same unto those who sat next to him, who conveyed, on both hands the predicant, the bread on plates, and the wine in cups to those who sat next unto them: they themselves broke the bread, being cut into long narrow pieces. When all these had received they departed, and others succeeded. . . . After all had received, a psalm sung, and then some short prayer read, and so concluded.[56]

The Church of England's practice, as laid out in the various sixteenth-century editions of the Book of Common Prayer, specified that congregants who wanted to receive the sacrament were to come forward to stand close to the table, with men and women in separate groups. After the consecration liturgy was completed, they were to kneel and join in a prayer of confession, receive the priest's absolution, and recite together a prayer of supplication. The Book of Common Prayer specified that the people were to kneel when receiving the bread and the wine. Although the 1552 edition of the Book of Common Prayer specified that the priest was to place the bread in the communicant's hand, previous and subsequent editions omitted this point.[57] Although kneeling to receive the bread and wine was the stated rule, the practice might well have varied somewhat, as surviving church interiors from the period have benches around the table, suggesting that some congregations may have held a seated Communion instead.[58]

Conflicts. Not surprisingly, the wide range of liturgical and ritual practices surrounding the sacrament offered many occasions for clashes. Among the conflicts that emerged in medieval Catholic churches over Communion was the rivalry between parish clergy and orders of friars. Since laypeople could make their confession to any

---

[56]Quoted in Spicer, "Sites of the Eucharist," 346-47.
[57]*The First Prayer-Book of Edward VI*, 249-52.
[58]Spicer, "Sites of the Eucharist," 350-51.

ordained priest, and since the friars included a number of priests, it was possible for people who so desired to make their annual confession to such a friar and not to their parish priest. Apart from professional rivalries, the problem was that the annual confession and Communion of the laity at Easter time was also when laypeople traditionally paid their tithes. Hence a shift away from parish priests to friars for confession and Communion could also jeopardize the parish clergy's financial bottom line. The church addressed this problem by the late 1200s by ordering that all laypeople had to fulfill their annual Communion obligation in their parish church.[59]

The conflicts that could occur during the celebration of Communion were many and various. In Anglican churches, conflicts could and did spring up when one person objected to their neighbor's presence at the sacrament due to a preexisting conflict or a conviction that their neighbor was not in a fit moral state to partake in the rite. Other people clashed with the priest when he refused to administer the sacrament to them. This decision could lead to public embarrassment and was particularly problematic for those who made a mental association between the offering they had just given and their right to receive the sacrament. For some, it seemed as though they were not getting what they had just paid for.[60]

Among the most common Communion clashes in Reformed churches were conflicts of precedence in the lines of people waiting their turn to go forward and receive the bread and wine from their pastor's hands. People were supposed to go forward separated by gender and in descending order of social rank, but these gradations could cause acrimony if someone thought he or she was more socially prominent than the person ahead of them in the line. In 1598 in Ganges in southeastern France, two women, members of leading families of this small town, got into a shoving match in the

---

[59]Macy, "Medieval Inheritance," 20-21.
[60]Haigh, "Communion and Community," 730-37.

processional line, as each felt she was from a more prominent family and hence should have precedence.[61]

Conflicts could also occur between confessional groups over differing liturgical practices during the celebration of Communion. In the German lands, Lutherans and Reformed church leaders and their congregations clashed over the presence of rituals and actions that the Lutherans held as intrinsic aspects of the sacramental celebration, but that the Reformed stigmatized as remnants of Roman Catholicism. These included the use of candles, vestments for the clergy, and the use of altars rather than Communion tables. The most divisive aspect, however, had to do with the pastor's actions just before distributing the Communion elements to the congregation: Did he keep the bread intact, or did he ritually break it before having the faithful partake? The Reformed, following the biblical passages in Matthew 26, Luke 22, and 1 Corinthians 11, made the breaking of the bread an intrinsic part of their Communion liturgy. The Lutherans kept the bread intact following the consecration until the point of distribution and viewed any pastor who did ritually break the bread as a crypto-Calvinist. Reformed theologians viewed the Lutheran unwillingness to break the bread following the consecration as a sign of the Lutherans' support for the doctrine of the real presence of Christ in the bread and the wine.[62]

CONCLUSION

This last instance of conflict surrounding the sacrament of Communion encapsulates many of the core issues that caused such deep divisions among early modern Christians. The sacrament was the occasion of an encounter with the holy, a place of reconciliation and communal

---

[61]Raymond Mentzer, "The Persistence of 'Superstition and Idolatry' Among Rural French Calvinists," *Church History* 65, no. 2 (1996): 220-33, esp. 230.

[62]Bodo Nischan, "The 'Fractio Panis': A Reformed Communion Practice in Late Reformation Germany," *Church History* 53, no. 1 (1984): 17-29.

solidarity, a sacred meal meant to root Christ's sacrifice and God's grace in believers' hearts. But this sacrament could also become a touchstone of group identity that ended up pushing confessional groups away from each other. Congregations might not have been able to explain the theological distinctives that their church leaders debated at length, but they knew and defended the Communion worship practices that made the sacrament genuine to them.

For Further Reading

Burnett, Amy Nelson. "The Social History of Communion and the Reformation of the Eucharist." *Past and Present* 211 (2011): 77-119.

DeMolen, Richard. "Childhood and the Sacraments in the Sixteenth Century." *Archiv für Reformationsgeschichte* 66 (1975): 49-71.

Haigh, Christopher. "Communion and Community: Exclusion from Communion in Post-Reformation England." *The Journal of Ecclesiastical History* 51, no. 4 (2000): 721-40.

Haigh, Christopher. "'A Matter of Much Contention in the Realm': Parish Controversies over Communion Bread in Post-Reformation England." *History* 88 (2003): 393-404.

Nischan, Bodo. "The 'Fractio Panis': A Reformed Communion Practice in Late Reformation Germany." *Church History* 53, no. 1 (1984): 17-29.

Range, Matthias. "'Wandelabendmahl': Lutheran 'Walking Communion' and its Expression in Material Culture." *Journal of Ecclesiastical History* 64, no. 4 (2013): 731-68.

Wandel, Lee Palmer, ed. *A Companion to the Eucharist in the Reformation.* Leiden: Brill, 2014.

SEVEN

The Visual Arts and Music

Every Christian should, when singing spiritual songs or psalms,
always sing more with the heart than with the mouth, so that the words
that are sung have also been eagerly absorbed by the heart.

PREFACE TO ANABAPTIST HYMNAL (CA. 1555)

THE EXPERIENCE OF WORSHIP in early modern worship was not limited to the spoken word, whether preached from the pulpit, articulated in prayer, or proclaimed in the celebration of the sacraments. Indeed, two crucial features of the practice of worship that were used by many confessional groups in the period and debated by all were the place of music and of the visual arts. Apart from in Zwingli's Zurich (where there was no singing or music of any kind in worship until 1598), Reformation-era Christians across the board made use of music in worship services. Music in early modern worship could include choral anthems, liturgies chanted by clergy, instrumental music (especially for preludes and postludes), and congregational singing. Singing could be unaccompanied or supported by instrumentalists. Leadership could be provided by cantors or trained singers. This rich variety in the possible forms of worship music

---

Preface to *Ein außbundt Schöner geistlicher Lieder* (c. 1555), in *Later Writings of the Swiss Anabaptists, 1529–1592*, ed. C. Arnold Snyder (Kitchener, ON: Pandora, 2017), 131.

helps explain why (as in the case of other aspects of worship) the provision of music in worship was not without controversy. What was the purpose and place of music in worship? Could or should everyone participate, or was music in church best left to those trained in that art? Should congregations sing hymn texts by human authors, or were the words of Scripture or scriptural paraphrases the only appropriate source of congregational song? Should singing be unaccompanied or was organ or other instrumental accompaniment permissible? Should people sing in unison or in parts? What was the best way to teach congregational singing, especially in communities where little to no such singing took place before the Reformation?

The questions and debates were even fiercer when it came to the visual arts. Fundamentally, various confessional groups came to radically different answers when deciding whether representative religious images were allowable in church. The spectrum ranged from clear encouragement to install religious art in places of worship, both for devotional and pedagogical reasons, to outright hostility against any form of religious art in churches, perceiving these images as a form of idolatry and a breach of the Ten Commandments. Those hostile to such depictions could and did engage in iconoclasm (the destruction of religious art), removing and eradicating what they saw as an affront to God's honor. Yet even these "cleansed" churches were not completely bare, as the urge to provide focal points for the eyes remained a constant.

In December 1551, the renowned composer of much of the music of the Genevan Psalter, Louis Bourgeois, was briefly imprisoned in Geneva, on the orders of the city government. The magistrates were displeased with Bourgeois for two reasons. First, he had made some corrections to the melodies of the Psalms, fixing previous printers' errors, but changing the music, thus upsetting those who had become familiar with the "wrong" notes. Second, and more significantly, his revised edition of the Psalter music included a very pointed preface, critiquing the singing practices of the Genevan congregations. Bourgeois's chief complaints centered on those who sang without having any real experience (or talent)—they sang too loudly, too slowly, or at a different tempo from those around them. In his preface, Bourgeois highlighted the problems, but also what he saw as the necessary solutions:

> Let no one who is not confident in doing this well take it upon himself to sing, and may those who know nothing be content to listen to the others and learn in silence, until they can sing in tune with those who do sing well. . . . Wherefore let each take note and let the ignorant in music lend their ears to those who do understand it: that is to say, that in singing they do not presume to force and elevate their voices as high as they might like, and that in simplicity of song and without dragging (as they are in the habit of doing), they imitate them, in order that all be well-ordered in the Church of God.[1]

Bourgeois's critique provides crucial evidence about the practice of congregational singing in Reformation-era worship. In Bourgeois's testimony we see that congregations in Geneva did sing, but that the results were not always what a trained musician might want. Indeed, some of his complaints may well resonate with church musicians today. Clearly, there was a gap between the hopes and expectations of church leaders and musicians regarding congregational song and the day-to-day reality.

↪

---

[1] Louis Bourgeois, "Announcement Concerning the Psalm Melodies," in Daniel Trocmé-Latter, "'May Those Who Know Nothing Be Content to Listen': Loys Bourgeois' *Advertissement* to the Psalms (1551)," *Reformation and Renaissance Review* 11, no. 3 (2009): 345-46.

During the Wonderyear of 1566 in the Low Countries, iconoclasm broke out beginning in August—beginning in the southern provinces and then spreading northward over the subsequent weeks and months. According to eyewitness accounts, the image-breaking in Antwerp began in the Church of Our Lady. The men involved attacked religious images of all kinds, including crucifixes, statues, and pictures, and damaged and desecrated the altars. Yet in the midst of all this destruction, nothing was looted or stolen, and no one was injured by flying shards or falling statuary. The toll of destruction was enormous: one account of the iconoclasm states, "They cast down or plundered these with such vehemence and headlong insolence that before midnight, they had reduced one of the largest, most glorious and splendidly adorned churches in Europe with its seventy altars to an empty and ghastly hulk."[2] The magistrates of Antwerp did very little to stop the iconoclasm in its first phase, concentrating instead on protecting civic buildings in case the image-breakers moved on to new targets. After three days of iconoclasm, the civic authorities finally intervened in force when the crests of the royal family and those of the knights of the golden fleece were damaged during iconoclasm in the Grote Kerk of Antwerp.[3]

This narrative highlights a number of important points about the role of religious art in places of worship. The iconoclasts did not view their work as wanton vandalism or mindless destruction. Instead, their aim was to cleanse the churches from what they saw as idolatry, to make the buildings fit for faithful Reformed worship. In this instance, as in many cases elsewhere, the local authorities made little attempt to actively prevent or stop the iconoclasm, though they drew

---

[2]Geeraert Brandt, *Historie der Reformatie en andere Kerkelyke Geschiedenissen in en ontrent de Nederlanden* (Amsterdam: Rieuwertsz and Boom, 1677) 1:345. Translated into English as G. Brandt, *The History of the Reformation and Other Ecclesiastical Transactions in and About the Low Countries* (London: Timothy Childs, 1720), 1:193.

[3]Brandt's account is available in an English translation on the Dutch Revolt site maintained by the University of Leiden, https://dutchrevolt.leiden.edu/english/sources/Pages/15660701.aspx (accessed May 2, 2019).

the line firmly at any attack against symbols of political authority displayed in church buildings.

Both of these vignettes provide examples of how music and the visual arts could be used but also challenged in worship. Those who supported the use of music and/or the visual arts in the context of communal worship offered a range of arguments in favor of these practices. Opponents presented equally vehement arguments against including one or both of these during the worship service or in the worship space. Yet apart from the arguments put forth on one side or the other, it is especially instructive to consider that the various confessional groups did not confine themselves to rigid all-or-nothing options. Instead, even within confessional groups over the course of the century from 1517, the use of music and visual arts in worship waxed and waned depending on a wide range of influences. These included theological stances, political pressures, interconfessional rivalries, and shifting power relations between church and state.

THE ROLE OF MUSIC IN WORSHIP

Catholics and Protestants agreed that music in public worship was a pressing issue. In many instances, the concerns over what music should be sung or played in worship were the same, regardless of confessional background. The Italian Catholic archpriest Bernardino Cirillo, in a letter dated 1549 and sent to a fellow priest in Rome, laid out his hopes regarding music to be sung at Mass:

> I wish that when a Mass is to be sung in church, and according to the underlying substance of the words, its music would be made of certain harmonies and numbers suited for moving our affections to religion and piety, and the same for psalms, hymns and the other paeans offered to God.[4]

---

[4]Chiara Bertoglio, "Cats, Bulls and Donkeys: Bernardino Cirillo on 16th-Century Church Music," *Early Music* 45, no. 4 (2017): 559-72, esp. 565.

Cirillo complained about the propensity of Mass composers to have all the parts of the Mass sung entirely in the same mode and sometimes at the very same time, taking no account of the different emotional effects of the various parts of the Mass. He added, "Let us see if such corruptions could be banned from the churches where they are, introducing in their place affecting harmonies, apt at moving [people] to religion and piety, and at inclining [them] to devotion."[5] Cirillo held that the right use of music in worship could affect people's level of devotion. His desire to use church music more effectively to shape people's life of faith was a goal shared by many church leaders in the early modern era.

Luther was among the strongest proponents of the use of hymns in corporate worship and was himself a prolific hymn writer. In the preface to the hymnal printed in Wittenberg in 1524, Luther laid out his main ideas about the importance of hymnody in worship. He highlighted the biblical examples of psalm-singing in the Old and New Testaments and in the early church, and he underscored the crucial role that sacred hymns could play in transmitting the gospel message. In his final paragraph, Luther emphasized the pedagogical importance of these hymns:

> And these songs were arranged in four parts to give the young—
> who should at any rate be trained in music and other fine arts—
> something to wean them away from love ballads and carnal
> songs and to teach them something of value in their place, thus
> combining the good with the pleasing, as is proper for youth.
> Nor am I of the opinion that the gospel should destroy and
> blight all the arts, as some of the pseudo-religious claim. But I
> would like to see all the arts, especially music, used in the service of Him who gave and made them.[6]

---

[5]Bertoglio, "Cats, Bulls and Donkeys," 566.
[6]Martin Luther, "Preface to the Wittenberg Hymnal," in *Luther's Works*, vol. 53, *Liturgy and Hymns*, ed. Ulrich S. Leopold (Philadelphia: Fortress, 1965), 316.

Although the argument that sacred music was important because it was spiritually healthier for people's ears and mind and soul than secular songs was reprised by many reformers, Luther's defense of the importance of music in worship is worth further analysis. He categorically rejected the idea that music, as one of the arts, was intrinsically unsuited to the practice of true religion. Indeed, in other writings, Luther tied Christians' strong convictions that they have been justified by faith to their desire to "willingly sing and speak about it so that others also may come and hear it."[7] Simply using speech was not sufficient: genuine believers joyously shared their faith in song. On biblical and pragmatic grounds, therefore, Luther strongly defended the use of music in worship and encouraged congregational song. Yet not everyone among his fellow reformers followed suit.

Indeed, other Protestant religious leaders took a radically different approach. The one most concerned about the power of music to distract from genuine worship was Zwingli. As a result no congregational singing or music of any kind was included in public worship in Zurich from 1525 through 1598. The other Swiss cities that had followed Zurich's lead in adopting Reformed theology and worship did however reincorporate singing into worship already by the 1530s and 1540s. It is worth noting that Zwingli was critiquing a particular kind of music used in worship in the pre-Reformation church. Already in the early 1520s, he criticized the priestly and choral singing that he had grown up with as being oriented toward performance, and grounded in pride and in the desire to be noticed, rather than focusing on honoring God. He said nothing, however, to condemn congregational song.[8]

Already from the early years of the Genevan Reformation, Calvin and his colleague Guillaume Farel were strong advocates of the importance of congregational singing, perceiving that this practice would

---

[7]Martin Luther, "Preface to the *Gesangbuch*" (1545), in *Liturgy and Hymns*, 333.
[8]Markus Jenny, *Zwinglis Stellung zur Musik im Gottesdienst* (Zurich: Zwingli Verlag, 1966), 8-13.

combat the spiritually cold worship services "which should cause us great shame and embarrassment."[9] Calvin's views on the role of music in public worship were most clearly expressed in his preface to the 1543 edition of the Genevan Psalter. He noted the power of music to enchant the human heart—therefore music needed to be harnessed and used appropriately to the honor and praise of God, rather than misused in dissolute songs. Calvin was convinced that the only genuinely appropriate source for texts to be sung in worship was Scripture, especially the book of Psalms. Channeling the emotional draw of music by selecting grave and measured melodies, and tying this music to the words of Scripture sung in the people's own language provided an ideal way to deepen devotion and help the congregation lift their hearts up to God.[10] Indeed, from Calvin's perspective, congregational psalm-singing bound believers ever more tightly to their Creator:

> Wherefore, when we have looked thoroughly everywhere and searched high and low, we shall find no better songs nor more appropriate to the purpose than the Psalms of David, which the Holy Spirit made and spoke through him. And furthermore, when we sing them, we are certain that God puts the words in our mouths, as if he himself were singing in us to exalt his glory.[11]

Hence Calvin strongly supported the use of music in worship in the form of unison unaccompanied congregational singing of words taken from Scripture and sung to appropriately majestic melodies. Unlike the visual arts in the worship space, which invariably led to distraction and the risks of idolatry, under the conditions listed above, the emotional power of music could be harnessed to bring the people closer to God.

---

[9]Christian Grosse, "L'esthétique du chant dans la piété calviniste aux premiers temps de la Réforme (1536-1545)," *Revue de l'histoire des religions* 227, no. 1 (2010): 13-31, esp. 19.

[10]Grosse, "L'esthétique du chant," 24-25.

[11]John Calvin, "Foreword to the Genevan Psalter 1542/3," in *Lifting Hearts to the Lord: Worship with John Calvin in Sixteenth-Century Geneva*, ed. Karin Maag (Grand Rapids, MI: Eerdmans, 2016), 146.

In the Church of England, Archbishop Thomas Cranmer provided theological and practical insights as to how best to use music in worship. Reacting to the very ornamented polyphonic choral singing that flourished in the late fifteenth and early sixteenth century, Cranmer wrote a letter to Henry VIII in 1544 when a revision of the liturgy for the English church was underway:

> After your highness hath corrected it, if your grace command some devout and solemn note to be made thereunto, [. . .] I trust it will much excitate and stir the hearts of all men unto devotion and godliness: but in my opinion, the song that shall be made thereunto would not be full of notes, but, as near as may be, for every syllable a note; so that it may be sung distinctly and devoutly.[12]

Cranmer's advocacy of musical settings that allowed the words to be understood clearly echoes the aims of Calvin and other reformers, whose emphasis was on transmitting and teaching the words of Scripture in an attractive yet clear way.

Psalms versus hymns. In the nineteenth and twentieth centuries, some denominations, especially in the Reformed and Presbyterian churches, have split over whether one should sing only scriptural texts (mainly the Psalms) in public worship, or whether hymn texts written by men and women were also allowable. This matter also divided churches in the Reformation era, although the divisions here were between confessional groups: early modern Lutherans and Anabaptists included hymns in worship, while some (but not all) Reformed only sang metrical psalms and scriptural paraphrases.

Indeed, the divisions between psalm-singing and hymn-singing were not hard and fast: there is evidence of Dutch Reformed psalters including a number of Lutheran-inspired hymns already in the sixteenth century. For instance, a volume of Dutch Psalms sung to

---

[12]Quoted in Andrew Shead, "Is There a Musical Note in the Body? Cranmer on the Reformation of Music," *Reformed Theological Review* 69, no. 1 (2010): 1-16, esp. 2.

Genevan tunes, published in 1574, also included a number of Luther's hymns in Dutch translation, including a version of "A Mighty Fortress."[13] Another good example of the blended practice of singing both psalms and hymns in corporate worship comes from the Swiss city of Basel. Inspired by the practice of congregational singing in Strasbourg, and undeterred by Zurich's worship services focusing solely on the spoken word, Reformed worship in Basel featured congregational singing already in 1526. One of the most popular books used by the Basel congregations in their singing was the *Christenlich Gsangbuech*, or "Christian songbook," brought out by the Zurich publisher Christoph Froschauer in 1559. It included all 150 Psalms set to music and eighty-five hymns from a wide variety of Protestant hymn writers.[14] By 1606, Basel's congregations used a book that included the metrical psalms in German by Ambrosius Lobwasser and an extensive set of Lutheran hymns. The book also had several settings of the hymns in four-part harmony. These were intended for trained church choirs, but congregations were still meant to join in the melody, which was moved from the tenor to the soprano line, to make the melody easier to hear and sing.[15]

The practice of psalm-singing. The most widely influential form of psalm-singing had its roots in the Genevan metrical psalms. A metrical psalm is simply a psalm text set in poetic meter, usually with a rhyming scheme. The text can then be set to music. John Calvin's earliest encounters with psalm-singing dated from his time in Basel in 1536 and most importantly his exile in Strasbourg from 1538 to 1541. Here Calvin heard the German-language congregations

---

[13]Jan Luth, "Luther im reformierten Gottesdienst," in *Luther and Calvinism: Image and Reception of Martin Luther in the History and Theology of Calvinism*, ed. Herman Selderhuis (Göttingen: Vandenhoeck & Ruprecht, 2017), 313-34, esp. 314-15.

[14]Kenneth Marcus, "Hymnody and Hymnals in Basel, 1526–1606," *Sixteenth Century Journal* 32, no. 3 (2001): 732.

[15]Marcus, "Hymnody and Hymnals in Basel," 737-38.

singing metrical psalms in their own language.[16] Here too Calvin first tried out the practice of having his congregation of French exiles sing rhymed paraphrases of the psalms. Indeed, some of the earliest editions of the metrical psalms in French had texts by Calvin, but these were quickly dropped in favor of better and smoother versions prepared by two men with a genuine talent for French poetry—namely, Clément Marot and Theodore Beza. The process of versifying all 150 Psalms and setting each of them to music was a gradual process, only complete in 1562. As well as the Psalms, the 1562 Psalter also offered a musical setting of the Song of Simeon and the Ten Commandments.[17] The musical mode for each psalm was carefully selected to match its content, with much of the music coming from simplified Gregorian chants.

In Reformed and Presbyterian churches that took up the practice of metrical psalm-singing in communal worship, the pattern remained consistent: congregations sang in unison and unaccompanied by instruments of any kind. Given the prevalence of instruments such as harps, lyres, and trumpets in the Psalms and in other Old Testament passages, it is appropriate to wonder why Calvin and other Reformed theologians insisted so strongly on unaccompanied singing. For Calvin, the musical instruments mentioned so frequently in the Old Testament were part of the old dispensation—they did not apply to Christian churches, where the accent was on making sure that everyone could understand the words being sung. As Calvin noted in his commentary on Psalm 71:22,

> To sing the praises of God upon the harp and psaltery unquestionably formed a part of the training of the law, and of the service of God under that dispensation of shadows and figures;

---

[16]Daniel Trocmé-Latter, *The Singing of the Strasbourg Protestants, 1523–1541* (Farnham, UK: Ashgate, 2015), 220-24.

[17]John Witvliet, "The Spirituality of the Psalter: Metrical Psalms in Liturgy and Life in Calvin's Geneva," *Calvin Theological Journal* 32, no. 2 (1997): 273-97, esp. 274-76.

but they are not now to be used in public thanksgiving. We are not, indeed, forbidden to use, in private, musical instruments, but they are banished out of the churches by the plain command of the Holy Spirit, when Paul, in 1 Corinthians 14:13 lays it down as an invariable rule, that we must praise God, and pray to him only in a known tongue.[18]

From Calvin's perspective, the sound of musical instruments that would otherwise accompany congregational singing seemingly obstructed or overshadowed the clear communication of the psalm paraphrases being sung.

In many instances, the singing was led by a precentor (*chantre*, *voorsinger*), whose task was to set the starting pitch and the tempo. In Geneva, the boys at the Latin school had an hour of psalm-singing a day, so they served for a time as the leaders of congregational song under the direction of the *chantre*. The same held true in early modern Scotland, where the boys who attended the song schools in Glasgow and St. Andrews, for instance, were to sit with their master around the pulpit to lead the singing of the Psalms during worship.[19] Everyone else was then meant to follow along. However, as Louis Bourgeois noted in our opening vignette, in many instances that ideal was very far from being realized. Indeed, later Protestant assumptions about how congregations must have relished the opportunity to join in song together, and how beautiful that singing must have sounded, are not always borne out by the evidence of contemporary sources. Some religious exiles did praise the sound of psalm-singing in Reformed worship. For instance, Martin du Mont, the young man from Antwerp studying in Strasbourg whom we met in the introduction, provided an eyewitness testimony to this practice:

---

[18]John Calvin, *Commentary on the Book of Psalms*, trans. James Anderson (Grand Rapids, MI: Eerdmans, 1949), 3:98.

[19]Andrew Spicer, "'Accommodating of Thame Selfis to Heir the Worde': Preaching, Pews and Reformed Worship in Scotland, 1560–1638," *History* 88 (2003): 405-22, esp. 418.

On Sundays . . . we sing a psalm of David or some other prayer taken from the New Testament. The Psalm or prayer is sung by everyone together, men as well as women with beautiful unanimity, which is something beautiful to behold. For you must understand that each one has a music book in his hand; that is why they cannot lose touch with one another. Never did I think that it could be as pleasing and delightful as it is.[20]

This account is particularly valuable in that it provides early evidence of the use of psalters in worship, most likely the 1539 Psalter produced in Strasbourg under John Calvin's leadership.

Others, however, seemed uncomfortable with what was to them a new aural experience. In his 1567 diary from his country parish outside Geneva, Pastor Charles Perrot noted how few of his rural congregation could sing the Psalms in worship with any degree of confidence—and that was fully thirty years after the Reformation had been officially adopted in the Genevan territory.[21] The bottom line was that the practice of singing metrical psalms in worship had to be taught: it was not obvious or self-evident to those who were meant to take part.

The practice of singing metrical settings of the Psalms in worship spread from Geneva to France, Scotland, the Netherlands, the German lands, and Hungary. In each case apart from France, the Psalms first needed to be versified into the local vernacular before being set to music. In most cases, the melodies assigned to particular psalms were retained in the new linguistic setting, so that the Dutch, Scots, Hungarians, German Reformed, and others were all singing Genevan psalm tunes. Many of the versions in other languages, such as Ambrosius Lobwasser's German translation, and Albert Molnár's version in Magyar for the Hungarian Reformed, were masterpieces—retaining

---

[20]Quoted in Witvliet, "Spirituality of the Psalter," 276.
[21]Charles Perrot, "Managing a Country Parish: A Country Pastor's Advice to his Successor" (1567), in Maag, *Lifting Hearts to the Lord*, 67.

the simple directness of the original version in the new language in texts that could easily be set to music.[22]

This practice did however lead to some controversy over time. In some places, especially in the Netherlands and in Scotland, protests grew by the end of the sixteenth century, complaining that the music was too difficult and too varied from psalm to psalm. In the Netherlands in the first decades of the seventeenth century, a pastor named Patroclus Römeling pointed out the weaknesses in Dutch Reformed psalm-singing in his day, especially the difficulties congregations were having in trying to learn so many different psalm melodies. His proposed solutions included limiting the total number of distinct tunes in the Dutch Psalter from 129 to no more than twenty-three.[23] The Scots solved the difficulty by the seventeenth century by singing as many psalms as possible in a small range of common meter tunes. Congregations then only had to learn twelve melodies that could be sung to a wide range of different psalms.[24] In Hungary, the grounds for protest were somewhat different. Some Hungarian Reformed church members complained about having to sing psalm paraphrases to imported Genevan melodies, instead of Hungarian hymns set to home-grown Magyar tunes. Other Hungarians disagreed, highlighting instead the importance of maintaining confessional bonds across linguistic barriers. These church leaders favored further reformation of Hungarian worship and church polity, bringing it closer to the Genevan model. From this perspective, psalms sung in the local language to Genevan melodies deepened the bond between the Hungarian Reformed and the wider Reformed community of faith.[25]

---

[22]Marcus, "Hymnody and Hymnals in Basel," 736-37.

[23]Jan Luth, "Remarks on the History of Congregational Singing in the Dutch Reformed Churches," in *Omnes Circumadstantes: Contributions Towards a History of the Role of the People in the Liturgy*, ed. Charles Caspers and Marc Schneiders (Kampen: J. H. Kok, 1990), 190.

[24]Karin Maag, "'No Better Songs': John Calvin and the Genevan Psalter in the Sixteenth Century and Today," *The Hymn* 68, no. 4 (2017): 21-26, esp. 25.

[25]Maag, "'No Better Songs,'" 25-26.

The practice of congregational singing of metrical psalms also took root in England during the reign of Elizabeth I. The English exiles under Queen Mary, many of whom had spent time in Geneva, began to sing metrical psalm settings in their worship services and brought the practice home with them upon their return to England. The psalter most commonly used in the Church of England was known as the Sternhold-Hopkins Psalter, named after Thomas Sternhold and John Hopkins, both of whom provided versified versions of the Psalms for the collection. Unlike in the case of the Genevan Psalter, which made use of a wide range of poetic meters and musical modes, the Sternhold-Hopkins Psalter kept to a very small number of meters and tunes.[26]

Congregational singing in worship. Whether singing psalms, hymns, or both, congregational singing was an integral part of corporate worship. Indeed, persecuted communities had to be cautious: the sound of congregational singing could alert authorities to their presence. So, for instance, the evidence about Anabaptist congregational singing especially in the sixteenth century is largely lacking, though surviving evidence suggests that they sang a hymn at the start and another hymn at the end of their worship service. Dutch Anabaptist hymnals included a wide variety of texts, including in some instances the Dutch metrical psalms by Peter Dathenus as well as martyr hymns, scriptural hymns, and spiritual hymns, sung to a relatively narrow range of melodies. Dutch Anabaptist congregations sang a capella until the late 1700s.[27]

In Lutheran churches, the use of music in worship went well beyond congregational singing. Luther's liturgies called for the priest to chant the Gospel reading and for trained choirs to sing the various key parts of the liturgy (the Kyrie, Gloria, Credo, Sanctus, and Agnus Dei) in polyphonic settings, often alternating with congregational

[26]Ramie Targoff, *Common Prayer: The Language of Public Devotion in Early Modern England* (Chicago: University of Chicago Press, 2001), 67-72.
[27]Nanne van der Zijp, "The Hymnology of the Mennonites in the Netherlands," *Mennonite Quarterly Review* 31, no. 1 (1957): 11-15.

singing of unison verses.[28] A congregational hymn (at times also sung alternating with the choir) was sung between the Epistle reading and the Gospel reading, and came to be known as the gradual hymn. It changed Sunday by Sunday, depending on the liturgical season and the themes of the Scripture readings.[29]

In Geneva and in the churches that followed Genevan worship practices, congregational singing took place twice during most worship services, once at the beginning of worship and once after the sermon. The 1562 Genevan Psalter included a chart that listed the breakdown of which psalms or parts of psalms should be sung on Sundays and Wednesday worship services over the course of twenty-five weeks. A careful use of the chart allowed the entire Psalter to be sung through twice a year. At the quarterly celebrations of the Lord's Supper, the psalm sung after the sermon was replaced by a musical setting of the Ten Commandments. After the prayer of thanksgiving at the end of the Lord's Supper liturgy, the congregation then sang the Song of Simeon.[30]

In the Church of England, the practice of music in communal worship followed different tracks depending on the setting for these worship services. In cathedrals and chapels, including the Chapel Royal, the practice of having trained choirs sing responses, anthems, and the various set parts of the liturgy continued to flourish. In parish churches, congregational singing primarily featured metrical psalms. Indeed, Cranmer's revised edition of the Book of Common Prayer, published in 1552, left little room for choirs and anthems due to his

---

[28]Robin Leaver, "Christian Liturgical Music in the Wake of the Protestant Reformation," in *Sacred Sound and Social Change: Liturgical Music in Jewish and Christian Experience*, ed. Lawrence Hoffman and Janet Walton (Notre Dame, IN: University of Notre Dame Press, 1992), 124-44.

[29]Robin Leaver, "Sequences and Responsories: Continuity of Forms in Luther's Liturgical Provisions," in *Worship in Medieval and Early Modern Europe: Change and Continuity in Religious Practice*, ed. Karin Maag and John Witvliet (Notre Dame, IN: University of Notre Dame Press, 2004), 300-328.

[30]See "A Chart from the Psalter in the 1567 Genevan Bible," in Maag, *Lifting Hearts to the Lord*, 94-95.

distrust of overly ornamented singing that made the words difficult
or impossible to understand.[31]

The organ controversy. Prior to the Reformation, larger churches
in urban areas commonly had an organ. When the Reformation was
adopted in the Swiss lands and in other areas that held to the Reformed faith, organs were either removed or left to decay. In Geneva,
the organ pipes were melted down and repurposed into tableware for
the Genevan charitable hospital. As noted above, Calvin objected to
the use of organs in worship, and indeed to any kind of instrumental
accompaniment to congregational singing, on the grounds that these
veered toward performance and detracted from the worship focus.
Yet the absence of instrumental accompaniment to congregational
singing did have unintended consequences over time—namely, the
gradual slowing down of the pace of singing. Without an instrument
to help with the tempo, congregations singing a cappella tended to
slow down. By the early seventeenth century, the problem of slowed-
down psalm-singing was so serious that Pastor Patroclus Römeling
submitted a formal complaint to the Synod of Dordt in 1618. He
noted that it was no longer possible to sing an entire psalm during a
worship service because everything was being sung so slowly. Instead,
congregations could barely squeeze in a couple of verses of the metrical paraphrase, where previously they had been able to sing through
the whole thing. Furthermore, he pointed out that the slow rate of
singing was distorting the words and exaggerating the syllables, so
that no one could make out what was actually being sung.[32]

In spite of these difficulties, the prohibition on instrumental accompaniment to congregational singing persisted, even though organs began to play again in some Dutch churches by the late sixteenth
century. In many of these communities, the organs were paid for and
installed in churches by the city authorities—hence their playing was

[31]Shead, "Is There a Musical Note in the Body?," 1-16.
[32]Luth, "Congregational Singing," 190.

regulated by the city leaders, who paid the organist's salary. The compromise that eventually resulted was that there would be no organ accompaniment of congregational singing during the worship service, but that organists could play preludes and postludes as musical bookends to the worship. Other Reformed churches were much slower to reintroduce any use of organs: in Zurich, organ music gradually became allowed only beginning in 1839.[33]

Although controversies did emerge over music in church, in most instances, church leaders agreed that music in worship was important, and the debates centered on what kind of music or singing was most appropriate. However, when it came to the visual arts and their place in worship spaces, controversies became much more heated.

THE ROLE OF THE VISUAL ARTS IN WORSHIP

Catholic perspectives. Although the world of late medieval Catholicism featured a rich tradition of religious images as focal points for devotion in churches, shrines, and places of pilgrimage, this reality should not obscure the fact that there were currents of thought within medieval Catholicism that warned against too great a focus on religious images in worship settings. In fifteenth-century England, for instance, a number of Catholic clergy and scholars articulated in texts and sermons their concerns about the dangers of misplaced popular image worship.[34]

Catholic theologians before and after the Reformation made clear distinctions between the veneration owed to images of Christ, of the Virgin Mary, or of saints, and the worship owed to God. Ordinary Catholics also understood this distinction, as evidenced in a letter written by a Welsh Catholic to his Protestant cousin in 1625. The Catholic Welshman attempted to explain to his relative that the bowing and

[33]Marcus, "Hymnody and Hymnals in Basel," 729.
[34]Peter Marshall, "Catholic Puritanism in Pre-Reformation England," *British Catholic History* 32, no. 4 (2015): 431-50.

kneeling before religious images was in line with the accepted practice of paying homage to the image or badges of office of the monarch:

> Will you then have liberty and hold it lawful, to honor the crown, sword, or stool of an earthly prince, and bar us from honoring the king of heaven, his crown of thorns, or that gracious throne of our redeemer the cross[?] . . . Will you needs bow with reverence to the dead picture of a temporal Queen, and rail at us for doing reverence to the image of Christ?[35]

In spite of his eloquence, the writer's attempt to explain Catholics' attitude of reverence toward religious images as representations of the holy was unlikely to dispel ongoing Protestant concerns about the risks inherent in having such images before the eyes of congregations in churches. Investigations into Protestant responses to visual art in the worship space in the early modern world do highlight, however, that Reformation theologians offered a range of views on the matter rather than a single stance.

Martin Luther's theological perspective on the presence and use of images in churches was shaped by his debates with those who strongly opposed giving any place to images in worship spaces. Already in 1522, Luther's colleague Andreas Karlstadt had written and preached against religious images in churches and had advocated iconoclasm on the grounds that religious images drew people in to idolatry. In response, Luther preached and wrote in defense of retaining images in churches. On the one hand, Luther argued that religious images fell into the category of adiaphora, or matters indifferent: according to him there was no scriptural warrant for their removal. He did not believe that there was any need for fervent action: the preaching of God's Word would erode people's attachment to religious images over time. On the other hand, Luther was concerned about any

---

[35]See David J. Davis, ed., "'The meanes of justification': A Catholic Letter on the Image Debate in Reformation Britain," *Reformation & Renaissance Review* 14, no. 3 (2012): 288-311, esp. 305.

incipient rise of radicalism. Insofar as the men whom Luther labeled as radical favored the forcible removal of these images, Luther became correspondingly convinced that these images ought to be retained, not least to preserve public order.[36]

> Their prophets stand, crying and arousing the masses, saying, heigh, hew, rip, rend, smash, dash, stab, strike, run, throw, hit the idols in the mouth. If you see a crucifix, spit in its face. This is to do away with images in a Karlstadtian manner, to make the masses mad and foolish, and secretly to accustom them to insurrection.[37]

Figure 7.1. Lucas Cranach the Elder, *Martin Luther* (1529)

Luther's colorful depiction of iconoclasm highlights his anxieties over its association with disorder. Hence in spite of his own stated opposition to the Catholic cult of images, he provided scriptural grounds for the retention of religious images in churches "for remembrance and as witnesses," testifying to God's acts among his people.[38] Luther

---

[36]Bridget Heal, *A Magnificent Faith: Art and Identity in Lutheran Germany* (Oxford: Oxford University Press, 2017), 16-20.

[37]Quoted in Heal, *A Magnificent Faith*, 20.

[38]Heal, *A Magnificent Faith*, 20.

himself had a long and close association with a number of artists based in Wittenberg, including Lucas Cranach the Elder and his family. Cranach was an early and ardent defender of Luther, and many of his paintings, including large-size altarpieces, adorned the churches of Wittenberg during Luther's tenure.[39]

Later Lutherans continued to uphold the legitimacy of retaining religious images in places of worship, especially when confronted with the decidedly more iconoclastic approach of rival German Calvinists in the late sixteenth and early seventeenth centuries. In some instances, Lutherans made a strong theological case for the important role played by religious art, as in the case of Johann Mathesius, who served as the Lutheran pastor in St. Joachimstal in Bohemia from 1545 until his death in 1565. Mathesius praised and encouraged the work of artists and craftsmen in adorning places of worship through their skills, which he saw as gifts of the Holy Spirit.[40]

Mathesius offered a very positive view of religious art and artists. Yet others among Luther's successors adopted a much more negative view of the role and place of religious images in worship, aware of the danger of ending up too close to a Catholic position in which images were venerated.[41] Among the hard-line Gnesio-Lutherans, Matthias Flacius and two colleagues in Jena wrote to Johann Friedrich, Duke of Ernestine Saxony in 1558, to articulate their reasons for opposing the presence of a pre-Reformation altarpiece in St. Michael's church in Jena. They were convinced that the altarpiece would "give simple Christians or secret papists, or at least their descendants . . . occasion and reason to pray with abominable sin to Joseph and Mary, who are carved and gilded on this panel." They testified that four years earlier they had seen "that on a feast day at meal time

---

[39]For more on Cranach's work in Wittenberg see Joseph Leo Koerner, *The Reformation of the Image* (Chicago: University of Chicago Press, 2004).

[40]Christopher Boyd Brown, "Art and the Artist in the Lutheran Reformation: Johannes Mathesius and Joachimstal," *Church History* 86, no. 4 (2017): 1081-1120.

[41]Heal, *A Magnificent Faith*, 68-69.

women here knelt before the high altar and prayed to the saints."[42]
Clearly for these Lutherans the dangers of misplaced devotion en-
gendered by the presence of religious art in the worship space far
outweighed any potential benefits.

At the root of the problem lay the fact that the images debate
within the Lutheran church was part of a larger unresolved controversy over the direction of the Lutheran faith following Luther's
death. Hard-liners and moderates allied themselves on different
sides of this and other issues, making acceptance or hostility toward
images in churches one of the identifiers in this ongoing conflict.[43]

In contrast, the theological perspective of the Swiss Reformed
regarding images in places of worship was very straightforward.
Based on their reading of the Ten Commandments, any religious
image was a potential doorway into idolatry, most especially if the
image was located in a place of public worship. The image could
distract people from the true worship of God and could cause them
to direct their prayers to someone other than God himself. Several
of the early Swiss Reformed theologians also made the argument
that the purchase and adornment of religious images was a misap-
propriation of funds that should have better been spent on the poor,
who were the living images of God. For instance, in a sermon
preached in Bern in January 1528 at the close of the public disputa-
tions that marked the official acceptance of the Reformation in that
Swiss city, Huldrych Zwingli summarized many of the Reformed
arguments against the use of images in worship settings. He
preached his sermon in Bern's minster, where altars, images, and
ornamented side chapels still stood in all their splendor. In his sermon, Zwingli built comparisons between what he depicted as the
grubby human sacrifice of the Mass and Christ's one-time sacrifice,
and stated that the church needed to be cleansed from all its filth so

---

[42]Heal, A Magnificent Faith, 55.
[43]Heal, A Magnificent Faith, 43-45.

as to turn its eyes to God alone, and not to the work of human hands. Yet Zwingli understood that the physical removal of images from places of worship would only be effective if the human inclination to idolatry was first addressed. "One should first remove the idols from one's heart, and then cast them away from one's eyes," he proclaimed.[44]

The Swiss Reformed perspective on the danger of religious images in worship settings was echoed in the French-speaking Reformed world. Calvin's theological perspective on the role of religious images in churches was clearly laid out in his *Institutes of the Christian Religion*. He categorically rejected such images, noting that attempting to depict God through visual arts was an insult to God's majesty and an open door to idolatry. He pointed out that those who create and set up religious images in the worship space turn people's attention to the work of human hands and away from God. He strongly repudiated the Catholic notion that religious images could serve an educational purpose for those unable to read. Calvin also used the opportunity to chastise his Catholic opponents for not doing more to teach the uneducated through solid biblical preaching instead of relying on human-made images to do so. Finally, he dismissed the Catholic distinction between image veneration and image adoration, commenting that such a practice was still idolatrous irrespective of its name.[45] Subsequent Reformed theologians followed Calvin's lead. The 1563 Heidelberg Catechism, for example, neatly summarizes these teachings in a pair of questions and answers on visual images in worship:

---

[44] Andreas Rüfenacht, "Bildersturm im Berner Münster? Berns Umgang mit sakralen Bildern in der Reformation—Symptom der städtischen Herrschaft," *Zwingliana* 44 (2017): 1-155, esp. 78-81.

[45] John Calvin, *Institutes of the Christian Religion*, ed. John T. McNeill, trans. Ford Lewis Battles (Philadelphia: Westminster, 1960), 1.11. Calvin did leave room for representative art depicting historical events or landscapes, so long as this artwork was displayed outside a church setting.

Q. May we then not make any image at all?

A. God can not and may not be visibly portrayed in any way. Although creatures may be portrayed, yet God forbids making or having such images if one's intention is to worship them, or to serve God through them.

Q. But may not images be permitted in churches in place of books for the unlearned?

A. No, we should not try to be wiser than God. God wants the Christian community instructed by the living preaching of his Word—not by idols that cannot even talk.[46]

In some ways, the Church of England's theological approach to the question of images in places of worship reflected the Reformed view. The set of three linked sermons on this issue in *Certain Sermons or Homilies* already indicate in their title the church's official stance at the start of Elizabeth's reign: "An Homily Against the Peril of Idolatry, and Superfluous Decking of Churches." Along with an analysis of the key scriptural passages warning against and prohibiting any making of images for use in worship, the first sermon warns that images mislead the simple into idolatry and turn the covetous away from worship and toward desiring the gold and silver adorning the images.[47] While the second sermon provides a lengthy historical presentation of various church fathers' and councils' positions on images in worship settings, the third sermon counters some of the main arguments made to support the use of religious images in churches. After rejecting any justification for depictions of God or of Christ in a visual form, the preacher then turns to images of saints. The sermon argues that any

---

[46]Heidelberg Catechisms Q&A 97 and 98, in *Heidelberg Catechism 450th Anniversary Edition* (Grand Rapids, MI: Faith Alive, 2013), 56.

[47]"An Homily Against the Peril of Idolatry, and Superfluous Decking of Churches (First Part)," in *Certain Sermons or Homilies, Appointed to Be Read in Churches* (London: printed for the Prayerbook and Homily Society, 1852), 157-69.

depiction of saints is necessarily a lie, because the images only repre-
sent the body and not the soul: "Wherefore they be no images of saints,
whose souls reign in joy with God, but of the bodies of saints, which
as yet lie putrefied in the graves."[48] The preacher also echoes the Swiss
reformers in condemning the adornment of images in churches to the
detriment of any care or concern for the poor, "the lively images of
God, commended to us so tenderly by our savior Christ."[49]

Thus early modern religious leaders displayed a range of perspectives regarding the appropriateness or danger of displaying religious
images in churches. Not surprisingly, the churches' practices regarding the visual arts in church were equally diverse.

The visual arts and church interiors. The amount of representative religious art displayed in churches in the early modern period
varied tremendously, even within the same confessional group. To a
certain extent, these differences were due to the amount of resources
a given community might have available to adorn their church. One
should not assume that a church with very few pieces of religious art
in it necessarily implies that the faith community using that church
for worship viewed the presence of religious art in the worship space
with disfavor. In other words, rather than considering or counting
the number of religious images in a given place of worship and using
that as a measure to assess whether the faith community in question
was nearer to the iconophilic or iconoclastic end of the spectrum, it is
more helpful to consider the kinds of visual art on display.

There is strong evidence that religious art in many late medieval
churches was both plentiful and valued by congregations, who were
willing to pay significant amounts of money for the upkeep, refurbish-
ing, or addition of statues, altars, and altarpieces in their places of
worship. For instance, evidence from the diocese of Exeter in England
in the early 1500s shows that parishioners in congregations across the

---

[48]"An Homily Against the Peril of Idolatry (Third Part)," 196.
[49]"An Homily Against the Peril of Idolatry (Third Part)," 237.

bishopric contributed to the painting and gilding of various statues of Jesus, the Virgin Mary, and assorted saints, the construction of crucifixes, and the building of rood lofts to display religious images above the screen that divided the nave from the high altar.[50]

In Lutheran areas, the place of religious art in churches varied tremendously. The strong role of local and regional authorities in issuing mandates and church orders meant that there was no uniform practice or agreement as to whether pre-Reformation imagery should be retained in or removed from churches, what kinds of religious images were acceptable and what ones had to be removed, or whether new religious artworks could be commissioned. For instance, while St. Anna's church in Annaberg in Saxony retained all six of its large-scale pre-Reformation altarpieces in its worship space well into the seventeenth century, the Nikolaikirche in Leipzig got rid of all its side altars already by 1540. In 1560, it added four Dutch tapestries and four banners featuring scriptural passages at the front of the church, surrounding the altar, and by the early 1600s replaced its pre-Reformation altarpiece on the high altar with a more Lutheran one.[51]

For their part, though they might be described at the time and afterward as barren, cold, or clean, Reformed churches still continued to make use of the visual arts, albeit within a fairly narrow set of parameters. One important way that Reformed churches made use of the visual arts without contravening any rules against potentially idolatrous images was to turn to texts. Where previously there had been frescoes or wall paintings depicting Christ, the saints, or biblical scenes, now words of Scripture appeared, written in very large and ornate script. In some cases, the words of Scripture were inscribed in spaces or on surfaces that had previously displayed religious images. For instance, in the parish church in Binham in

---

[50]Robert Whiting, "Abominable Idols: Images and Image-Breaking Under Henry VIII," *Journal of Ecclesiastical History* 33, no. 1 (1982): 30-47, esp. 33-35.
[51]Heal, *A Magnificent Faith*, 48.

Norfolk, England, passages from the 1539 English Bible were painted onto a whitewashed surface that covered up images of St. Michael, St. Catherine, and Christ as the Man of Sorrows. In Northamptonshire, the parish church of St. Mary reversed a panel featuring an image of Judas betraying Jesus with a kiss, and instead used the blank surface to display the words of the Ten Commandments.[52]

The disappearance of images: Iconoclasm or orderly removal? As depicted in the second vignette at the beginning of this chapter, in some areas the presence of religious images in the worship space became a flashpoint between rival confessional groups, leading to iconoclasm. A particular target for the Reformed were any and all images directly associated with Catholic worship practices, especially surrounding the Mass. So images on or near altars and any ritual objects associated with the Mass were on the frontline for removal, whereas images that were present in the worship space but not directly linked with the celebration of the Mass had a greater chance of survival. Examples from England, where images were removed from parish churches during the reign of Edward VI, show that the process of cleansing churches from what was seen as "spiritual fornication" involved the disappearance of statues, altars, relics, shrines, and rood lofts. Memorial stones to the dead were allowed to remain even though the practice of holding memorial Masses ended. In some instances, the inscriptions on the memorials that had called for prayers for the souls of the deceased were however carefully excised from the stone.[53]

As some recent scholars have pointed out, iconoclasm did not take place as a result of a decisive confessional shift in favor of the Reformed, but rather was a tool used in situations where the eventual confessional outcome was still uncertain. In other words, iconoclasm was more of a

---

[52] Alexandra Walsham, "Recycling the Sacred: Material Culture and Cultural Memory after the English Reformation," *Church History* 86, no. 4 (2017): 1121-54, esp. 1137.

[53] Walsham, "Recycling the Sacred," 1126.

means of pressure than an expression of victory.[54] In other territories, images were removed from churches in an orderly fashion under the orders of the local government, who informed donors who had paid for the religious images to be set up to come pick them up, take them out of the public worship space, and bring them home. Such was the case in the Swiss Protestant city of Bern, for instance, where this process of image removal mandated by the government was completed by 1530.[55] In some cases, when the image was not freestanding and hence could not easily be removed, it was altered to take away its sacral character. For instance, the Christopher Tower of the Heiliggeist Church in Bern had a larger-than-life wall painting of St. Christopher bearing the Christ child on one of the inner walls of the tower. This image had been commissioned by the city and was completed between 1496 and 1498. In 1536, the image was altered in several key ways. The figure of the Christ child was erased, and St. Christopher was given a helmet, a halberd, and a two-handed sword, turning him into the figure of Goliath instead.[56] This creative refashioning of the image took away its tie to the cult of saints, and turned it (apparently) into an acceptable image in the eyes of the Reformed Bernese leaders.

It is worth noting that even in cases when images were damaged and destroyed, rather than removed or reworked, one should not conclude that Reformed Christians were necessarily iconophobic or opposed to imagery or the visual arts in general. The key focal points for iconoclasm were three-dimensional anthropomorphic figures in churches, since these seemed most likely to attract misplaced worship.[57] Two-dimensional images in worship spaces, such as frescoes, wall paintings, or stained-glass windows, might be covered over or replaced in a broader aim to remove visual distractions for the congregation, but

[54]Rüfenacht, "Bildersturm," 4.

[55]Rüfenacht, "Bildersturm," 11.

[56]Rüfenacht, "Bildersturm," 14.

[57]See the careful study on these issues by Adam Morton, "Images and the Senses in Post-Reformation England," *Reformation* 20, no. 1 (2015): 77-100, esp. 85.

these did not tend to attract such concern over the dangers of idolatry. A good example of images remaining in a previously Catholic church building taken over for Reformed worship is in the Grote Kerk (also known as St. Bavo Kerk) in Haarlem in the Dutch province of Holland. Although religious statues and altarpieces were removed, the church retained its fifteenth-century painted organ shutters depicting the resurrection of Christ and its pre-Reformation brass lectern with an allegorical carving of a pelican pecking its own breast. The pelican was thought to offer its own blood to feed its hungry young, thus symbolizing Christ's sacrificial offering of himself for the faithful.[58]

Responses to iconoclasm. One of the best ways to gauge the Catholic response to iconoclastic acts in churches is to investigate what happened when churches that had been damaged in iconoclastic attacks were restored to Catholic hands. This was the case, for instance, in the southern Netherlands, where churches whose interiors were damaged during the iconoclasm in the Wonderyear of 1566 were repaired and made ready for Catholic worship once again in the following months and years. In Flanders, for instance, orders given by the Duke of Alva and Margaret of Parma to fix what had been broken were quickly carried out, with local governments and guilds commissioning and paying for new altars and altarpieces.[59] Some of the newly installed images did however reflect the ongoing tension over the appropriateness of religious art in the worship setting. For example in the church of Notre Dame in Antwerp, the reconsecration of the altars hit a snag when suffragan bishop Martin de Cuyper objected to the depiction of Moses, Christ, and the Ten Commandments on one

[58]Henry Luttikhuizen, "The Art of Devotion in Haarlem Before and After the Introduction of Calvinism," in Maag and Witvliet, *Worship in Medieval and Early Modern Europe*, 281-99, esp. 284-85. On the medieval understanding of pelicans as allegorical images of Christ's sacrifice, see Anastasia Pineschi, "The Pelican, Self-Sacrificing Mother Bird of the Medieval Bestiary," *The Iris: Behind the Scenes at the Getty* (blog), May 11, 2018, http://blogs .getty.edu/iris/the-pelican-self-sacrificing-mother-bird-of-the-medieval-bestiary.

[59]Andrew Spicer, "After Iconoclasm: Reconciliation and Resacralization in the Southern Netherlands, ca. 1566–85," *Sixteenth Century Journal* 44, no. 2 (2013): 411-33, esp. 418.

of the altarpieces. It seems the bishop was concerned about the prominent display of the commandment prohibiting the making of graven images on the altarpiece. Although the altar was consecrated, the altarpiece in question was subsequently quietly removed.[60] In this instance, the content of the image was controversial because it could itself be read as a warning about the dangers of religious art becoming a vector for idolatry.

Religious art and Protestant artists. One issue that remained largely unresolved was the outcomes of the Reformation for artists and craftsmen who made their living producing works for churches. Was it allowable for a Protestant artist or craftsman to make and sell religious artwork or to accept a commission to provide religious art for a place of worship? From a Lutheran perspective, artists and craftsmen were free to create objects and images to be placed in churches, so long as these images were not intended to be venerated or associated in any way with the cult of relics. So Pastor Mathesius in St. Joachimstal stated in a sermon on Exodus 31:11,

> I have considered this at length so that I might offer artists instruction from God's word about what they are able to make for other people in good conscience. For just as Bezaleel was able to work on the adornment of the Tabernacle, in accord with God's command, and Solomon's goldsmiths were able to make crown, scepter, throne, and shield out of silver, so may every pious artist help to adorn our churches with beautiful panels, paintings, carvings, chalices, etc.[61]

For Mathesius, artwork that honored God in its beauty and message was warmly welcomed in a church worship setting.

In contrast, the Reformed perspective on what artists and craftsmen could contribute to worship spaces was much more limited.

---

[60]Spicer, "After Iconoclasm," 420-21.
[61]Brown, "Art and the Artist in the Lutheran Reformation," 1116.

Since Reformed churches were not open to religious art in churches, the only ones commissioning or purchasing such works were Catholics or Lutherans. By and large, Reformed religious authorities were in agreement that such activities were not permissible, since in doing so, the artists and craftsmen were effectively encouraging idolatry. So for instance the French Reformed national synods meeting in Orléans in 1562 and in Verteuil in 1567 both put rules in place barring Reformed artists and craftsmen from making and selling anything that would foster idolatry or superstition.[62]

Conclusion

As this chapter has shown, the dividing lines between Catholic and Protestant thinking and practice regarding music and the visual arts in the worship setting were not hard and fast. In fact, the preconceptions that Protestants sang and Catholics did not, or that Catholic churches were full of images and Protestant churches had none, do not match the much more complex reality of adaptations, recycling, and borrowings when it came to religious art and music in early modern churches. What is clear is that theologians and church leaders were keenly aware of the impact of both music and the visual arts on the faithful, and sought to find ways to harness that power to direct worshipers' eyes, ears, and hearts toward God.

For Further Reading

Bertoglio, Chiara. "Cats, Bulls and Donkeys: Bernardino Cirillo on 16th-century Church Music." *Early Music* 45, no. 4 (2017): 559-72.

Brown, Christopher Boyd. "Art and the Artist in the Lutheran Reformation: Johannes Mathesius and Joachimstal." *Church History* 86, no. 4 (2017): 1081-1120.

---

[62]Philip Benedict, "Calvinism as a Culture? Preliminary Remarks on Calvinism and the Visual Arts," in *Seeing Beyond the Word: Visual Arts and the Calvinist Tradition*, ed. Paul Finney (Grand Rapids, MI: Eerdmans, 1999), 19-45, esp. 35.

Caspers, Charles and Marc Schneiders, eds. *Omnes Circumadstantes: Contributions Towards a History of the Role of the People in the Liturgy*. Kampen: J. H. Kok, 1990.

Finney, Paul, ed. *Seeing Beyond the Word: Visual Arts and the Calvinist Tradition*. Grand Rapids, MI: Eerdmans, 1999.

Heal, Bridget. *A Magnificent Faith: Art and Identity in Lutheran Germany*. Oxford: Oxford University Press, 2017.

Koerner, Joseph Leo. *The Reformation of the Image*. Chicago: University of Chicago Press, 2004.

Maag, Karin, ed. *Lifting Hearts to the Lord: Worship with John Calvin in Sixteenth-Century Geneva*. Grand Rapids, MI: Eerdmans, 2016.

Maag, Karin. "'No Better Songs': John Calvin and the Genevan Psalter in the Sixteenth Century and Today." *The Hymn* 68, no. 4 (2017): 21-26.

Shead, Andrew. "Is There a Musical Note in the Body? Cranmer on the Reformation of Music." *The Reformed Theological Review* 69, no. 1 (2010): 1-16.

Spicer, Andrew. "After Iconoclasm: Reconciliation and Resacralization in the Southern Netherlands, ca. 1566–85." *Sixteenth Century Journal* 44, no. 2 (2013): 411-33.

Walsham, Alexandra. "Recycling the Sacred: Material Culture and Cultural Memory After the English Reformation." *Church History* 86, no. 4 (2017): 1121-54.

Witvliet, John. "The Spirituality of the Psalter: Metrical Psalms in Liturgy and Life in Calvin's Geneva." *Calvin Theological Journal* 32, no. 2 (1997): 273-97.

Zijpp, Nanne van der. "The Hymnology of the Mennonites in the Netherlands." *Mennonite Quarterly Review* 31, no. 1 (1957): 11-15.

EIGHT

WORSHIP OUTSIDE CHURCH

God is to be worshiped everywhere, in spirit and truth;
as, in private families daily, and in secret, each one by himself.

WESTMINSTER CONFESSION OF FAITH (1646)

ALTHOUGH THIS VOLUME HAS PRIMARILY FOCUSED on various aspects
of communal worship in church, early modern Christians did not
limit their practice of prayer and praise solely to the assigned days
and times for public worship. Indeed, church leaders across the confessional spectrum advocated and expected daily worship by individuals and families in their homes and communities, as noted in the
Westminster Confession of Faith, quoted above.

Yet simply mandating household and individual worship was not
enough. Whether Catholic or Protestant, individuals and families had
to be taught how to engage in these worship practices and pass them on
to the next generation. Various works were produced, including catechisms, prayer books, and psalters, all designed to provide resources
for the inculcation of a regular rhythm of individual and familial turning to God. By providing models for prayer and petition, these works
were meant both to shape individual and household worship and to

---

The *Confession of Faith of the Assembly of Divines at Westminster*, tercentenary ed. (London:
Presbyterian Church of England, 1946), 21.6.

guard against any slippage into what many religious leaders termed superstitious worship practices. Meanwhile, traditional cultic practices associated with holy times of the year or holy places sometimes overlapped with and sometimes cut across religious authorities' expectations for worship away from the more supervised space of the church. The end result was that worship outside church took on a much more variegated character compared to worship in church. Some of these devotional practices were clearly shaped by religious leaders' efforts to channel household and individual faith into model Christian worship, while other parts were much more influenced by a continuing tradition of folk religion that proved resistant to the clergy's control.

⌒

Several generations of the Adornes family, based in Bruges in the Low Countries, had made pilgrimages to Jerusalem beginning in 1269, with a father-and-son pair (Anselm and Jan Adornes) following suit in 1470–1471. Their pilgrimage took fourteen months in total. While they spent most of their time in Jerusalem, engaging in prayer and devotions at sites associated with Christ's Passion, they also made stops at other holy sites along the way, including the monastery of St. Catherine at Mount Sinai. Pilgrimages were a well-known devotional practice in the Middle Ages (although most did not travel so far afield). However, the Adornes clan did not simply bask in the spiritual glow of these repeated journeys to walk where Jesus walked. Instead, the family built a private chapel in Bruges that re-created the Jerusalem pilgrimage, providing those who could not find the time or the money to go so far the opportunity to engage in a spiritual pilgrimage that brought them to the holy sites of Jerusalem through an act of spiritual imagination. Constructed between 1470 and 1483 on the site of an earlier family chapel also known as the Jerusalem chapel, this building in Bruges included a bas-relief depicting the hill of Calvary, relics, images of objects associated with Christ's sufferings, and a chamber in the crypt containing a life-size effigy of Christ in the tomb. As in the Church of the Holy Sepulchre in Jerusalem, this chamber was only accessible via a very narrow and low door. Although this chapel was ostensibly private and for the use of the Adornes family, it crossed private-public boundaries by being open to local pilgrims, who could receive an indulgence of forty days for their visit.[1] The Adornes family's Jerusalem chapel in Bruges offers a striking example of pious laypeople's profound sense of sacred connection with holy sites, to the point of extensive investment in imaginative re-creations of pilgrimage experiences, set within their local communities.

∽

In the first decades of the seventeenth century, the English Puritan pastor William Hinde wrote a hagiographic account of the life and faith of his brother-in-law, the Puritan layman John Bruen (1560–1625). Although Hinde's deep admiration for his subject means that his assessments of Bruen's piety should be weighed carefully, Hinde does provide testimony about the practice of worship in Bruen's household. According to Hinde, family devotions took place in Bruen's home twice a day, in the morning and the evening. Before the morning family worship got underway, Bruen would prepare himself to lead the gathering:

> It was his ordinary course to rise very early in the morning, before the rest of his family, betwixt three and four of the clock in summer, and at or before five in the winter, so that by this his vigilancy and industry, he gained the liberty and opportunity most commonly of an hour or two before he rang the bell, to awaken the rest of his family: which time he bestowed most graciously, first in private prayer for himself, and for every soul in his family, making mention of some more particularly by

---

[1]Mitzi Kirkland-Ives, "*Capell nuncapato Jherusalem noviter Brugis*: The Adornes Family of Bruges and Holy Land Devotion," *Sixteenth Century Journal* 39, no. 4 (2008): 1041-64.

name, as their occasions or afflictions might move him there-
unto; and giving thanks to God therewithal, for such mercies
and comforts as both he and they had received that night past,
and formerly also from his hand. Secondly, in meditation upon
some part of God's Word and work, wherewith he did season
his mind and refresh his heart, endeavoring so to set the watch
aright in the morning, that the clock might go all the better the
day after. Thirdly, he did as he had occasion, usually write out
fair, some part of such Sermons, as he had by running hand,
taken from the mouth of the Preacher, for renewing and increasing of the benefit, and comfort which he had reaped and
received by the same. . . . Thus did he awake with God in the
morning, that he might the better awake unto righteousness,
and walk before God in holiness and uprightness all the day
after, even until the evening.[2]

This account of Bruen's morning prayers offers a window into the
practice of individual devotion in some Puritan households, which
included prayer, reading and meditating on Scripture, and reflection
on sermons. It is worth noting that his prayer was not focused solely
on himself and on his own spiritual life, but on his household. The
importance of daily worship to shape and guide the course of each
day also comes through very clearly in this account.

ↄ

Both of these vignettes highlight key aspects of worship that took
place outside the community's church buildings: individuals, families,
and households like the Adornes and the Bruens incorporated their
devotional practices into their daily lives and clearly did not limit
themselves only to worship on Sundays at church. Indeed, their

---

[2]William Hinde, *A faithfull remonstrance of the holy life and happy death of John Bruen of Bruen-
Stapleford, in the county of Chester* (London: Stephens and Meredith, 1641), fol. F1v-F2r.

significant investments of time and money signal just how important these home-based worship practices were in their lives of faith. Although the distance between the Catholic Adornes family's pilgrimage reenactment in their Jerusalem chapel in Bruges and the Puritan John Bruen's private devotions may seem great, both testified to the vitality of lay worship and to the common desire to draw near to God beyond the bounds of regular church attendance. This chapter will consider a range of worship practices that took place outside of church, beginning with the widest-ranging, active, and public activities of worship, and gradually moving to a more and more intimate setting, ending up beside a believer's deathbed.

ON THE ROAD: SHRINES AND PILGRIMAGES

The late medieval Christian landscape abounded with sacred places: shrines, holy wells and springs, chapels, and other sites where Christians could encounter the holy. In many instances, these sites overlapped with older pagan sites of worship. Whether part of a deliberate policy to make a visible statement about the power of Christianity over against an older pagan faith or in an attempt to help people transition from one faith practice to another, these holy sites were understood by laypeople and religious leaders alike as powerful places, where healings and other miracles could and did take place.[3] Certain shrines became closely associated with the healing of specific diseases or conditions. Touching a particular rock or drinking from a holy fountain or a well was part of the ritual. For instance, the shrine of Our Lady of Walsingham in Norfolk, England, was thought to provide healing for those suffering from headaches or stomach issues. Here pilgrims knelt on a stone beside the fountain, and put their

---

[3]See Alexandra Walsham's careful analysis in *The Reformation of the Landscape: Religion, Identity, and Memory in Early Modern Britain and Ireland* (Oxford: Oxford University Press, 2011), esp. 36-79.

offering of money in the water before they departed.[4] Medieval religious leaders did not endorse all shrines and holy places. In fact, if there were concerns that the people traveling to the shrine were misdirecting their worship or venerating an object rather than a holy person, authorities could step in and shut down the shrine. For instance, in 1410, the bishop of Hereford Robert Mascall condemned ritual practices at a shrine in Turnastone. According to the bishop's records, he had received word that people were worshiping a stone and a well, and that "they take away with them the mud of the same, and treat it and keep it as a relic, to the grave peril of their souls and a pernicious example to others."[5] In this case at least, church leaders held that any ritual activities connected to this site were more likely to mislead people into false worship than help them in their life of faith.

Worries over shrines' propensity to mislead the faithful grew exponentially once the Reformation got underway. Religious leaders were particularly keen to remove any potential spiritual power from these sites in the landscape, especially when these sites stood on the other side of confessional borders and could attract the faithful back into "superstition." Protestant arguments against pilgrimages, like their rejection of religious images, stated firmly that these activities wasted money and time, and that the faithful were better off staying home, caring for their families, and fearing God.[6] In his 1520 treatise on good works, Luther proclaimed,

> On this is based the wonderful and righteous judgment of God, that at times a poor man, in whom no one can see many great works, in the privacy of his home joyfully praises God when he fares well, or with entire confidence calls upon Him when he fares ill, and thereby does a greater and more acceptable work

---

[4]Walsham, *Reformation of the Landscape*, 52.
[5]Walsham, *Reformation of the Landscape*, 69.
[6]Carlos Eire, *War Against the Idols: The Reformation of Worship from Erasmus to Calvin* (Cambridge: Cambridge University Press, 1986), 96.

than another, who fasts much, prays much, endows churches, makes pilgrimages, and burdens himself with great deeds in this place and in that.[7]

Luther's critique of many devotional practices of his day, including pilgrimages, contrasted these with faithful day-by-day trust in God. Yet in some instances, Protestant populations continued to turn to pilgrimages, especially ones directed at shrines in their local area that reputedly had healing powers. For instance, both in Geneva and in Reformed areas of France, consistories dealt with a number of cases of Protestant families carrying out pilgrimages to such shrines in their search for healing.[8]

In a Catholic context, the early modern period proved to be a time of resurgence for pilgrimages, albeit with some differences compared to medieval practices. From the sixteenth to the eighteenth centuries, Catholic pilgrimages tended to be more regional than long-distance, more directly controlled and overseen by religious orders and clergy, and more focused on the Virgin Mary, Christ, and the major saints as opposed to more locally known holy persons.[9] However, some long-distance pilgrimage destinations still flourished, including Rome and Mont-Saint-Michel in France. Indeed, the French shrine served as a rallying point for French Catholics during and after the religious wars of the sixteenth century, since the archangel Michael (to whom the shrine was dedicated) was one of France's patron saints. From the early seventeenth century onward, the Benedictine order that ran the shrine increased its emphasis on the Eucharist as the central feature of the pilgrimage experience, investing heavily in altars and vestments, and

[7]Martin Luther, *A Treatise on Good Works* (1520), sec. 20, Project Gutenberg, January 24, 2008, www.gutenberg.org/files/418/418-h/418-h.htm.

[8]Marianne Carbonnier-Burkard, "Pélerinages et réforme protestante," *Revue d'histoire et de philosophie religieuses* 88, no. 2 (2008): 129-45, esp. 141-42.

[9]Elizabeth Tingle, "Long-Distance Pilgrimage and the Counter-Reformation in France: Sacred Journeys to the Mont-Saint-Michel 1520–1750," *Journal of Religious History* 41, no. 2 (2017): 158-80, esp. 159-60.

much less in relics, compared to the medieval period.[10] Accounts of pilgrims' religious activities survive for this period, shedding helpful light on the acts of individual and collective worship that shaped the pilgrimage experience. In the mid-seventeenth century, for instance, a group of pilgrims traveled to Mont-Saint-Michel from Caen, a distance of over eighty miles. They began by singing the Latin hymn *Veni creator* in church in Caen, stopping along their journey to attend two of the daily offices in other churches along the way. When they crossed over to Mont-Saint-Michel at low tide, the group sang hymns to the Virgin Mary and prayed to St. Michael. Upon arrival in the abbey church, they joined in a responsive prayer and attended a sung Mass, followed by an opportunity to view the relics held by the abbey and a tour of the pilgrimage complex. Along their way back to Caen, the group attended Mass in three different churches before gathering one more time in Caen for yet another Mass.[11]

Therefore, while Catholic practices of pilgrimages persisted from the medieval through the early modern world, the practice was strongly discouraged in Protestant areas, albeit with some resistance from local populations who continued to want to turn to these local sources of holiness, especially when on the search for healing.

IN THE COMMUNITY: FEAST DAYS AND FESTIVALS

Another fascinating intersection point between worship shaped by religious authorities and popular religious practices occurred during the celebrations of feasts and festivals. Many of these events featured worship services in church, along with religious processions and popular celebrations. The medieval church calendar listed numerous such feast days, honoring Christ, the Virgin Mary, and various saints, from locally venerated figures to those whose cult extended far and wide. In some places, the coming of the Reformation simply put an end to these combinations

---

[10]Tingle, "Long-Distance Pilgrimage," 166-68.
[11]Tingle, "Long-distance Pilgrimage," 165.

of worship and festivities. In other locations, the practice of marking the day continued but in new guises. Consider for instance the feast day of St. George, celebrated in England from the Middle Ages onward on April 23. In many locations, the medieval celebration of St. George's Day featured a Mass, a procession, and a play in which the character dressed up as St. George defeated the dragon and rescued the maiden about to be sacrificed to appease the dragon's appetite. In Norwich, the procession featured members of St. George's guild, the mayor and aldermen, and a representative group of clergy from the city's churches.[12] Although the elements of the celebration varied from place to place and from era to era, the commemoration of St. George offered individuals and communities the opportunity to highlight both their devotion and their civic status. St. George's feast day continued to be observed through the end of Henry VIII's reign, even though other saints' days were expunged from the religious calendar.[13] In the reign of Edward VI, injunctions against religious processions and confraternities put an end to many of the observances of St. George's Day. While Catholic practices were officially revived under Queen Mary, the celebrations of St. George's Day did not seem to gain much traction, and by the reign of Elizabeth, very few elements of the traditional celebrations remained. In Norwich, the guild of St. George had survived by changing its name to the Company and Fellowship of St. George, and shifted its observance away from April 23, finally settling on the month of June. Although they still held the procession, the figure of St. George was absent, as was the figure of the maiden. The only survivor was the dragon, whose threatening power was replaced by a rather more comedic stance. The festivities still included a worship service (although no prayers were offered to or for the saint), a feast, and the selection of new members and officers for the Company.[14]

---

[12]Muriel McClendon, "A Moveable Feast: Saint George's Day Celebrations and Religious Change in Early Modern England," *Journal of British Studies* 38, no. 1 (1999): 1-27, esp. 11-13.

[13]McClendon, "A Moveable Feast," 15-16.

[14]McClendon, "A Moveable Feast," 21-23. By the early seventeenth century, the dragon's nickname was Snap.

The shift from the emphasis on worship and social activities during feast days and festivals toward more of a focus on sociability and less on worship occurred across the board in Protestant areas that still retained memories of their pre-Reformation practices. Retaining the celebration but downplaying the worship element was one way that authorities found a path forward between the dangers of allowing for an otherwise superstitious practice and banning the activity altogether.

AT SCHOOL

School-based worship proved to be one of the most fertile areas for inculcation of officially sanctioned worship practices, shaping both the faith of the students themselves and spreading from them to their families and the wider community. Indeed, one of the chief strategies of the efforts spearheaded by the Jesuits to gain back areas of central and eastern Europe that had adopted the Lutheran or Reformed faith following the Reformation was to set up day schools and especially residential schools. These educational institutions combined excellent academics and daily Catholic worship practice for all pupils.

In Protestant areas, the school day also set out regular times for worship, combining an emphasis on developing a regular practice of prayer and devotion along with an instructional focus aimed at ensuring that students internalized the fundamentals of their faith. In Lutheran Saxony, for instance, the school ordinances of 1580 carefully laid out the goals of education: "In these Christian schools, three goals must be pursued: the first is the fear of God and true faith and religion; the second is outward discipline, and the third, that the students become learned and intelligent people."[15] The primary emphasis on teaching the faith meant that teachers were to establish the truths of Christianity in their pupils' hearts so effectively that these truths

---

[15]"Schulordnung aus der Kursächsischen Kirchenordnung, (1580)," in *Die evangelischen Schulordnungen des sechzehnten Jahrhunderts*, ed. Reinhold Vormbaum (Gütersloh: Bertelsmann, 1860), 230-96, esp. 274.

would decisively shape the course of the students' entire lives. In practice, that meant regularly reading out and teaching from the Bible and
Luther's *Small Catechism*. Instructors were also to teach the students
to pray, with specific forms of prayer to be recited when getting up in
the morning, before and after lessons, before and after meals, and before going to sleep at night.[16] In Lutheran Württemberg, the ordinances for the Latin school and for the monastery school (for boys
who would later study for the ministry) also carefully laid out regular
times of worship, from daily prayers in the Latin school to a round of
worship services for the students who lived at the monastery school.
These included a dawn prayer service at four or five in the morning,
morning prayers at eight or nine, and evening prayers at four. These
worship services included Scripture readings, responses, and prayers.[17]
This daily rhythm of worship underscored the authorities' desire to
have the regular practice of worship become second nature for their
students, especially those who were meant to continue on into ordained ministry. As noted in the earlier chapter on going to church,
the religious authorities' hopes to have the community come together
for worship on weekdays as well as on Sunday were largely unsuccess-
ful due to the competing pressures of making a living. But where the
authorities had free rein, as in a school setting, the implementation of
worship as a daily practice came swiftly to the fore.

Using schools as a means to train youngsters into a pattern of daily
devotion that would hopefully shape their lives in the longer term also
emerged in Reformed areas. In Geneva, for instance, each morning at
the start of classes the boys who attended the city's Latin school recited
in turn the prayer for students included in the Genevan Catechism.
The morning's classes finished with the recitation of the Lord's Prayer.

---

[16]"Schulordnung," 274-75.
[17]Charlotte Methuen, "Securing the Reformation Through Education: The Duke's Scholarship System of Sixteenth-Century Württemberg," *Sixteenth Century Journal* 25, no. 4
(1994): 841-851, esp. 846-47.

At the end of the school day, the whole school gathered together and students recited in turn the Lord's Prayer, the Ten Commandments, and the Apostles' Creed. All pupils also joined in an hour of psalm-singing daily, thus anchoring the Psalms in their hearts and minds but also preparing them to serve as worship leaders when these same metrical psalms were sung during church services.[18] Reformed leaders also made explicit connections between what the students learned in school and the provision of household worship, even at basic levels. For instance, as late as 1650, the pastor of Aberdeen in Scotland advocated that parents "put their children to schools, that they might be instructed to read that the family worship might be promoted both in town and parish and that every family might have one at least within it that might read."[19] In this case, the training the child received was not only meant to shape him but also to help family worship flourish by opening access to the text of Scripture and devotional works to all in the household through the student's ability to read.

AT HOME

Whether Catholic or Protestant, religious leaders knew that the household was the crucial location that decisively shaped families' religious practice, including children and servants. Thus heads of household were regularly reminded of their duty to hold family devotions and provide a model of worship to their family and their neighborhood. Fathers were meant to serve as "pastors" to their household "church." The regular practice of home-based worship was thought to encourage piety and good morals, and to train the younger and less

---

[18]Statutes of the Genevan Academy (1559), in Karin Maag, "Change and Continuity in Medieval and Early Modern Worship: The Practice of Worship in the Schools," in *Worship in Medieval and Early Modern Europe: Change and Continuity in Religious Practice*, ed. Karin Maag and John Witvliet (Notre Dame, IN: University of Notre Dame Press, 2004), 117-18.

[19]Quoted in Shona MacLean Vance, "Godly Citizens and Civic Unrest: Tensions in Schooling in Aberdeen in the Era of the Reformation," *European Review of History* 7, no. 1 (2000): 123-77, esp. 128 (spelling modernized).

educated members of the household in worship. For example, in 1621, the Walloon Calvinist pastor Jean Taffin described parents' religious obligations vis-à-vis their households as follows:

> All fathers and mothers of families must oversee their children and other servants to such an extent that their homes constitute any number of small churches, from which all vices and immorality are banished and driven out, so that the house of God can be holy and that God can be praised, served, worshiped, and called upon at night and in the morning and at meal times. Families who follow these practices will no doubt experience the truth of God's promises, that he will be with them as in his temple, and that he will bless them with all the mercies promised to his Church.[20]

Not only did Taffin link the regular daily practice of worship in the household to public worship held in churches, but he also asserted that God would bless these worshiping households in the same way as he blessed the congregations that gathered for public worship week by week. In Taffin's view at least, these practices of family worship were not simply a training ground for the more important public worship, but they in fact created a community of faith that reaped the same divine benefits as a duly constituted church.

In England, the recommended practice was to gather for household worship twice a day, mornings and evenings, though if only one gathering time a day was feasible, the morning time was preferable to the evening, because it prepared people for their day, and their attention was more focused than in the evenings when they were weary. Family devotions were usually meant to last about a quarter of an hour, typically including prayers, a Scripture reading, and perhaps the singing of a psalm. These gatherings were to be led by the head of

---

[20]Jean Taffin, *Traicté de l'amendement de vie* (Geneva: Chouet, 1621), fol. Ddi r-v (translation mine).

the household, usually the father/husband, but in his absence or incapacity, women could and did lead family devotions.[21] Indeed, the role of wives and mothers as family worship leaders transcended confessional and national borders. For instance, in his memoirs about his time as an apprentice to a grocer in Geneva in the early 1560s, André Ryff recalled how the grocer's household gathered daily for worship:

> Each morning and again every evening, Master Jean, his wife, his brother-in-law, and the whole household knelt down in the main room, and there the mistress prayed in a very loud voice, reverently thanking God for his gracious gifts and his blessings, and praying to him with fervor, asking him to grant us his Spirit, his protection, his blessing, and his mercy.[22]

This account highlights the daily rhythm of worship in the grocer's household and the central role of prayer in the family's worship practice. It is worth noting in this instance that although the male head of the household and other male relatives were present, the mother of the family led the devotions twice a day, without this female worship leadership seemingly causing any controversy, whether for her male relatives or in the mind of their young apprentice.

One of the most important vectors for household worship was through singing. In Lutheran areas, successive editions of the *Gesangbuch*, or hymnal, proved to be by far the most likely book owned by Lutheran households. Wills and after-death inventories provide evidence of the book's popularity both as an individual possession and as a treasured item passed down through generations. Various editions of the *Gesangbuch* were deliberately set up to encourage use in family devotions. For example, the 1646 edition published in Hanover organized

---

[21] Alec Ryrie, *Being Protestant in Reformation Britain* (Oxford: Oxford University Press, 2013), 365-74.

[22] André Ryff, "Memories of a Boy from Basel," in *Lifting Hearts to the Lord: Worship with John Calvin in Sixteenth-Century Geneva*, ed. Karin Maag (Grand Rapids, MI: Eerdmans, 2016), 66.

all the hymns into a handy chart, "so that whoever wants to pray at home with his kin, in his household church [*Hauskirche*] can sing through the whole work in six weeks or otherwise by following this guide."[23] Families sang the hymns and recited the prayers included in this book both during times of private devotion and when the household gathered for worship.[24] John Bruen's Puritan household also sang psalms when they gathered for family worship both morning and evening. According to his biographer, Bruen would select the psalm and start the singing, while the rest of the household "in a sweet accord and harmony joining with him, as if they had desired to sing *David's* Psalms, not only with *David's* harp, but even with *David's* heart also."[25]

The other main feature of household and individual worship was prayer. Prior to the Reformation, the practice of prayer in households could vary from individual and group recitation of set prayers such as the Pater Noster and the Ave Maria to regular participation in liturgies designed for household use and set out in books of hours, including the Little Office of the Blessed Virgin Mary. These texts, designed specifically for laypeople, echoed the pattern of the daily monastic prayer offices and included verses from the Psalms, responses, and prayers.[26]

As in the case of prayer in church, a certain amount of tension emerged between those who favored set prayers for use in household worship and those who wanted to encourage extemporaneous prayer. In England, the set prayers for use at home provided in the Book of Common Prayer were supplemented from the 1540s onward by numerous publications from clerical and lay writers, offering a wide variety of set prayers for every possible occasion and circumstance.

---

[23]Patrice Veit, "Piété, chant, et lectures: les pratiques religieuses dans l'Allemagne protestante à l'époque moderne," *Revue d'histoire moderne et contemporaine* 37, no. 4 (1990): 624-41, esp. 627.

[24]Veit, "Piété, chant, et lectures," 624-41.

[25]Hinde, *A faithfull remonstrance*, fol. F4r (emphasis original).

[26]Margot Fassler, "Psalms and Prayers in Daily Devotion: A Fifteenth-Century Devotional Anthology from the Diocese of Rheims: Beinecke 757," in Maag and Witvliet, *Worship in Medieval and Early Modern Europe*, 15-40, esp. 29-30.

Christians were to pray individually in private (in their "closet") (Mt 6:6) and during family devotions, gathering the whole household together. Many of the works also recommended praying before and after going to church, before and after receiving Communion, and at times of crisis such as sickness, accidents, or when a member of the household was nearing death.[27] The moderate Anglican clergyman John Wilkins underscored the appropriateness of set prayers for household and individual worship in his 1651 work on the gift of prayer:

> As for those weaker Christians and new Converts, who have not their hearts enlarged with an ability to express their own wants and desires, 'tis both lawful, and convenient for such to help themselves, not only in their *families*, but even in their *secret* performance of this duty, by the use of some good book or prescribed form, until by further endeavour and experience, they may attain unto some measure of this gift.[28]

Wilkins saw set prayer in household and individual worship as an excellent first step, though he did not want people to remain at this stage, particularly if there was any risk that they were doing so out of spiritual laziness. As Wilkins explained, it would be as if someone who needed crutches for an injury kept on using the crutches even after the injury healed, and became permanently dependent on these aids.[29]

By the 1590s, some clergy increasingly wanted to encourage extemporaneous prayer in household and devotional worship, modeling the practice in their own praying at church and at home, writing books that offered guides to extemporaneous prayer, and recommending free

---

[27]Ian Green, "New for Old? Clerical and Lay Attitudes to Domestic Prayer in Early Modern England," *Reformation and Renaissance Review* 10, no. 2 (2008): 195-222.

[28]John Wilkins, *A discourse concerning the gift of prayer Shewing what it is, and how far it is attainable by industry, with divers useful and proper directions to that purpose, both in respect of matter, method, expression* (London: Gellibrand, 1651), fol. B1v (emphasis original).

[29]Wilkins, *A discourse concerning the gift of prayer,* fols B2r-v.

prayer based on the structure of the Lord's Prayer.[30] A range of books offered guidance on how to prepare one's heart and mind for private prayer, ideally articulated in one's own words. As the Suffolk clergyman Elnathan Parr noted in his 1636 treatise,

> As for private prayer of one Christian alone, it is more expedient that it be uttered without a book; and the most complete performance of that duty is, when a Christian is not only able to repeat and apply to his own soul and conscience a prayer conceived by another, but also upon fit matter, and heads suitable to the occasion, to conceive and utter prayers of his own.[31]

Although Parr warned against praying thoughtlessly without due preparatory meditation and reading of Scripture, he sought to provide guidelines for individuals to develop their own capacity to voice their prayers to God without relying on set texts.

WORSHIP WITH THE SICK AND THE DYING

Whether individuals and families prayed on a daily basis depended a great deal on their level of devotion and the pressures of daily life. But household worship came to the fore in times of trial, especially when someone in the house lay sick or near death. In many instances, these situations brought the church into the household via the members of the clergy who played a key role in many of the rituals around the bed of the person who was ill or dying. For Catholics, Lutherans, and Anglicans, a final confession, absolution, and reception of the sacrament of Communion was an integral part of a good Christian death, and these elements could only occur if a member of the clergy was present to carry out these rituals. Because the Reformed largely rejected any sacramental action in the case of sickness or death, the presence of clergy was not required, but

---

[30]Green, "New for Old?," 206-15.

[31]Elnathan Parr, *Abba Father: or a Plaine and short Direction concerning the framing of private Prayer* (London: Samuel Man, 1636), fol. A4v (spelling modernized).

Reformed accounts of sickbed and deathbed scenes still often featured a pastor administering consolation through prayers and Scripture readings. In all cases, however, apart from sudden deaths, the act of dying was rarely private, and the presence of various household members, family, servants, friends, and neighbors meant that worship activities enfolded more than the one suffering individual. In other words, in the case of the sick and the dying, one should bear in mind that the practice of worship in these settings tended to be a group activity.

Worship rituals centered on the spiritual care of the dying person varied depending on the family's confessional allegiance. According to the fourteenth-century ritual of Breslau, assuming sufficient notice given to the priest that someone was on their deathbed, Catholic rituals began with a procession led by the priest bearing the consecrated elements, accompanied by acolytes carrying lit candles, a crucifix, holy water, and the holy oil. At the bedside, the priest sprinkled holy water on the dying person and recited verses from James 5:14-15. After leading in prayer and hearing the person's confession of sin, the priest offered absolution, presented the crucifix to be kissed, prayed, and recited the seven penitential psalms. After anointing the dying person with holy oil, the priest again prayed, and then administered a final partaking in the consecrated host (the viaticum).[32]

Martin Luther's attitude toward worship rituals at the bedside of the dying evolved over time. By 1520, in *The Babylonian Captivity of the Church*, he rejected the notion that extreme unction was a sacrament and that it was reserved for the dying. Based on his reading of James, he criticized the Catholic Church's use of the ritual, stating categorically,

> It is evident, therefore, that they have arbitrarily and without any authority made a sacrament and an extreme unction out of the misunderstood words of the apostle, which they have

---

[32]Susan Karant-Nunn, *The Reformation of Ritual: An Interpretation of Early Modern Germany* (London: Routledge, 1997), 140-42.

wrongly interpreted. And this works to the detriment of all other sick persons, whom they have deprived on their own authority of the benefit of the unction that the apostle enjoined.[33]

The German reformer did, however, recognize the power of the ritual, and did not call for it to be banned: "We do not deny, therefore, that forgiveness of sins and peace are granted through extreme unction; not because it is a sacrament divinely instituted, but because he who receives it believes that these blessings are granted to him."[34] Although extreme unction was retained at first in Lutheran deathbed rituals, it had disappeared by the 1530s, leaving confession, absolution, and participation in Communion as the main features of worship for the dying. Lutheran church ordinances laid out in considerable detail how pastors should conduct these rituals. In 1539, for instance, Duke Heinrich of Saxony instructed his clergy to begin by instructing the person and then to offer absolution, followed by Communion and prayer. The penitential psalms were replaced by other psalms and Scripture readings, including John 3:16. Again, the instructions, readings, exhortations, and prayers were not focused solely on the person dying, but also and at times more so on the household members present in the room. For instance, one set of ecclesiastical ordinances from Augsburg in 1555 had the pastor announce in a sermon at the bedside,

It is a special work of God's love, dear Christians, toward us poor, sinful humans that God presents to us, in addition to his dear and holy Word, daily examples of sick and dying people, in order thereby to keep us in a state of repentance and not to let us quickly and in large numbers to be ripped away in his fury, as every day we so richly deserve. Therefore, we

---

[33]Martin Luther, *The Babylonian Captivity of the Church* (1520), in *The Annotated Luther*, vol. 3, *Church and Sacraments*, ed. Paul Robinson (Minneapolis: Fortress, 2016), 122.
[34]Luther, *The Babylonian Captivity*, 125.

Christians should be glad to be around the sick and the dying, in order to take their example to heart.[35]

Clearly in this instance, the pastor's words were not directed at the person who was dying but at the other laypeople present in the room at the time. Lutheran church orders could also move laypeople from audience to active participants in the ministry of pastoral consolation. For instance, an unusual church ordinance issued in 1540 in the Lutheran territory of Brandenburg authorized laypeople (in the absence of a priest) to recite the words of the eucharistic liturgy in the presence of the dying person, albeit without actually consecrating bread and wine or administering Communion. Instead, by hearing the words of the sacrament recited, the dying person was to commune spiritually.[36] This approach both underscored the importance of Communion as an intrinsic part of a person's final worship practices, and reinforced the notion that the household could function like a miniature church.

The Anglican Book of Common Prayer of 1549 laid out in detail the liturgy to be conducted by the clergy at the bedside of the sick, including the reading of Psalm 143, a series of antiphons and responses, a set prayer, and an admonition to confession. The priest then asked the sick person to assent to each article of the creed in turn and then heard the person's confession before pronouncing the absolution. Then followed a shorter prayer and the recitation of Psalm 71, followed by a blessing. Anointing with oil was offered as an option, followed by Psalm 13. The liturgy then continued with the sacrament of Communion. The instructions noted that the sick could share in the sacrament on days when Communion was celebrated in church by having the priest reserve some of the consecrated bread and wine from the public service to bring to the sickbed. On days when the sacrament was not celebrated in

---

[35]Quoted in Karant-Nunn, *The Reformation of Ritual*, 153.

[36]Ronald Rittgers, "Pastoral Care as Protestant Mission: Ministry to the Sick and Suffering in Evangelical Church Ordinances," *Archiv für Reformationsgeschichte* 103 (2012): 149-81, esp. 163.

church, the instructions directed the clergy to consecrate the elements at the person's home. The person requesting Communion was urged to ask others to join in the sacrament in his or her home: "The sick person shall always desire some, either of his own house or else of his neighbours, to receive the Holy Communion with him, for that shall be to him a singular great comfort, and of their part a great token of charity."[37] Although couched in terms that suggest the aim was simply to ensure that the sick or dying person benefited from the strength of community support, the desire to distinguish the Anglican Communion of the sick from the Catholic rite clearly lay behind these rubrics.

Among the Reformed, pastoral care for the sick and the dying involved worship that was both less clergy-led and less sacramental. Because of their strong rejection of Communion in any other context apart from in church in the presence of the whole congregation, the Reformed rituals of worship for the sick and the dying did not tend to feature any partaking of the sacrament in the home. For instance, in 1581, the Dutch Reformed Synod of Middelburg responded to a question asking whether Communion of the sick was allowable. In response, the synod delegates stated, "The sacraments are to be administered only in the general assembly, in the location where the congregation ordinarily meets."[38] However, some Reformed leaders did leave room for bringing Communion to the bedside of those who were sick or dying. Most significantly, in a letter to Caspar Olevianus, written in 1563, John Calvin laid out at some length his reasoning favoring this practice.

> I know that issue is undecided, while the grounds for and against are not lacking. But by the nature, the purpose, and the right use of the sacrament, I believe that I can rightly conclude that one may not well rob someone who is suffering from a lengthy

---

[37] *Book of Common Prayer 1549* (repr., New York: Church Kalendar Press, 1881), 258-68, esp. 267.

[38] *Acta van de Nederlandsche synoden der zestiende eeuw*, ed. F. L. Rutgers (The Hague: Martinus Nijhoff, 1889), 445 (translation mine).

sickness or is in danger of life from such a privilege. . . . When a
believer sees that he must leave this world, it cannot be any other
way than that he is frightened and assaulted by manifold tempta-
tion, and then he shall rightly desire to arm himself, in order that
he may be able to stand up in this warfare. May one then rob him
of this entirely unique means of salvation that so strengthens his
trust that he joyfully faces the battle and triumphs? . . . But
although a pure administration of the Lord's Supper cannot
take place without communion, one may not regard the communion of the sick as a deformation, because actually it is not a
private communion. For in reality it is only a part of the public
celebration. . . . I would recommend that the Lord's Supper
rarely, by way of an exception, be administered to the sick, and
surely not without careful knowledge of the real situation of
the member. And in order also that the celebration of the Lord's
Supper be not removed from the institution of Christ neither
depart from it in the least, I regard it as desirable that it be
observed only in the circle of believers and not without preaching
the Word or liturgy, exactly as it is observed publicly.[39]

In this letter of advice to his German colleague, Calvin made a strong
case for the pastoral importance of providing some means of carefully
vetted access to the Lord's Supper for the sick, for their spiritual comfort. It is worth noting Calvin's insistence on having any Communion
for the sick follow the full practice for Communion services at church,
once again shifting the household from a private to a quasi-public
space. Although the church orders of Reformed communities did not
explicitly advocate home-based Communion for the sick and the
dying, other evidence suggests that it was possible to do so. The main

---

[39]John Calvin, letter to Caspar Olevianus, December 1563, in *Corpus Reformatorum*
20:200-201 (Latin). English translation available from L. W. Bilkes, "Restricting the Celebration of the Lord's Supper to Worship Services," Free Reformed Churches of North
America, November 29, 2001, http://frcna.org/component/k2/item/7542-/7542-.

concern was to ensure that the ritual replicated the sacramental celebration in church. For instance, the Huguenot pastor Charles Drelincourt, in the preface to his second volume of *Les visites charitables* (1657), responded to the Catholic charge that the Reformed cruelly refused the sacrament of Communion to the sick and the dying. In his answer, Drelincourt noted that the Reformed in Paris could not receive Communion at home due to the prohibition of the government regarding Huguenot worship within the city boundaries. He went on,

> But there are churches in our denomination who do not refuse to do so for those suffering from long-term illnesses. They create a small congregation, a kind of church, at the sick person's home, where several of the faithful take communion along with the person who is ill. If we had permission to do so in the city of Paris, we would make no objection to doing the same, and provide this consolation to the sick.[40]

Drelincourt's work, intended as a pastoral care manual for Huguenot clergy, primarily advocated prayer and Scripture-based assurances to the sufferer. He also encouraged those who were present at the bedside to join in the work of providing spiritual comfort to the one who was ill or dying, edifying and consoling that individual through their words.[41]

CONCLUSION

From large-scale and wide-ranging events such as pilgrimages and religious feast days to the focal point of a believer's last hours, early modern people interwove worship practices into their daily experience. Religious leaders encouraged training in worship in schools and homes, hoping to inculcate a regular rhythm of worship to deepen and shape the devotional life of the population. At the same time, various aspects

---

[40]Charles Drelincourt, *Les Visites charitables ou consolations chrétiennes pour toutes sortes de personnes affligées* (Geneva: Antoine and De Tournes, 1667), vol. 2, fol. (ō)2v (translation mine).
[41]Drelincourt, *Les Visites charitables*, vol. 2, fol. (ī)1r.

of worship outside church were also largely outside the clergy's control, especially the very public (such as popular religious festivals) and the very private (such as individual devotions). Whether reflecting personal piety, a desire for spiritual protection, or a need for help in times of crisis, people's worship practices spanned a range from officially endorsed to strongly condemned activities. In this sphere, perhaps more than in any other, laypeople had the most leeway to construct worship practices that best responded to their outlook and their needs.

For Further Reading

Eire, Carlos. *War Against the Idols: The Reformation of Worship from Erasmus to Calvin* (Cambridge: Cambridge University Press, 1986).

Green, Ian. "New for Old? Clerical and Lay Attitudes to Domestic Prayer in Early Modern England." *Reformation and Renaissance Review* 10, no. 2 (2008): 195-222.

Karant-Nunn, Susan. *The Reformation of Ritual: An Interpretation of Early Modern Germany*. London: Routledge, 1997.

McClendon, Muriel. "A Moveable Feast: Saint George's Day Celebrations and Religious Change in Early Modern England." *Journal of British Studies* 38, no. 1 (1999): 1-27.

Rittgers, Ronald. "Pastoral Care as Protestant Mission: Ministry to the Sick and Suffering in Evangelical Church Ordinances," *Archiv für Reformationsgeschichte* 103 (2012): 149-81.

Ryrie, Alec. *Being Protestant in Reformation Britain* (Oxford: Oxford University Press, 2013).

Tingle, Elizabeth. "Long-Distance Pilgrimage and the Counter-Reformation in France: Sacred Journeys to the Mont-Saint-Michel 1520–1750." *Journal of Religious History* 41, no. 2 (2017): 158-80.

Walsham, Alexandra. *The Reformation of the Landscape: Religion, Identity, and Memory in Early Modern Britain and Ireland*. Oxford: Oxford University Press, 2011.

CONCLUSION

In December 1565, the General Assembly of the Church of Scotland issued a call for nationwide services of fasting and repentance, scheduled for the following May. In an extensive preface, the Scottish church leaders laid out the reasons why the nation needed to humble itself before God. These challenges included Mary Queen of Scots' continued Catholicism and the open celebration of the Mass in otherwise Reformed Scotland, and rising Catholic pressure against Protestants across Europe. On two successive Sundays in May 1566, congregations across Scotland were to come together in church for three hours in the morning and another two in the afternoon. Everyone who could do so was to fast from eight in the evening on Saturday to five o'clock in the afternoon on the Sunday. "Gorgeous apparel" was prohibited, and games of any kind were to be avoided. The order of worship for the morning services included a confession of sins led by the pastor, Scripture readings including the Ten Commandments, silent prayer for a quarter of an hour or more at a time, a lengthy sermon, prayers, and the singing of Psalm 51 in its entirety. In the afternoons, the pastor was to preach from Psalm 119 or from 1 John 1:5. The afternoon worship service also featured more prayers and the singing of Psalm 6.[1]

---

[1] *Book of Common Order of the Church of Scotland*, ed. George Washington and Thomas Leishman (Edinburgh: Blackwood, 1868), 150-84.

Though more detailed than most, this call for a time of worship in metaphorical sackcloth and ashes was one of many issued in the Reformation era. Here and elsewhere we see that the reaction to calamities, whether political, religious, or natural, was to gather the community together for worship, in prayer and repentance, to acknowledge past sins and commit to renewed faithfulness to God's ways. Thus for church leaders at least, the practice of communal worship offered a much-needed response to times of stress and danger.

For Reformation-era Christians, whether out of personal commitment or external compulsion, or a combination of the two, worship lay at the heart of their life of faith. At church on Sundays and perhaps also on weekdays, at school and at home, they engaged in prayer, singing, hearing sermons, and rituals that marked their passage through life, from their baptism all the way to the prayers, readings, and ritual actions that took place around their deathbed.

At the end of this study, a few key points stand out. The first notable feature is just how similar the expectations of religious and political leaders were when it came to the practice of worship in the Reformation era. Whether Catholic, Lutheran, Anglican, or Reformed, clergy and government leaders alike expected punctual attendance, quiet and reverent attention, and active participation in worship services. They all condemned those who arrived late or left early, who gossiped or chatted with their neighbors, or who failed to turn up at all. The authorities' emphasis on the correct attitudes and behaviors at public worship is part of the larger framework of social disciplining that grew in strength throughout the early modern era.

The second point worth noting is just how quickly new patterns of worship became engrained in congregations, and became markers of confessional identity for them. By the end of the sixteenth century, less than a hundred years after the start of Luther's reformation, Lutherans faced with growing pressure from German Calvinists in Brandenburg, for example, increasingly staked their identity as

Lutherans on distinctive worship practices, such as baptismal exorcisms, or not breaking the Communion bread during its consecration, but only at the moment of distribution. These seemingly small ritual actions carried great weight and served as markers that allowed clergy and congregations to declare their confessional allegiance through their worship choices.

The third key feature is how even in a context that might be expected to foster spiritual equality at the very least, social class and rank still shaped people's experience of worship. From being able to insist on baptisms in one's home rather than in a cold and potentially germ-ridden church, to taking advantage of lineage and past practice to bury one's deceased relatives in the floor of the church, to engaging in major conflicts over precedence in processions and in seating in church, rank and status carried weight in the Reformation-era practice of worship.

Finally, this study has allowed readers to hear, even if only briefly, some of the voices and stories of the people who worshiped inside and outside church in the Reformation era. The liturgies and ordinances and church orders only provide part of the picture. It is my hope that the accounts and words of those who lived through this period of change and continuity has shed some light on the experience of worshiping in the Reformation era and contributes to fruitful ongoing conversations about the practice of worship today.

NAME INDEX

Subject Index

SCRIPTURE INDEX

Finding the Textbook You Need

The IVP Academic Textbook Selector
is an online tool for instantly finding the IVP books
suitable for over 250 courses across 24 disciplines.

ivpacademic.com